362.7
2a

The Teenage
Pregnant Girl

The Teenage Pregnant Girl

Edited by

JACK ZACKLER, M.D.

Assistant Commissioner
Chicago Board of Health, Retired; Diplomate, American
Board of Obstetrics and Gynecology

and

WAYNE BRANDSTADT, M.D.

Chicago Board of Health
Fellow American College of Physicians; Diplomate, American
Board of Preventive Medicine

CHARLES C THOMAS · PUBLISHER
Springfield · Illinois · U.S.A.

Published and Distributed Throughout the World by

CHARLES C THOMAS • PUBLISHER

Bannerstone House

301-327 East Lawrence Avenue, Springfield, Illinois, U.S.A.

© *1975, by* CHARLES C THOMAS • PUBLISHER

ISBN 0-398-03152-5

Library of Congress Catalog Card Number: 74-3362

*With THOMAS BOOKS careful attention is given to all details of
manufacturing and design. It is the Publisher's desire to present books that are
satisfactory as to their physical qualities and artistic possibilities and
appropriate for their particular use. THOMAS BOOKS will be true to those
laws of quality that assure a good name and good will.*

Printed in the United States of America

C-1

Library of Congress Cataloging in Publication Data

Zackler, Jack, comp.
 The teenage pregnant girl.

 1. Unmarried mothers—United States—Addresses,
essays, lectures. 2. Pregnant school girls—United
States—Addresses, essays, lectures. 3. Illegitimacy
—United States—Addresses, essays, lectures.
I. Brandstadt, Wayne, joint comp. II. Title.
ɪDNLM: 1. Illegitimacy. 2. Pregnancy—In adoles-
cence. WQ200 Z16t 1974ɪ
HV700.5.Z3　　362.7'8'982　　74-3362
ISBN 0-398-03152-5

CONTRIBUTORS

Peter Barglow, M.D.: Associate Professor of Psychiatry and Director of Psychiatric Residency Training, The Medical School, Northwestern University, Chicago.

Dorothy Chevalier, M.S.W.: Director of Social Services, Mount Zion Hospital and Medical Center, San Francisco.

Phillips Cutright, Ph.D.: Professor, Department of Sociology, Indiana University, Bloomington.

Ruth T. Gross, M.D.: Chief of the Department of Pediatrics, Mount Zion Hospital and Medical Center, San Francisco.

Marion Howard: Former Director, Consortium on Early Childbearing and Childrearing, Boston.

Howard N. Jacobson, M.D.: Director, The Macy Program; Chairman, Committee on Maternal Nutrition, Food and Nutrition Board, National Research Council; Boston Hospital for Women and Harvard Medical School, Boston.

James F. Jekel, M.D., M.P.H.: Associate Professor of Public Health, Department of Epidemiology and Public Health, Yale University Medical School, New Haven.

Donald Keith, M.B.A.: Research Assistant, Illinois Family Planning Council, Chicago; Associate Director, Department of Obstetrics, Cook County Hospital, Chicago.

Louis Keith, M.D.: Associate Professor of Obstetrics and Gynecology, The Chicago Medical School, University of Health Sciences, Chicago.

Janet C. King, Ph.D.: Assistant Professor of Nutrition, Department of Nutritional Sciences, University of California, Berkeley.

Lorraine V. Klerman, Dr.P.H.: Associate Professor of Public

Health, Florence Heller Graduate School for Advanced Studies in Social Welfare, Brandeis University, Waltham.

Harriet F. Pilpel, J.D.: General Counsel, Planned Parenthood—World Population, New York.

Mrs. Lee Ryan, A.C.S.W., M.S.W.: Director, Crittenton Comprehensive Care Centers, Chicago.

Mrs. Georgiana M. Selstad: Director, Health and Hospital Nursing Department, Ventura Health Service Agency, Ventura, California.

Mrs. Ruth Sharpe, A.C.S.W., M.S.W.: Social Work Supervisor, Crittenton Comprehensive Care Centers, Chicago.

Judith Weatherford Shouse, M.S.S.: Formerly Clinical Social Worker, Adolescent Maternity Center, Children's Hospital, San Francisco.

Robert C. Stepto, M.D., Ph.D.: Professor and Chairman, Department of Obstetrics and Gynecology, The Chicago Medical School, University of Health Sciences, Chicago; Chairman, Division of Obstetrics and Gynecology, Cooke County Hospital, Chicago.

Patti Tighe, M.D.: Department of Psychiatry, Pritzker School of Medicine, University of Chicago.

Myrtle White, R.N.: Assistant Director of The Comprehensive Child Care Project, Mount Zion Hospital and Medical Center, San Francisco.

FOREWORD

I<small>N RECENT YEARS</small> there has been a marked increase in teenage pregnancies which presents many problems to the young mothers, their parents and their doctors and is of deep concern to those working in public health. It is imperative that all those involved in the care of these teenage pregnancies have a better understanding of the problems which develop. Interest in bringing the various phases of these problems together in a single volume grew out of my activities with the federally supported Maternal and Infant Care Project No. 502.

It has become abundantly clear that attitudes must be adjusted and programs must be established, while bearing in mind that our efforts are to be geared primarily (1) to the PREVENTION of future recurrences and (2) to the assurance of the opportunity to experience the full potential of life for both the mother and child.

Recognized authorities in the various fields dealing with the general problems related to teenage pregnancy have contributed chapters. The result is a comprehensive coverage of this timely subject.

J.Z.

CONTENTS

The Teenage
Pregnant Girl

CHAPTER I

THE RISE OF TEENAGE ILLEGITIMACY IN THE UNITED STATES: 1940-1971

Phillips Cutright

INTRODUCTION

THIS CHAPTER documents the increase in illegitimacy among teenagers in the United States over recent decades. Illegitimate births to girls under twenty years swelled from about 48,000 in 1940 to an estimated 239,000 in 1971. In part, the increased number of births is a function of the increase in the number of unmarried teenagers, but the probability of an illegitimate birth has also increased. For example, the illegitimacy rate of unmarried girls aged fifteen to nineteen was about 8 per 1,000 in 1940; by 1960 the rate was 16 per 1,000. The 1971 rate is estimated at nearly 24 per 1,000 unmarried teenagers.

Having documented the increase in the illegitimacy rate, we seek to explain it. We begin by discussing the immediate causes responsible for increasing illegitimacy. Surveys conducted in 1971 and in the 1940's sought to ascertain the proportion of unmarried teenagers who were no longer virgins. Comparisons of these studies have been used to support the claim that the rise of illegitimacy is a result of increasing sexual activity. We will examine the validity of such comparisons. A second set of data used as evidence of rising sexual activity is the venereal disease rate. Trends in VD rates should fit the trends in illegitimacy if both figures are, in fact, an index of changing sexual activity.

A third set of data, derived from studies of vital documents and measures of health conditions, provide an alternative meth-

NOTE: This research was supported by the Commission on Population Growth and the American Future, Public Health Service grant MH 15567 of DHEW and by Indiana University.

3

od of discussing causes of rising illegitimacy. This analysis focuses on changes in spontaneous and induced fetal loss, changes in fecundity due to a decline in the age of menarche, and changes in "first child sterility." Consideration is also given to changes in breastfeeding practices as a cause of increasing illegitimate births among teenagers.

Our analysis of immediate causes of changes in the teenage illegitimacy rate then shifts to more remote factors that are believed by some to be the true causes of rising illegitimacy. We examine urbanization, the AFDC program, and measures of economic status.

THE TREND IN TEENAGE ILLEGITIMACY

Much confusion in past discussions of illegitimacy has been generated by claims that we really do not know whether illegitimacy has increased. Underregistration of births to nonwhites in past years and continuing undercount by Census of women are two major barriers to accurate calculations of illegitimacy rates. However, it is possible to correct these errors in official statistics, and this has been done in Table I-I.[1]

Alleged higher rates of concealed illegitimacy among whites than nonwhites (due to falsification of birth records or forced marriages are cited as factors that make illegitimacy figures and/or racial comparisons meaningless. However, careful examination of these unsupported claims[1] allows us to reject them. Some writers have argued that rates of nonmarital sexual activity among young girls in the white and nonwhite population are actually equal, that the observed differences in illegitimacy rates are the result of differential patterns of induced abortion, contraceptive use, and forced marriages. These claims have little weight, as is shown below. In sum, when we look at trends in either white or nonwhite teenage illegitimacy rates, we are looking at changes in reasonably valid measures of the changing probability

---

1. P. Cutright, "Illegitimacy in the United States, 1920-1968," in C. F. Westoff and R. Parke, Jr., eds., *Demographic and Social Aspects of Population Growth* (Washington, D. C., Government Printing Office, 1972) , Appendix A.

TABLE I-I

ILLEGITIMATE BIRTHS PER 1,000 UNMARRIED WOMEN UNDER
20 YEARS, AND AGED 15 TO 44,* BY COLOR:
UNITED STATES, 1940-1971

Color and Age	1940	1950	Year 1960	1968	1971†
Nonwhite					
14	13	19	20	21	—
15-17	38	53	56	67	—
18-19	61	93	114	112	—
15-19	45.5	65.6	73.9	82.0	89.1
15-44	39.7	69.1	90.2	80.2	67.5
White					
14	0.5	0.8	1	1	—
15-17	2	3	4	6	—
18-19	5	8	12	17	—
15-19	3.5	5.1	6.6	9.7	12.1
15-44	3.6	5.8	9.3	12.4	13.5
All					
15-19	8.3	12.8	15.6	19.8	23.5
15-44	7.9	14.1	21.7	23.2	22.7

Source: Cutright, P., "Illegitimacy in the United States, 1920-1968," *op. cit.*, Tables 2 and 3.

* Rate for ages fifteen to forty-four standardized on 1960 age distribution of unmarried women. Rate for age fourteen related births to unwed mothers under fifteen to the number of unmarried women aged fourteen. Rates for fifteen to nineteen years exclude births to girls under fifteen.

† 1971 estimated by applying 1965-1968 change to the succeeding three year period.

that an unmarried teenage girl will deliver an illegitimate child from one year to another.

Table I-I shows the change in the risk of an illegitimate birth to young girls and to unmarried women aged fifteen to forty-four, over a three-decade period.* Our teenage rate for 1971 is based on a projection of the change between 1965 and 1968. Offi-

* In 1920 and 1930 the illegitimacy rate for both white and nonwhite women was about the same as that of 1940. This suggests that the teenage rates during the period 1920 to 1940 were stable and similar to the relatively low 1940 rates. Since pregnancies among whites and nonwhite brides were also stable during the 1920 to 1940 period we conclude that coital activity among young unmarried women was relatively stable during this period.[2]

2. *Ibid.*, Tables 2, 9, and 10.

cial estimates of illegitimate births after 1968 were not available in July, 1973 when this paper was completed. It makes little difference whether the percentage change or the absolute 1965-1968 change in the rate is used to make this projection.*

Among nonwhites the illegitimacy rates show a marked increase over the period covered whereas among whites the increase in rates is rather steady but small.

IMMEDIATE CAUSES OF RISING ILLEGITIMACY

The immediate causes of changes in illegitimacy rates are changes in (1) nonmarital sexual activity, (2) voluntary controls over conception (contraception), (3) voluntary controls over gestation (induced abortion), (4) involuntary controls over conception (fecundity or ability to conceive if sexually active), and (5) involuntary controls over gestation (spontaneous fetal loss, including stillbirth).

Causes of changes in illegitimacy that affect, for example, changes in sexual activity are referred to here as "remote causes." Discussion of some possible remote causal factors is deferred to later sections. Our task now is to review the evidence regarding each immediate cause to see whether it has changed in a direction that would account for increasing illegitimacy.

CHANGE IN VOLUNTARY CONTROLS OVER ILLEGITIMACY

STUDIES OF NONMARITAL SEX AMONG UNMARRIED TEENAGERS. Reports from a national study of unmarried girls provide a reliable measure of teenage sexual activity in 1971. These statistics invite comparison with Kinsey studies for earlier years.[3-7] Indeed, *Time*

---

*See Table I-VIII. In this table the rates for states overstate the actual nonwhite rates because correction for census undercount of unmarried women can be made only for national data.

3. M. Zelnik and J. Kantner, "Sexuality, Contraception and Pregnancy among Young Unwed Females in the United States," in C. F. Westoff and R. Parke, Jr., *op. cit.*

4. J. Kantner and M. Zelnik, "Sexual Experience of Young Unmarried Women in the United States," *Family Planning Perspectives*, 4:9-18 (October, 1972).

5. M. Zelnik and J. Kantner, "The Probability of Premarital Intercourse," *Social Science Research*, 1:335-341 (September, 1972).

has already claimed that the 1971 data show coitus among whites to be double the rate reported by Kinsey.[8]

When originally published, the Kinsey studies were subject to a barrage of technical criticisms because the respondents were unlike the population in general. For example, some 80 percent of the Kinsey sample of whites, but only about 17 percent of the comparable white female population with similar years of birth, had attended college. Among nonwhites, the Kinsey sample reported 41 percent attended college, while Census would indicate a figure closer to 7 percent.[9] Since women with higher years of education reported lower levels of coitus at early ages than did women with fewer years of school, the unadjusted total from the Kinsey study will underestimate the sexual experience of young unmarried girls in the U. S. population.

There is a large difference in the religious composition of the Kinsey sample and the population in general. Nearly 29 percent of the Kinsey white sample, but only 3 percent of the white population, were Jews. Kinsey underrepresented both Catholics and Protestants. Because early coital experience was lower among Jews than in either of the two other religious groups, the sample's religious composition biases the Kinsey estimates of white coital activity downward.[10]

Efforts to adjust the Kinsey sample statistically to fit national data have found that Kinsey respondents differ from the population, even when matched on one or another characteristic. For example, Tietze and Martin[11] found that Kinsey's sample reported far fewer births than did the comparable U. S. population.

To use Kinsey data as a benchmark against which the 1971 survey data might be used to measure change in teenage coitus over

---

6. A. Kinsey, W. Pomeroy, C. Martin and P. Gebhard, *Sexual Behavior in the Human Female* (Philadelphia, W. B. Saunders Company, 1953).

7. P. Gebhard, W. Pomeroy, C. Martin, and C. Christensen, *Pregnancy, Birth and Abortion* (New York, John Wiley & Sons, Inc., 1966 [First published in 1958]).

8. *Time*, August 21, 1972, pp. 34-40.

9. Kinsey, *et al., op. cit.,* Table 1.

10. *Ibid.,* Table 90.

11. C. Tietze and C. Martin, "Foetal Deaths, Spontaneous and Induced, in the United States," *Population Studies*, 11:170-176 (1957).

the years, it would be necessary to standardize the Kinsey materials to represent the U. S. population in 1940. This statistical manipulation would require (1) adequate sample size within educational, racial, religious, and geographical categories; (2) confidence that Kinsey's subsample categories were representative of the population and (3) similarity in the methods used to obtain information by Kinsey and the 1971 survey. These assumptions cannot be satisfied. For example, the 1971 survey does not rely on retrospective data—rather it asked teenagers about their current and recent sexual activity. In contrast, the bulk of Kinsey respondents were older women who were asked to recall their sexual histories. The effect of this and many other methodological differences on the responses of women in the two studies cannot be estimated.

An effort by the Institute for Sex Research to reexamine the data used in early published reports has led to rather substantial downward adjustment of the number of usable interviews. Using these "clean" data we requested tabulations of Kinsey's respondents, where the respondent was aged twenty or under at interview, unmarried, and not a student—the latter restriction in order to get some idea of the completed educational level. These restrictions limited sample size to fifty-three black and 919 white respondents. However, 789 of the white and forty of the black cases were women with some college attendance. Clearly there are insufficient cases at any educational level among blacks to satisfy the requirement that subcategories in Kinsey's sample be large enough to represent subgroups of the national population. Among whites there were just sixteen girls with less than twelve years of school and forty-four with only twelve years.

A second feature of the Kinsey sample is the high level of contraceptive use by those who admitted sexual activity before marriage. Among the 144 sexually active unmarried teenage whites, 94 percent claimed to use contraception and most of these were in a "much" use code, a category that is at the top of a four-point scale designed to gage the regularity of use. Further, for what it is worth, nearly the same high level of use is found at all educational levels. This remarkably high level of use also is found within the black sample—84 percent of the nineteen sexually active unmarried claimed to use contraception. These high levels of contraceptive use and the high regularity of use claimed by the sexually active are unusual, given information from other studies of contraceptive use at the time among the unmarried and the married.[12-14]*

It is impossible to reconstruct the teenage sexual behavior of the U. S. population from Kinsey's data due not only to small sample size within subgroups, but also to selective biases that were at work. The suggested bias toward unusually high levels of contraceptive use is at least partially supported by the low levels of fertility among older women in the sample.[15] We conclude, reluctantly, that there is no early benchmark against which the 1971 study can be compared.

Some results of the 1971 survey bear reporting. In 1971 about 23 percent of never-married whites aged fifteen to nineteen reported having coitus, while 40 percent of whites aged nineteen years said they had experienced coitus. Among black never-married teenagers, 54 percent of those aged fifteen to nineteen reported coitus, while 81 percent of black girls aged nineteen had experienced coitus.[16]

VD RATES AS A MEASURE OF CHANGING SEXUAL ACTIVITY

Although we have no direct evidence of a change in coital activity, one is often confronted with the suggestion that venereal disease rates are an indirect measure of changing coitus. Since VD is usually sex-related, does not the rise in VD rates prove that

---

12. Cutright, *op. cit.,* Table 8.

13. R. Farley, *The Growth of the Black Population* (Chicago, Markham Publishing Company, 1970) , Chapter 8.

14. S. Polgar, "Sociocultural Research in Family Planning in the United States: Review and Prospects," *Human Organization,* 25:321-329 (Winter, 1966) .

* Contraceptive use among Kinsey's unmarried teenagers was higher than the level reported by older married Protestant wives in the 1940 representative survey of the Indianapolis population and higher than was reported by Protestant wives in 1955 and 1960.

15. C. Tietze and C. Martin, *op. cit.,* p. 174.

16. J. Kantner and M. Zelnik, *op. cit.,* Table 1.

sexual activity has increased? Indeed, it is commonly held that increasing sexual activity is the *cause* of the rising VD rate.[17]

Understanding the association, or lack of it, between trends in VD rates and sexual activity of unmarried women as reflected in illegitimacy rates is hampered by inadequate reporting of known cases of VD to the public health reporting network by private physicians, by lack of data on the marital status of women whose cases are reported, and by the failure of authorities to adjust the trend over the years to account for demographic factors and better coverage of the population by the reporting network. Since 1940, this network has improved with the expansion of public health VD clinics to areas that lacked such facilities in the past and through changes in state laws that began to require reporting of the results of marriage license blood tests. If only better reporting were at work, the trend in VD rates since 1940 would have been in only one direction—up.

Syphilis rates are higher among unmarried than among married women.[18, 19] This suggests that as the proportion of married women increase, syphilis rates should decline and vice versa. This possibility has not received the attention it deserves.

Our preliminary view of long-run movements in VD and illegitimacy rates in Figure I-1 displays the trend in gonorrhea and primary and secondary syphilis per 100,000 women since 1940 or 1941. Against these two widely used measures of VD we plot the trend in the rate of illegitimate births per 1,000 unmarried women aged fifteen to forty-four. Because VD rates are not age standardized, we do not use age standardized illegitimacy rates.

If VD rates and illegitimacy rates were subject to a common causal factor (for instance, coital activity) one would expect them to move up and down together or remain stable over the same periods. The graph (Figure I-1) indicates that the actual

17. *New York Times*, M:25 (September 9, 1972) . *Time, op. cit.*

18. H. Carter and P. Glick, *Marriage and Divorce: A Social and Economic Study* (Cambridge, Mass., Harvard University Press, 1968) , Table 11.12.

19. NCHS, "Findings on the Seriological Test for Syphilis in Adults: United States, 1960-1962" (Washington, D. C., U. S. Government Printing Office, 1965) , Series 11, No. 9. Table 10.

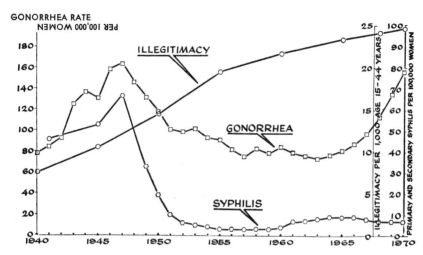

Figure I-1. The Trend in Female VD and Illegitimacy Rates: United States, 1940-1970. Sources. Table I-I. VD Fact Sheet (Annual), Female VD rates prior to 1949 estimated using the ratio of women to total population in 1949-50, U. S. Public Health Service, DHEW Publication, Washington.

trends have, over the past three decades, shared no consistent movements. We conclude that (1) different types of VD rates may or may not move in the same direction over the same period; (2) the illegitimacy rate may or may not move in the same direction as one or another VD rate over the same period; (3) the simple assumption that either VD rate is a response to changing sexual activity need not be accepted without empirical evidence; (4) the view that illegitimacy and VD rates move together can be rejected; (5) the theory that change in coital activity is the cause of changes in both VD and illegitimacy rates should be returned to its proponents with a request for some supporting evidence; and (6) VD rates do not provide a reliable proxy measure for changing patterns of coital activity.

In Figure I-1 we presented female VD rates, computed without regard to age or color. Color specific VD rates are available since 1956 and these trends, when plotted against color specific illegitimacy rates, yield about the same results as we found above using the rates without regard to color.

Although we believe that the trend in VD rates for all women is likely to reflect common trends among both married and unmarried women, it is possible to establish this point only approximately and only with data for 1956 and later years. The national VD reporting system data were first broken down by age, color, and sex in 1956 and have been reported in that detail—but without a marital status breakdown—since that time. Still, because so few girls fifteen to nineteen are married, it seems reasonable that the bulk of the female teenage VD cases are unmarried. Actually, a comparison of the teenage VD trend for a given measure of VD shows, after 1956, a common trend with the rate for girls under fifteen years, as well as the trends for older women.

Table I-II derived from Figure I-1, answers the question, Did the gonorrhea or primary and secondary syphilis rates for teenage girls move in the same direction as the teenage illegitimacy rate over a given period? For female teenagers, we find no consistent pattern between the rate for gonorrhea or syphilis and the illegitimacy rate.

There are causal factors other than coital activity changes that help explain changes in VD rates over some periods. For example, prior to the mid-1950's improved reporting may explain in part the rise in VD to its post World War II peak, while the decline in the rates after 1947 has been viewed as a result of the introduction of penicillin by VD clinics. The happenstance theory contends that the widespread use of penicillin by private physicians and VD clinics contributed to the sharp post World War II decline. This theory also helps explain why the VD rates—or at

TABLE I-II

DID CHANGES IN TEENAGE ILLEGITIMACY RATES MOVE IN THE SAME
DIRECTION AS CHANGES IN TEENAGE VD RATES AFTER 1956?

Change Period	Whites		Nonwhites	
	Gonorrhea	*Syphilis*	*Gonorrhea*	*Syphilis*
1956-60 .... Yes		Yes	No	Yes
1961-65 .... Yes		No	No	Yes
1966-68 .... Yes		No	Yes	No
1969-70 .... Yes		No	Yes	No

least the gonorrhea rate—moved up in the late 1950's, since it was at that time that prescription of penicillin was restricted in the treatment of patients without VD.

Another school of thought attempts to explain part of the rise in gonorrhea during the 1960's as a result of a shift in contraceptive methods. The increased use of the Pill and IUD are accompanied by a decline in the use of condom, jelly, and douche. If the latter methods tend to prevent the spread of VD, a decline in their use may cause the rate to increase. At the moment it is enough to note that while no single causal factor appears to explain the trend in both VD rates over the entire period, there do exist some reasonable explanations of the trends that do not rely solely on the idea that changes in coital activity are the overwhelming causal factor behind shifts in VD rates.*

CHANGES IN CONTRACEPTION AND ABORTION

We turn now to an alternative method of estimating changes in nonmarital sexual activity—a step that forces us to move through the other immediate causes of illegitimacy in search of an explanation for the rise in the rates since 1940.

HAS EFFECTIVE USE OF CONTRACEPTION DECLINED? Studies of contraceptive efficacy among nonwhite unmarried women in the 1920's and 1930's show virtually no effective use in the population.[20, 21] Thus, effective contraceptive use among blacks cannot have declined since 1940. Among unmarried whites we can be less certain, although it seems clear that contraceptive effectiveness is much lower than many people believe.

From the Zelnik and Kantner study we find that 20 percent of white and 15 percent of black sexually active teenagers claim to use contraception "always." This does not mean that 20 or 15 percent of the population at risk of pregnancy is actually protected,

---

* My thanks to Edward M. Brecher for suggestions regarding a study of VD and illegitimacy. See his "Women Victims of the VD Rip-Off," *Viva* 1 (October, November, 1973), for a review of the current status of anti-VD efforts in the U. S.

20. R. Pearl, "Third Progress Report on a Study of Family Limitation," *Milbank Memorial Fund Quarterly*, 14:258-284 (July, 1936).

21. Farley, *op. cit.*

because an even *higher* percent of unmarried girls pregnant at the time of interview claimed to have been regular users of contraception.[22] Of currently pregnant girls who did not want to become pregnant 24 percent of whites and 17 percent of blacks claimed to be regular users of contraception.[23] If contraception was preventing many pregnancies we would expect fewer pregnant than nonpregnant sexually active girls to be contraceptive users. This appears not to be the case.

Elsewhere we have contrasted contraceptive efficacy among young white and black wives in the 1965 National Fertility Study and concluded that effective use among young couples is quite low, even with the advantages of married life.[24] Another reason to doubt an increase in effective use is that the male has traditionally been responsible for protection against illicit pregnancy. The recent shift from male to female methods—a change that occurred primarily after the Pill was introduced—has led to a decline in male use by married couples and may also depress male use outside marriage. Data from the 1971 survey indicate heavy reliance, by both black and white teenagers claiming to use contraception, on ineffective methods and very little current use of the Pill, although about a fourth of girls who have ever used contraception claim to have used the Pill at some time.[25] Perhaps only 8 or 9 percent of sexually active teenagers were using the Pill effectively at the time of their most recent coitus, a figure that will grossly exaggerate protection by the Pill over an extended period.

Of a group of girls of all ages taking the Pill in the Atlanta family planning program 24 percent became pregnant within 18 months. Pregnancy rates among the younger patients were double

---

22. M. Zelnik and J. Kantner, Sexuality, Contraception and Pregnancy among Young Unwed Females in the United States, *op. cit.*, Table 10.

23. *Ibid.*, p. 372.

24. P. Cutright, "The Teenage Sexual Revolution and the Myth of an Abstinent Past," *Family Planning Perspectives*, 4:28-29 (January, 1972).

25. M. Zelnik and J. Kanter, "Sexuality, Contraception and Pregnancy among Young Unwed Females in the United States," *op. cit.*, Table 13.

the failure rates of those twenty to twenty-nine years old.[26] The increase of Pill use from zero prior to 1961 to 8 or 9 percent in 1971 should not be taken as evidence of increasing effective use, since increases in Pill use are linked (at least among the married) to declines in the more effective traditional methods, e.g. condom and diaphragm. The rise of illegitimacy is not a function of declining contraceptive use, nor is it likely that the rise has been dampened by a notable increase in effective contraception by sexually active teenagers. This conclusion may need to be qualified if applied to white teenagers having premarital sex only with a fiance.

HAS INDUCED ABORTION AMONG UNMARRIED TEENAGERS DECLINED? If it were true that induced abortion was more heavily used in the past than it was in 1970-1971, then some portion of the higher teenage illegitimacy rate in 1971 would be due to a decline in abortion use. The only available indicators of long run trends in induced abortion use are derived from death certificates on which the detailed cause of maternal death is specified. For a population of women suffering maternal death, those whose deaths were due to abortion and those whose deaths were due to other causes may be separated. The ratio of the number of abortion deaths to other deaths yields the abortion death ratio. The trend over the years in this ratio provides a measure of use of induced abortion (primarily illegal abortion) by pregnant women.

In the United States the abortion death ratio by marital status, color, and age is available only for the 1949-1951 period. The marital status detail is unavailable in other years, although age and color detail are available.[27] In the 1949-1951 period, for example, the abortion death ratio for unmarried whites under twenty was 43.9. There were about forty-four abortion-related deaths for every 100 maternal deaths from other causes. In contrast the abortion death ratio for married teenage whites under

---

26. C. Tietze and S. Lewitt,, "The IUD and the Pill: Extended Use Effectiveness," *Family Planning Perspectives*, 3:53-55 (April, 1971).

27. P. Cutright, "The Teenage Sexual Revolution and the Myth of an Abstinent Past," *op. cit.*, Tables 4 and 5.

twenty was only 6.3. The abortion death ratio was nearly seven times higher among unmarried than among married white teenagers. In the same years the abortion death ratio for nonwhite teenagers was 21 for unmarried and 7.2 for married women. The abortion death ratio for young unmarried nonwhites was nearly triple the ratio among married nonwhite women under twenty.

Higher abortion death ratios to the unmarried at each age are found within both the white and the nonwhite population. The higher abortion death ratio among white teenagers compared to nonwhite teenagers indicates more frequent use of induced abortion by pregnant unmarried white girls in the 1949-1951 period. This does not mean that the induced abortion rate per 1,000 unmarried teenagers was higher among whites.[28, 29] A higher white than nonwhite likelihood of aborting an illicit pregnancy does not imply that the induced abortion rate per 1,000 unmarried women is higher among whites than nonwhites. Assume two unmarried female populations fifteen to nineteen, one with a pregnancy rate of 40 and the other with a pregnancy rate of 140. If 50 percent of the pregnancies in the first population are voluntarily aborted, while only 25 percent are aborted in the second population, the induced abortion rate per 1,000 women in the first population will be 20, while in the second it will be 35. Because pregnancy rates per 1,000 women in the white and nonwhite unmarried populations are so different (see Table II-I), one cannot conclude that the absolute effect of induced abortion on depressing the illegitimacy rate is less for nonwhites than for whites, in spite of the conclusion that pregnant unmarried whites are more likely than pregnant unmarried nonwhites to abort.

Assuming that trends in induced abortion will be shared by the

---

28. J. P. Abernathy, B. G. Greenberg and D. C. Horvitz, "Estimates of Induced Abortion in Urban North Carolina," *Demography*, 7: Table 1 (1970). J. Sklar and B. Berkov, *The Role of Legal Abortion in Fertility Decline: The California Experience* (Berkeley, Cal., Institute of International Studies, August, 1973), Tables F and H.

29. J. Pakter and F. Nelson, "Abortion in New York City: The First Nine Months," *Family Planning Perspectives*, 4:5-11 (July, 1971).

married and the unmarried population, we can estimate abortion death ratios for unmarried whites and nonwhites from 1939 through 1965. We have not made these estimated ratios specific to teenagers, although the age distribution of unmarried mothers is such that the abortion death ratio to all unmarried women is close to the ratio for women under twenty.

For both whites and nonwhites the abortion death ratio was much higher in 1939-1941 than it was in 1949-1951. The likely decline in abortion use during the 1940's was accompanied by a rising illegitimacy rate. A sharp rise in abortion death ratios of both white and nonwhite women occurred after the mid-1950's. This suggests that induced abortion use increased. The abortion death ratio in the 1962-1965 period was about equal to the ratio for 1939-1941. This suggests that the probability of induced abortion among the pregnant unmarried population in the mid-1960's was little different from the probability around 1940.

Comparisons of illegitimacy rates and changes in abortion death ratios in other populations show that periods of increasing abortion death ratios are usually accompanied by increasing illegitimacy rates.[30] This apparent anomaly may occur because abortion death ratios increase along with a rising illicit pregnancy rate. If the increase in abortions is not equal to that in pregnancies, the illegitimacy rate can increase in spite of increased abortion use. Thus, we conclude that illegally induced abortion increased after 1955 among both white and nonwhite unmarried women, but this increase was not sufficient to control the rise in illegitimacy. The probability of induced abortion among pregnant unmarried white and nonwhite girls in the mid-1960's was little different from the level in 1939-1941. Therefore, the rise in illegitimacy rates between 1940 and 1965 was not due to a decline in induced abortion use.

If the rise in illegitimacy is not a function of declining voluntary controls over fertility among the sexually active (i.e. contraception and induced abortion), the immediate cause of rising

---

30. P. Cutright, *Illegitimacy: Measurement and Analysis* (Cambridge, Mass., Joint Center for Urban Studies, Mimeo, 1970) , Chapter 4.

illegitimacy must be changes in involuntary controls over fertility (i.e. declining spontaneous fetal loss, declining sterility, and increasing fecundity) or increasing sexual activity.

CHANGE IN INVOLUNTARY CONTROLS OVER ILLEGITIMACY

INCREASING FECUNDITY AMONG TEENAGE GIRLS AFTER 1940. A number of studies indicate the mean age of menarche among teenagers in the 1960's was about one year earlier than it was for teenagers around 1940. A large study of age at menarche done during the early 1960's found the mean age to be 12.5 years, and the estimate for around 1940 is 13.5.[31] The 1965 National Fertility Study found no difference in mean age at menarche between white and nonwhite women and we therefore apply the same age at menarche to both populations.[32]

Virtually no women are fecund before first menses, and regular ovulation does not begin for some time thereafter. One estimate of the time of partial sterility after first menses is 2.3 years.[33] We use a period of 2.5 years of partial fecundity after first menses prior to attainment of full fecundity in the following analysis.

Tanner's review[34] of the historical literature on mean age at menarche concluded that the mean age was about 16.5 in 1870. It had declined (in Europe) to 14.5 by 1930, and moved on down to 13.5 in the 1950's. Over the past six decades mean age at menarche in the U. S. has been about one year below the European level and has shown a parallel decline. Tanner and others claim that the major factor responsible for the decline is improvements in nutrition and health that increase the rate of physical growth and thus decrease the age at menarche. An enormous difference in the fecundity of young girls as a function of mean age at

---

31. L. Zackarias, R. Wurtman and M. Schatzoff, "Sexual Maturation in Contemporary American Girls," *American Journal of Obstetrics and Gynecology*, 108: 108 (1970).

32. N. B. Ryder and C. Westoff, *Reproduction in the United States, 1965* (Princeton, N. J., Princeton University Press, 1971), p. 304.

33. Zackarias, *et al., op cit.*, Table II.

34. J. Tanner, Earlier Maturation in Man, *Scientific American*, No. 1, 218:26, (1968).

menarche has been observed. Under European conditions around 1870, only 23 percent of girls were fully fecund on their eighteenth birthday while under current conditions in the United States 23 percent are already fecund on their fourteenth birthday, and 95 percent are fully fecund at age eighteen.*

An increase in fecundity due to a one year decline in the age of menarche occurred in the United States after 1940. For example, the one year decline implies that at age fifteen there was an increase from 23 to 54 percent fully fecund—a change of 31 percent. At age eighteen, however, only 2 percent of girls were affected. Thus, girls aged fourteen through sixteen are much more likely to be fecund, while little change exists among girls age seventeen and older.† Therefore, illegitimacy among younger teenage girls may have increased after 1940 due to increases in fecundity alone.

One curious finding from the 1965 National Fertility Study is that girls who menstruate earlier than the average also require less time to become pregnant.[35] They are quicker to conceive their first as well as later births than other women. A woman with first menses later than the average takes more time to conceive than does the average woman. Furthermore, if women menstruating at an earlier age than average are more likely to have sexual relations at an earlier age than other women, they would be a group in a double bind. Some evidence from the Kinsey study[36] indicates that sexual relations do start earlier among women menstruating early. The magnitude of the effect of early rather than average or late age at menarche on nonmarital coitus by age twenty is notable; 22 percent of girls menstruating at ages 12.9 or under had coitus by age twenty compared to only 17.7 percent of those menstruating at age thirteen years or later. One effect, then, of a decline in age of menarche may be to increase the rate of sexual activity at an early age. In this chapter, however, we only

---

* An upper limit of 95 percent is imposed because about 5 percent of women are never able to conceive or to carry a fetus to a viable age.

† See P. Cutright, "Teenage Sexual Revolution and the Myth of an Abstinent Past," *op. cit.,* p. 26 for methods used to make these estimates.

35. N. B. Ryder and C. F. Westoff, *op. cit.,* p. 337.

36. Kinsey, *et al., op. cit.,* Table 85.

examine the impact of increased teenage fecundity as this characteristic affects illegitimacy, independent of changes in sexual activity.

THE DECLINE OF SPONTANEOUS FETAL LOSS AFTER 1940

Recent studies of populations of closely observed married women have resulted in sharp upward revisions of traditional estimates of spontaneous fetal loss. For example, registered late fetal deaths (twenty weeks or more gestation) for white and nonwhite married women in 1960 were 13.6 and 25.2 per 1,000 live births.[37] In contrast, the Shapiro, *et al.* study[38] of the population of married women in the Health Insurance Program of Greater New York reported a ratio of 230 and 460 spontaneous fetal loss of four or more weeks gestation per 1,000 live births among married whites and nonwhites, respectively, around 1960. Since fetal loss is higher among unmarried than married women,[39] estimated spontaneous fetal loss at four or more weeks gestation for unmarried women around 1960 is even higher— about 386 per 1,000 live births for whites and 552 for nonwhites. Among teenagers spontaneous fetal loss is lower than among older women. For example, late fetal loss among white and nonwhite unmarried teenagers is only 80 percent of fetal loss to unmarried women of all ages.[40] To estimate the change in the level of spontaneous fetal loss between 1940 and 1960 among unmarried teenagers, we start by estimating the level for all unmarried women in 1940. This is done by using the same number that, in 1960, was necessary to inflate registered late fetal loss to equal estimated true fetal loss at four or more weeks gestation. Apply-

---

37. R. Grove and A. Hetzel, *Vital Statistics Rates in the United States, 1940-1960,* National Center for Health Statistics (Washington, D. C., Government Printing Office, 1968) , Table 36.

38. S. Shapiro, H. Levine and M. Abramowicz, "Factors Associated with Early and Late Fetal Loss," *Advances in Planned Parenthood,* VI Excerpta Medica International Congress Series, 1971.

39. R. Grove and A. Hetzel, *op. cit.,* Table 36. National Center for Health Statistics, *Infant, Fetal and Maternal Mortality: United States, 1963* (Washington, D. C., Government Printing Office, 1966) , Table 17.

40. National Center for Health Statistics, 1966, *op. cit.,* Table 17.

ing these same multipliers (16.8 for whites and 18.6 for non-whites) results in estimated true spontaneous fetal loss in 1940 of 702 and 1,191 per 1,000 live births to white and nonwhite unmarried women.

Deflating these numbers to 80 percent and calculating the 1940 to 1960 change in spontaneous fetal loss yields an estimated *decline* of 252 and 511 spontaneous abortions per 1,000 live births to white and nonwhite unmarried teenagers.* This enormous increase in the ability of pregnant girls to reach term should be one factor behind the rise in illegitimacy after 1940. We have no data for the years after 1960 but the decline in late fetal loss since that time suggests further declines in spontaneous fetal loss at four or more weeks—a decline that is *not* included in our estimates of the effect of declining spontaneous fetal loss on illegitimacy changes after 1940.

The approximate validity of this method of estimating changes in spontaneous fetal loss depends, in part, on the assumption that change in late fetal loss will be accompanied by similar changes in early fetal loss. If early fetal loss, for some reason, was constant, while late fetal loss was variable, then our analysis would be of doubtful value. Tietze[41] has suggested that late fetal loss (and the racial difference in late fetal loss) is the result of environmental conditions that can change, while early fetal loss is the result of indigenous or other factors that are constant and presumably do not vary by race, an indicator that serves here as a proxy for the environmental factor. However, inspection of the Shapiro unpublished data[42] shows that racial differences in late fetal loss do not vanish as one moves to earlier gestation periods. In fact, the excess of nonwhite to white early fetal loss is greater than is the excess of late nonwhite to late white fetal loss.

---

* See P. Cutright, "Illegitimacy in the United States, 1920-1968," *op. cit.*, for details on procedures used in arriving at the 1940-1960 changes in spontaneous fetal loss.

41. C. Tietze, "Teenage Sexual Revolution," *Family Planning Perspectives*, 4:6 (April, 1972).

42. P. Cutright, "Reply to Tietze," *Family Planning Perspectives*, 4:6 (April, 1972).

Thus, although indigenous factors account for part of the total count of early as well as late fetal loss, environmental factors still may play a heavy role in early fetal loss.

THE DECLINE OF "FIRST CHILD STERILITY." Changes in involuntary sterility which prevents a first birth can be estimated from census data. In a review of these data, Farley argues that since very few married women wish to remain childless, changes in the percent of ever-married women who reach age forty-five without bearing a child can be used as a measure of change in this form of involuntary sterility. Farley's review of census data shows that only 6 or 8 percent of white and nonwhite married women who reached age forty-five around 1880 were childless. After 1880 childlessness increased rapidly—some 29 percent of nonwhite and 18 percent of white wives reaching age forty-five in the 1950-1954 period were childless.[43] Childlessness decreased rapidly after 1950-1954 and is expected to be about 6 percent among ever-married women aged forty-five in the 1970's.

If we compare the childlessness of women reaching age twenty in the 1940-1944 period with the expected childlessness of the 1970-1974 cohort age twenty, we find a decline of 12 percent childless among nonwhites and 5 percent among whites. The effect of this change and other measures of improved health on illegitimacy will be discussed later.

BREASTFEEDING AND ILLEGITIMACY. Gitta Meier[44] has suggested that a decline in breastfeeding after 1940 may be responsible for some part of the rise in illegitimacy, since prolonged breastfeeding lengthens the postpartum period of subfecundity. The component of the teenage illegitimacy rate that could be effected by a decline in breastfeeding would apply only to second and higher order births. Because around 90 percent of white and about 70 percent of nonwhite illegitimate births to women under twenty are first births,[45] most of the teenage illegitimate births could

43. R. Farley, *op. cit.*, pp. 109-111 and Table 4-5.

44. Private communication to the author, July 25, 1972.

45. National Center for Health Statistics, *Trends in Illegitimacy in the United States, 1940-1965* (Washington, D. C., Government Printing Office, 1968), Table 7.

not be influenced by a lactation variable. For the minority of births that might be affected, large effects could exist only if (1) the decline in breastfeeding were very large; (2) coital activity among parous unmarried women was high (thus leading to short birth intervals in the absence of breastfeeding; and (3) a large difference in pregnancy rates actually existed as a function of breast rather than bottle feeding.

Around 1960 some 43 percent of women breastfed their first child at some time.[46] Since we do not know what proportion of women breastfed after the first birth in 1940, but can assume that some portion did so, the decline is probably much less than 50 percent.* Ryder and Westoff[47] report that the central pregnancy rates in the first six months following birth among non-users of contraception was 890 among bottle-feeding and 557 among breastfeeding mothers. Pregnancy does occur frequently among noncontraceptors who are breastfeeding. Finally, pregnancy intervals are very wide between first and second illegitimate births. In one study the authors found that only 32 percent of young unwed mothers who did not later marry had a second birth within thirty-six months of the first birth.[48] Pregnancy intervals among fecund noncontraceptors are a function of coital frequency, while birth intervals in the same population will also be affected by patterns of fetal loss. One can estimate a variety of birth intervals for noncontracepting fecund women with varying levels of spontaneous or induced fetal loss and fecundability.[49] These birth intervals are very wide for the total population of unmarried women and will only be marginally reduced

---

46. N. B. Ryder and C. F. Westoff, *op. cit.,* p. 335.

* H. F. Myer, "Breast Feeding in the United States," *Clinical Pediatrics* (December, 1968) p. 709, reports a decline of 20 percentage points between 1946 and 1966 in the percentage of mothers breastfeeding on leaving the hospital.

47. *Ibid.,* Table XI-36. (Rates are for women with a first birth.)

48. F. Furstenberg, Jr., G. S. Masnick, and A. Rickets, "How Can Family Planning Programs Delay Repeat Teenage Pregnancies?" *Family Planning Perspectives,* 4: Table 1 (July, 1972).

49. R. G. Potter and J. M. Sakoda, "A Computer Model of Family Building Based on Expected Values," *Demography,* 3:450-461 (1966).

by changes in breastfeeding. Thus, we reject the hypothesis that a substantial shift in teenage illegitimacy rates after 1940 was caused by a decline in breastfeeding.

THE EFFECT OF IMPROVED HEALTH ON THE TREND IN TEENAGE ILLEGITIMACY. For women fifteen to nineteen we now ask, What would the 1940 illegitimacy rate have been had spontaneous fetal loss been no higher in 1940 than it was in 1960? What would the 1940 rate have been had girls been as fecund then as now? and What would the 1940 rate have been had the level of first child sterility been as low then as it is now? The results of these calculations are shown in Table I-III. To estimate the effect of declining fetal loss we multiply the observed number of 1940 illegitimate births by the *change* in the spontaneous fetal loss ratio. The effect of this adjustment is to increase the *expected* 1940 nonwhite rate by 23.2 and the white rate by 0.8 births per 1,000 unmarried teenagers, had 1960 rather than 1940 spontaneous fetal loss levels existed in 1940.

To estimate the effect of increasing fecundity due to a one year decline in the age of menarche we calculate (using more exact data than can be shown here) that 24 percent more girls aged fifteen to seventeen and just 2 percent more aged eighteen to nineteen were affected. When 1940 illegitimacy rates adjusted for spontaneous fetal loss are applied to the number of subfecund girls in 1940 that would have been fecund had the 1960 age at menarche been operative in 1940, we can calculate that the 1940 teenage rate was depressed by 9.6 for nonwhites and 0.6 for whites.

TABLE I-III

EFFECT OF HEALTH CONDITIONS IN 1940 RATHER THAN IN 1960'S
ON LOWERING 1940 TEENAGE ILLEGITIMATE RATES
PER 1,000 BY COLOR

| Color | Age | Health Conditions | | | Total |
		Higher Spontaneous Fetal Loss	Lower Teenage Fecundity	Higher First Child Sterility	
Nonwhite	15 to 19	−23.2	−9.6	−4.6	−37.4
White	15 to 19	− 0.8	−0.6	−0.2	− 1.6

TABLE I-IV

CHANGE IN 1940-1971 TEENAGE ILLEGITIMACY RATES PER 1,000
RELATED TO IMPROVED HEALTH AND OTHER
CAUSES, BY COLOR

Color	Age	Total Observed Change*	Health Related Change†	Nonhealth Causes	Percent of Change to Health Causes	Percent of Change to Nonhealth Causes
Nonwhite	15 to 19	43.6	37.4	6.2	86%	14%
White	15 to 19	8.6	1.6	7.0	19%	79%

* Observed changes are from Table I-I.
† These changes are from Table I-III.

To adjust for the higher 1940 levels of first child sterility we
first find the number of women in 1940 who were sterile that
would not have been sterile at 1940 levels of first child sterility.
Since this type of sterility primarily affects first births and 30 percent of nonwhite and 10 percent of white 1940 teenage births are
estimated to have been second or higher order births, the estimated number of added births to these hypothetically no longer
sterile women is reduced accordingly. Illegitimacy rates in 1940,
adjusted for spontaneous fetal loss and fecundity changes, are
applied to the number of women in 1940 who would have been
able to bear a first child had they enjoyed the 1940 level of first
child sterility. The number of added births to these women is
then reduced by 30 and 10 percent for nonwhites and whites, respectively, to account for second and higher order births. Table
I-III shows that the higher level of first child sterility in 1940
may have depressed the 1940 teenage rate by 4.6 among nonwhites
and 0.2 among whites.

The combined effect of health condition changes on depressing
the 1940 illegitimacy rate is 37.4 for nonwhites and 1.6 for
whites. Table I-IV compares the observed change in 1940-1971 illegitimacy rates with the change due to improved health. After
subtracting the health related change from the observed change,
we find that 6.2 of the 43.6 rate increase among nonwhites and

7.0 of the 8.6 rate increase among whites is *not* accounted for by improved health conditions. Since we discount a decline in contraceptive or induced abortion as factors that might explain this yet-to-be-explained component of the increased rates, it is likely that errors in adequately estimating the effect of improved health or increases in sexual activity are the most likely causes.

INCREASING NONMARITAL AND PREMARITAL COITUS. The magnitude of a change in nonmarital teenage sexual behavior, however, should not be over-estimated. In Table I-IV we see that even if we claim that all of the unaccounted for change is allocated to increased sexual activity, we are only talking about an increase in rates of 6.2 and 7.0 per 1,000 women for nonwhites and whites. When we think of these rates in percentage terms, rather than as rates per 1,000, we note that the increase supposedly due to sex affects just 0.6 and 0.7 percent more nonwhite and white teenagers in 1971 than was the case in 1940. Less than 1 percent more girls in either group are having an illegitimate child in 1971 as a result of higher coital activity in 1971 compared to 1940. Even if as many as one in five girls who are sexually active at some time during a year become pregnant, remain unmarried, and progress to term, the change in sexual activity implied by the change in illegitimate rate possibly related to higher coital activity would involve less than 4 percent of girls aged fifteen to nineteen.

A TEENAGE SEXUAL REVOLUTION? Thinking about changes in sexual activity among teenagers is facilitated by considering two types of sexually active unmarried girls. The first are those having nonmarital sex; these are in a sexual relationship that will not terminate in marriage. The second type are those having premarital sex; they will marry the sexual partner whether pregnant or not.

Increases in teenage illegitimacy rates have been paralleled by similar increases in the proportion of young brides already pregnant at the time of marriage. Between the early 1940's and the early 1960's, Census reports an increase in bridal pregnancy from 11 to 26 percent among young white brides and 33 to 40 percent among young nonwhite brides.[50]* If health conditions have been responsible for a similar proportion of the change in bridal pregnancy that we have allocated to illegitimacy, then about 12 percent of the total 15 percent point gain among whites is not related to health factors. Among nonwhites about 1 percent of the 7 percent increase in bridal pregnancy is related to nonhealth factors. The 12 percent increase in bridal pregnancy among white brides possibly due to increased premarital sex may be contrasted with the 0.7 percent fertility increase among whites who do not become brides. Among nonwhites there is little difference in the percent of brides pregnant and progressing to term and nonbrides pregnant and carrying the fetus to term that can be related to increased sex. In both cases the figure is 1 percent or less.

Among brides the percent of the sexually active who become pregnant and carry the fetus to term is higher than is the case among those having nonmarital sex. Data from a sample of white teenage brides married in Pennsylvania in 1967 indicate that half of teenage brides with premarital sex were pregnant at the time of marriage.† If this estimate applies to white teenage brides, the gain in bridal pregnancy related to increased sex

---

50. U. S. Bureau of the Census, Marriage, Fertility and Childspacing, June, 1965, *Current Population Reports,* Series P-20, No. 186 (Washington, D. C., Government Printing Office, 1969) , Tables 21 and 22.

* In theory the increase in the proportion of brides pregnant at marriage could reduce illegitimacy. Some writers have interpreted differences in illegitimacy rates as a function of differences among populations in the probability of legitimation of out-of-wedlock conceptions that are carried to term; such group differences are interpreted as the result of group differences in social stigma and related pressures. There is virtually no empirical support for this view and a good deal of evidence contradicts it. Therefore, we do not discuss legitimation of out-of-wedlock pregnancy by marriage as a cause of the level or trend in illegitimacy rates. For an elaboration of this view with some data see P. Cutright, "Illegitimacy in the United States, 1920-1968," *op. cit.,* pp. 403-407.

† Data from that study were generously given to me for analysis by Dr. Carlfred Broderick. Of the sixty teenage brides, fifty-one reported coitus before marriage and thirty said they were pregnant at marriage. The small size of this sample and its uncertain representativeness (50 percent were pregnant at marriage, a level of bridal pregnancy higher than that reported by other investigators using larger samples) suggest caution, hence our deflated estimate to 50 percent pregnant among the sexually active, rather than the observed level of nearly 60 percent.

would be multiplied by about two in order to calculate the increase in the percent of teenage brides with premarital sex between the 1940's and 1960's. This step results in an estimate of 12×2 or an absolute 24 percent increase in premarital sex among young white brides and a 2 percent gain for similar nonwhites. The 24 percent increase in coital activity among white brides-to-be may be contrasted to the possible 4 percent increase among those who do not become brides. Among nonwhites the difference is negligible. Thus, the teenage group apparently experiencing the largest gains in coitus after 1940 are white girls engaging in premarital sex with their future husbands.

It is possible that some decline in contraceptive use among young couples before and after marriage occurred after 1940, thus accounting for part of the increase in bridal pregnancy. Polgar[51] notes that the percent of white couples reporting use of contraception before the birth of their first child declined from 64 percent during the 1930's to 42 percent in the 1950's. The percent of young married white couples with no children reporting use increased from 42 percent in 1955 to 55 percent in 1960. The figure for 1965 was just 56 percent.[52] Ryder and Westoff reported still lower early use in 1965 than in 1941 in spite of differences between the two samples that tend to minimize the decline.

SOME REMOTE CAUSES OF ILLEGITIMACY

The study of immediate causes and their impact on illegitimacy rates does not explain *why* voluntary controls over conception or gestation have or have not changed; it merely documents change. Why has sexual activity increased at all? Why is the level what it is? In this concluding section we investigate some common theories put forward to explain illegitimacy rates in terms of urbanization, the AFDC program, and poverty. Changes in these remote causes of illegitimacy are tested to see if they explain the trend or racial differences.

URBAN AND RURAL DIFFERENCES IN TEENAGE ILLEGITIMACY. One explanation of the rise in illegitimacy in recent years has focused

---

51. S. Polgar, *op. cit.*, Table 1.
52. N. D. Ryder and C. F. Westoff, *op. cit.*, Table V-8.

on the movement of the American population from rural to urban areas. In particular, the movement of rural Negroes to urban areas has been seen as a contributing factor in the rise of nonwhite illegitimacy, presumably because the social constraints of the small rural community and rural values inhibit sexual intercourse and thus control illegitimacy. The transition to urban areas or, perhaps, simply living in ghetto areas of cities is thought to be conducive to high nonwhite illegitimacy rates.

Although we have no adequate measures of the impact of migration to urban areas on the migrant, we can compute urban and rural illegitimacy rates for states in which large numbers of nonwhites and whites still reside in rural areas. Outside the South there are no states with a large rural nonwhite population; therefore, the following analysis is restricted to whites and nonwhites in southern states for the year 1960.

Table I-V shows the mean age-specific illegitimacy rates by color for eight states, and the age-standardized rate for women fifteen to forty-four. We see, in the top panel, that the age standardized illegitimacy rates for nonwhites in rural and urban areas are nearly equal. Nonwhites remaining in rural areas seem little different from urban nonwhites, but when we look at teenage rates, an interesting pattern emerges. Among nonwhite teenagers in each of these states, urban rates were higher than the

TABLE I-V

URBAN AND RURAL ILLEGITIMACY RATES PER 1,000 BY COLOR
AND AGE OF MOTHER: EIGHT STATES, 1960*

Color	Place	Age of Mother	
		15 to 19	*15 to 44†*
Nonwhite	Urban	100.6	111.0
	Rural	76.6	109.2
	U/R ratio	131.3	101.6
White	Urban	7.2	9.5
	Rural	5.2	8.6
	U/R ratio	138.5	110.5

* Illegitimate births from *Vital Statistics of the United States, 1960,* Table 2.22. States included are Alabama, Florida, Louisiana, Mississippi, North Carolina, South Carolina, Texas, Virginia.
† Rates fifteen to forty-four are age standardized.

teenage rates in rural areas. For all eight states combined, the urban to rural ratio indicates an urban rate 31 percent higher than the rural teenage rate. It is likely that the higher urban rate means that a higher proportion of teenagers in urban than rural areas are having nonmarital sex—not that the teenage urban girl is less likely to use contraceptives or induced abortion. We conclude that one plausible effect of urban vs. rural residence in these states is to create a higher level of sexual activity among young urban nonwhites. Kantner and Zelnik[53] report 30 percent of farm, compared to 52 percent of lifetime urban nonwhite teenagers having coitus at some time.

Among whites the urban age standardized rate is about 10 percent higher than is the rural rate. The higher urban rate is entirely the result of much higher urban than rural teenage rates. We can probably attribute the higher urban teenage rate to higher rates of nonmarital coitus. For example, the 1971 survey[53] reports 9 percent of rural farm but 24 percent of urban teenagers having coitus at some time.

Table I-V only documents differences in teenage age rates by place of residence; it does not prove that rural to urban migrants are more likely than urban lifetime residents to have illegitimate children. Thus we have no evidence that urbanization is a factor in rising illegitimacy. A suggestion that migrants may have higher illegitimacy than girls who remain in rural places and also than lifetime urban residents is found in the 1971 survey. The percent of black and white girls who had lived on a farm at some time and had coitus was 69 percent and 32 percent, respectively.[53] These figures are well above the average for all teenage girls— 54 and 23 percent, respectively. On the other hand, only a small proportion of girls were migrants—12 percent of blacks and 9 percent of whites. Finally, 84 percent of white and black girls were urban residents in 1971. Thus urban location cannot explain much of the racial difference in teenage illegitimacy, although it is probably a factor that is related to variation among white and nonwhite teenage illegitimacy rates in the different states.

---

53. J. Kantner and M. Zelnik, *op. cit.*, Table 5.

AFDC AND ILLEGITIMACY IN THE UNITED STATES. Simple comparisons of the number of Aid to Families with Dependent Children (AFDC) families against the illegitimacy rate has little clear meaning because the illegitimacy rate measures illegitimacy for the unmarried population at risk, while the total count of AFDC families is not specific to the unmarried population at risk. There are numerous examples of years when illegitimacy rates increased while AFDC rolls were stable or in decline; also, we have examples of periods in which illegitimacy rates were stable or in decline while the number of AFDC families was rapidly increasing. If one used increases in numbers of AFDC families over short-run periods as a measure of changing access and use of AFDC by eligible female-headed families and saw such changes as a stimulus for illegitimacy, the historical record would provide comparisons that would either support or disprove the hypothesis that increased access and use of AFDC will increase illegitimacy rates.

THE EFFECT OF ILLEGITIMACY ON AFDC: 1961-1969. In 1961 there were 649,000 illegitimate children on AFDC; the number had risen to about 1.6 million in 1969. Of the increase of 951,-000, about 26 percent was due simply to the increase in the *number* of illegitimate children* under eighteen years of age between 1961 and 1969, and 74 percent to greater use of AFDC in 1969 as compared with 1961.[54]

In May 1969, the monthly AFDC benefit per recipient was about $45.16. Applying this figure to gauge the annual cost of AFDC benefits for unwed mothers and illegitimate children results in an estimate of about 1.1 billion dollars in 1969. This was about one-third the benefit cost of the AFDC program in 1969.[55]

THE EFFECT OF AFDC ON ILLEGITIMACY: 1940-1970. To find that illegitimacy will affect the cost of the AFDC program does not mean that the program will be a cause of illegitimacy. Although this explanation for the rise in illegitimacy rates since

---

* Deceased, legitimated, and adopted illegitimate children not included.

54. P. Cutright, "Illegitimacy in the United States, 1920-1968," *op. cit.*, Table 24.

55. P. Cutright, *Studies in Public Welfare, No. 12, Part 1*, Illegitimacy and Income Supplements, Joint Economic Committee of the Congress, Subcommittee on Fiscal Policy (Washington, D. C., Government Printing Office, 1973) .

1940 is popular, little systematic effort to test the hypothesis exists.

Adequate testing of the AFDC program as a cause of illegitimacy cannot readily use national trend data that would relate benefit levels and changing benefits to illegitimacy rates. This is true because the AFDC benefit varies greatly among the states, a fact that requires use of state illegitimacy rates and state benefit data. This complication, however, provides the analyst with the means for more adequate testing of program effects, because the variation among the states in benefits is great. We begin by first testing the view that changes in state illegitimacy rates between 1940 and 1950 were related to changes in state AFDC benefits.

BENEFIT CHANGE AND ILLEGITIMACY RATE CHANGE: 1940-1970

Eighteen states have sufficiently large numbers of nonwhites and whites as well as illegitimacy data for 1940, 1950, and 1960 to allow computation of state color-specific illegitimacy rates.

TABLE I-VI

PATTERN OF CHANGE IN AFDC BENEFITS* AND CHANGE IN
ILLEGITIMACY RATES† PER 1,000 BY COLOR, 1940-1960

Change in Annual AFDC Benefit Per Recipient		Change in Illegitimacy Rate Per 1,000 Aged 15-44, 1940 to 1960	
1940-50	1950-60	White	Nonwhite
High	High‡	4.3	61.9
Low	High§	5.5	58.1
High	Low‖	5.9	63.9
Low	Low¶	2.7	64.0

* Benefit data by states from U. S. *Social Security Bulletin,* various years adjusted to 1958 dollars. "Large" benefit gain between both periods was $51 or higher, with a mean gain in "large gain" states of $92 (compared to $23 in small gain states) between 1940 and 1950. Mean gain in large gain states between 1950 and 1960 was $89 compared to $19 in the small gain states. A change in the annual benefit per recipient of, say, $51 means that the annual benefit at the end of the decade period was $51 a year higher than it was at the beginning of the decade.

† State illegitimacy rates are age-standardized and were calculated from state birth data, adjusted for underregistration of births and census counts for unmarried women 15 to 44.

‡ Virginia, West Virginia, Illinois, New Jersey.

§ Kentucky, Louisiana, North Carolina, Ohio, District of Columbia.

‖ Florida, Tennessee, Texas, Pennsylvania, Michigan.

¶ Alabama, Missouri, Mississippi, South Carolina.

The analysis of change over the years in these states compares changes in age-standardized illegitimacy rates for whites and non-whites among states with large or small benefit changes between 1940-1949 and 1950-59. In Table I-VI four types of states are distinguished—those with (1) consistently high benefit changes, (2) those with high then low changes, (3) those with low then high changes, and (4) those with consistently low benefit changes. These figures reveal no steady effect of the pattern of benefit change and illegitimacy rate change. There is no relationship between changing benefit levels and changes in illegitimacy rates. For example, nonwhite rates in states with consistently rising benefits increased by about 62, while the rates in states with consistently low benefit changes increased by 64.

AFDC BENEFITS AND ILLEGITMACY: 1960 AND 1970

State illegitimacy rates in 1960 and 1970 may be compared only after married but separated women are included in the denominator along with single, widowed, and divorced women. Rather than using age-standardized data we are, for the first time, able to show the teenage rate distinct from the rate for women fifteen to forty-four.

From Table I-VII we conclude that no effect of AFDC benefits on illegitimacy rates existed among whites in 1960. For nonwhite women the middle stratum tends to have higher rates than either the highest or the lowest stratum. Part of this effect may be due to the inclusion of Delaware in the middle stratum; its rates may be somewhat unreliable because it has little more than 5,000 non-white women in the population at risk. A second row for the middle stratum is shown with Delaware excluded. Comparing the highest with the lowest stratum we find equal teenage rates and rates for women aged fifteen to forty-four lower in the high- than in the low-benefit states. The fact that the high-benefit states in 1960 have lower illegitimacy rates for women fifteen to forty-four does not suggest that the high AFDC benefit is a direct cause of lower illegitimacy.

The level of benefits in 1970 and average illegitimacy rates by age and color for all states for which such figures are available are shown in Table I-VIII. The comparisons between extreme states should make one exceedingly wary of assuming that Table I-VIII confirms the hypothesis that the 1970 nonwhite teenage rate is higher in high- than in low-benefit states because the benefit levels differ.

Among the factors left uncontrolled in the preceding analysis are differences among states in urban or rural residence, a characteristic which was associated with teenage illegitimacy rates among both whites and nonwhites in 1960. No similar data for 1970 are available, but there seems little reason to believe that the effect of being in an urban vs. a rural location diminished between 1960 and 1970. Some portion of the difference in teenage

TABLE I-VII

ILLEGITIMACY RATES PER 1,000 AND AFDC MONTHLY FAMILY BENEFITS,* BY AGE AND COLOR: 1960

1960 AFDC Benefit	Mean Monthly Benefit	Number of States	Illegitimacy Rates, by Age	
			15 to 19	15 to 44
		White		
High†	$180	8	7.1	9.0
Middle‡	$116	9	7.8	10.2
Low§	$ 74	9	6.9	8.9
		Nonwhite		
High†	$159	6	93.9	71.6
Middle‡	$102	7	98.1	90.1
	($103)	(6)	(86.0)	(82.3)
Low§	$ 67	7	93.6	89.9

* Monthly family benefits in 1967 dollars.

† For whites, high benefit states are District of Columbia, Iowa, Illinois, New Jersey, Minnesota, Oregon, Washington, and Wisconsin..

For nonwhites, high benefit states are District of Columbia, Illinois, New Jersey, Michigan, Pennsylvania, and Indiana.

‡ For whites, middle benefit states are Michigan, Pennsylvania, South Dakota, Indiana, Louisiana, West Virginia, Virginia, Missouri, and Delaware.

For nonwhites, middle benefit states are Louisiana, West Virginia, Virginia, Missouri, Delaware, Georgia, and Kentucky.

§ For whites, low benefit states are Georgia, Kentucky, North Carolina, South Carolina, Tennessee, Texas, Florida, Alabama, and Mississippi.

For nonwhites, low benefit states are North Carolina, South Carolina, Tennessee, Texas, Florida, Alabama, and Mississippi.

TABLE I-VIII

ILLEGITIMACY RATES PER 1,000 BY AFDC MONTHLY FAMILY
BENEFITS, BY AGE AND COLOR: 1970*

1970 AFDC Benefit	Mean Monthly Benefit*	Number of States With Age-Specific Data	Illegitimacy Rates, by Age	
			15 to 19	15 to 44
		White		
High	$193	8	11.1	13.5†
Middle	$120	9	12.9	15.1‡
Low	$ 71	8	9.7	10.9
		Nonwhite		
High	$189	6	118.0	82.9†
Middle	$101	6	103.7	80.4§
Low	$ 68	7	92.2	80.9
Extreme States		*White*		
Highest	$218	N. J.	7.5	9.4
Lowest	$ 40	Miss.	8.7	9.6
		Nonwhite		
Highest	$218	N. J.	116.0	81.7
Lowest	$ 40	Miss.	98.8	107.6

* Based on 1967 dollar evaluation.
† Includes one state lacking age-specific data.
‡ Includes five states lacking age-specific data.
§ Includes three states lacking age-specific data.
N.B. For whites the high-benefit states are New Jersey, Illinois Minnesota, New Hampshire, Wisconsin, Michigan, District of Columbia, South Dakota, Pennsylvania, and Washington; middle-benefit are Iowa, Virginia, West Virginia, Oregon, Delaware, Arizona, Texas, North Carolina, Kentucky, Colorado, Nebraska, Indiana, Oklahoma, and Missouri; low-benefit are Tennessee, Georgia, Arkansas, Florida, Louisiana, South Carolina, Alabama, and Mississippi.

For nonwhites the high-benefit states are New Jersey, Illinois, Wisconsin, Michigan, District of Columbia, Virginia, Pennsylvania; middle-benefit are Delaware, Texas, North Carolina, Kentucky, West Virginia, Tennessee, Nebraska, Indiana and Missouri; low benefit are Alabama, Arkansas, Georgia, Florida, South Carolina, Mississippi.

illegitimacy between high and low benefit states in 1970 may be a function of urbanization.*

Table I-VIII indicates that the 1970 rates of teenage illegitimacy, higher in high- than low-benefit states, are not accompanied

* The note to Table I-VIII lists the states in the various benefit strata. Clearly nonwhites in high benefit states are nearly all urban while those in the southern low benefit states are more likely to be in rural areas.

by a similar difference among older women. If older women are not stimulated by high benefits, why should one expect teenagers to be affected by benefit levels? Similarly, if younger whites and older whites and nonwhites are not affected by benefits, why should one think that only young nonwhites would respond to high benefits in 1970? Why did this group not have a similar response in 1960? We are forced to conclude that the cause of the difference in nonwhite teenage rates between high- and low-benefit states in 1970 must be found in differences between the two types of states that are not a function of the AFDC program and that variation among the states in AFDC benefit levels are not a cause of state difference in illegitimacy rates. Although illegitimacy is a major cause of AFDC expenditures, the program is not a cause of illegitimacy.

WHY BENEFITS DO NOT CAUSE ILLEGITIMATE BIRTHS. Recent studies on economic explanations of fertility develop the theory that income (measured in a variety of ways) and fertility should be positively related because children cost money.[56, 57] Since a program such as AFDC assumes the most obvious costs of childrearing, a naive view would argue that by moving the costs of illegitimacy toward zero, the program will stimulate illegitimacy. Since our analysis indicates that this is not the case, we must ask why the economic theory fails.

The economic theory of fertility is qualified by the provision that it will work only when childbearing is rational and deliberate, i.e. under conditions of perfect control over fertility. Since this condition is not at all true in the case of most illegitimate births, there is no reason to believe that a plausible basis for an economic theory of illegitimate fertility exists. Thus, an effort to control illegitimacy by cracking down on welfare is unlikely to have any more effect in the future than similar efforts have had in the past. It is also important to point out that increasing AFDC benefits will probably not reduce illegitimacy rates.

---

56. W. C. Robinson and D. E. Horlacher, "Population Growth and Economic Welfare," *Reports on Population/Family Planning*, New York, Population Council (February, 1971), pp. 1-39.

57. G. Cain, *Issues in the Economics of a Population Policy for the United States*, Madison, Wisconsin, Institute for Research on Poverty (Mimeo, 1971).

THE EFFECT OF AFDC ON REDUCING PUNISHMENTS
RELATED TO ILLEGITIMACY

Thinking about the possible effects of AFDC or guaranteed income supplements on illegitimate childbearing may be clarified by comparing the effect of alternative public programs and private efforts on reducing the different types of negative sanctions related to illegitimacy. Table I-IX lists the more prominent types of punishments, social and economic. The degree to which each punishment will be experienced by the pregnant unmarried women or the unwed mother will vary according to her age and economic status at the time of pregnancy.

If the woman does not experience pregnancy and illegitimate childbirth she will not be sanctioned, unless the economic reward for illegitimate childbearing exceeds the reward for avoiding it. Even if economic status were improved for a poor young woman, a glance at the other consequences of illegitimacy suggests that the net effect would still be negative. Table I-IX indicates that at present there is no way to assess the relative importance of one or another punishment. For example, use of birth control or abstinence means that illegitimacy is avoided. Thus the consequence

TABLE I-IX

EFFECT OF BIRTH CONTROL, INCOME SUPPLEMENTS, AND RELEASE
OF ILLEGITIMATE CHILD ON PUNISHMENTS FOR THE UNWED MOTHER

Types of Punishment	*Birth Control or Abstinence*	*Income Supplements*	*Adoption or Release*
Negative effects during pregnancy and childbirth	—*	0†	0
Sole responsibility for 16 to 18 years of child care	—	0	—
Social sanctions related to unwed status	—	0	0
Declining chance for marriage	—	0	—
High risk of female family head status	—	0	—
Declining economic status during pregnancy	—	0	0
Lower economic status after birth	Varies‡	Varies‡	Varies‡
Increase in poverty gap due to added children	—	Varies‡	—

* Indicates strong relief from the punishment.

† Indicates no effect on the punishment.

‡ Indicates that the risk of lower economic status after birth is a risk dependent on the economic status prior to the birth, the likely future economic status had the birth not occurred, and the size of child benefits offered by the income supplement program.

is to eliminate all the effects of illegitimacy (expressed by the negative signs). The same elimination of effects of some punishments can be obtained if the woman releases the child for adoption. This course of action, primarily used by whites rather than nonwhites, allows the unwed mother to avoid the sanction of sixteen to eighteen years of sole responsibility for child care, puts her back into the marriage market, and allows her to avoid the status of female head of a family or subfamily. In most cases release of the child for adoption also allows the low income unwed mother to avoid a decline in economic status. Avoiding childbirth or giving up the child allows women above the income supplement line to maintain their economic position. AFDC or other income supplements cannot affect this group.

Giving up a child after birth has no effect on social sanction related to illegitimacy, the negative feelings and material effects experienced during pregnancy and childbirth, or likely wage loss during pregnancy.

In contrast, AFDC or an alternative income supplement program can have no effect on any punishments except those involving the decline in economic position for women whose prepregnancy income was low enough to allow them to improve their economic status by bearing a child. Even so, the income supplement for this group of unwed mothers does not remove the sanction of sole responsibility for child care over a period of sixteen years or more. It does nothing to improve the woman's chances for marriage and normal family life, nor does it affect the other negative consequences of unwed motherhood.

From this perspective, AFDC or any plausible income supplement program can only alleviate some immediate and longer term economic consequences of bearing an illegitimate child. This does not suggest that future amelioration of the economic consequences for low-income women will stimulate illegitimacy, any more than that past alleviation through the AFDC program has stimulated it.*

---

* Hypothetical effects of AFDC on increasing female family headship by reducing adoption or legitimation of children by marriage are rejected elsewhere. (See P. Cutright, *Studies in Public Welfare, No. 12, Part I, op. cit.*) It is unlikely that the AFDC program reduces the use of birth control or increases sexual activity, thus promoting illegitimacy.

POVERTY, INCOME AND TEENAGE ILLEGITIMACY

In all populations for which illegitimacy rates by economic groups exist or can be inferred, the lower economic groups have higher illegitimacy rates than do groups with superior economic status. The United States is no exception.

Although a national survey of the economic status of unwed teenage mothers at the time of birth does not exist, it is possible to provide rough estimates. We can then calculate approximate teenage illegitimacy rates by color and economic status and thus test the hypothesis that differences in the illegitimacy rates among color groups are a function of the economic status of these subsets of the U. S. population of unmarried women.

A study of the percent of 1967 births in California[58] for which medical expenses were paid from public funds, provides the first set of data. For example, 51 percent of teenage white illegitimate, but only 19 percent of teenage white legitimate births had medical costs paid from public funds. Among blacks, 77 percent of teenage illegitimate and 55 percent of teenage legitimate births were paid from public funds. Because public financing of births is restricted to the low-income population, it is clear that teenage unwed mothers are more likely than wed teenage mothers to be poor, hence eligible for public payment for the medical costs of their births. A second interesting pattern is that among both blacks and whites, the likelihood of having a birth paid from public funds declines with increasing age among wed mothers but remains constant among unwed mothers. The younger unwed mother is about as likely as her older counterpart to be poor, while the older the married woman, the less likely she is to be poor. This interpretation is supported by direct national measures of the poverty status of married and unmarried women.[59]

The California data may underestimate the percent of teenage unwed mothers who are poor. First, it is unlikely that every poor unwed mother delivering in California in 1967 had her birth

---

58. B. Berkov, "Illegitimacy Fertility in California's Population," in K. Davis and F. Styles, *California's Twenty Million* (Calif., Institute of International Studies, 1971) , Table 5.

59. P. Cutright, "Illegitimacy in the United States, 1920-1968," *op. cit.*, Appendix A.

paid from public funds. Second, it is unlikely that any appreciable number of nonpoor unwed mothers had their births paid from public funds. Third, the economic status of California is well above that of the nation, and one might expect that a smaller proportion of California's unwed mothers would be poor than is the case in the nation as a whole.

Thus, we would expect that an alternative estimate of the poverty status of unwed mothers would be somewhat higher than that indicated above. Campbell[60] estimated that 62 percent of white and 82 percent of nonwhite illegitimate births in the years 1960-1965 were to mothers below the poverty line. In the following analysis we estimated that 60 percent of white and 80 percent of nonwhite illegitimate births to teenagers in the 1964-1966 period were to girls below the poverty line. From the 1967 Survey of Economic Opportunity we tabulated the number of unmarried women, by age, color, and 1966 poverty status. The economic status of unmarried women, when applied to our estimates of the number unmarried in 1965, provides the appropriate denominator from which illegitimacy rates can be estimated for each economic group.

THE EFFECT OF POVERTY STATUS ON RACIAL DIFFERENCES IN ILLEGITIMACY

Table I-X shows the illegitimacy rates before and after standardization for poverty. The difference between the observed white and nonwhite rates is 64.6; this difference would be expected to decline to 35.4 if nonwhites shared equal economic status with that enjoyed by whites. If poverty status were equal for the two racial groups, we would expect the nonwhite rate would decline from 72.4 to 43.2, a decline of 29.2 or 40.4 percent of the observed nonwhite rate. Put another way, about 45 percent (29.2/64.6) of the observed racial difference in 1964-1966 is directly related to the higher risk of poverty in the nonwhite population.

---

60. A. A. Campbell, "The Role of Family Planning in the Reduction of Poverty," *Journal of Marriage and the Family* (May, 1968) , p. 30. Tables A-1 and B-1, median estimates.

TABLE I-X

TEENAGE ILLEGITIMACY RATES PER 1,000 BEFORE AND AFTER
STANDARDIZATION FOR POVERTY, BY COLOR: UNITED STATES, 1964-66

Color	Poverty Status Low Income	Nonpoor	Total
Percent of unmarried women 15 to 19			
White	14.0	86.0	100.0
Nonwhite	56.8	43.2	100.0
Observed illegitimacy rate per 1,000 15 to 19			
White	33.5	3.6	7.8
Nonwhite	101.9	33.6	72.4
Expected nonwhite rate with white poverty distribution			
Nonwhite	101.9	33.6	43.2

One might expect that in the process of actually moving to equality of poverty status the nonwhite poverty specific rates would also decline, rather than remain fixed at the current level, as we have assumed in this exercise. Table I-X documents large differences in illegitimacy rates among teenagers who were poor and those not poor. We do not expect the problem of teenage illegitimacy to disappear with further gains in income. The reason for this apparent contradiction is that the post World War II period has seen an enormous reduction in the proportion of the population living below the poverty line, while simultaneously being a period of rising teenage illegitimacy rates. Further gain in family income, with the resulting decline in the percent of white or nonwhite teenagers living below a fixed poverty line, does not lead to the prediction that the illegitimacy rate to white or nonwhite teenagers will decline.

CHANGES IN THE ECONOMIC STATUS OF WHITES AND BLACKS: 1950-1970. For example, using the percent of white families living below a fixed poverty line (defined as the percent with less than $3,000 a year, corrected for price changes), we find that 20 percent of white families in 1950, but only slightly over 7 percent in 1970, had this little income. Similarly, the proportion of nonwhite families below this line declined from 50 percent in 1950 to 20 percent in 1970. The same percentage of black families had less than $3,000 in 1970 as we found for whites in

1950.[61] Both white and nonwhite illegitimacy rates increased over this period.

Corrected for price changes the median black family income was $6,516 in 1970 compared to $3,014 in 1950, an increase of $3,502. The median white family income in 1970 was $10,236 compared to $5,601 in 1950, an increase of $4,635. Although the black median income more than doubled, the gap between the purchasing power of the average black compared to white family increased; the median white family had $2,587 more than the median black family income in 1950. By 1970 the advantage of the white had increased to $3,720.[61]

RELATIVE INCOMES. In sum, the trend in white and black income since 1950 can be used to prove that economic position of both whites and blacks has dramatically improved or that the position of blacks relative to whites has become worse. The latter conclusion is based on the widening difference in purchasing power between the average white and the average black family. If blacks view income in the same way as whites do, it would be reasonable for them to see their rising purchasing power in a relative perspective and consider their position relative to whites as becoming poorer.

Since World War II, Gallup polls have repeatedly asked adults to estimate the smallest amount of money a family of four needs to get along in the respondents' community. Whites and blacks in similar communities give similar responses, a finding that should not surprise anyone. What is surprising is that this estimated smallest amount of money is constantly going up. The public does not define poverty in terms of a fixed measure of poverty. The public definition of poverty moves with the trend in median family incomes. Whatever the median, the smallest amount of money needed to avoid poverty will be about 60 percent of that median.[62] This finding is of potential importance in understanding the relationship of poverty, income, and income distribution to illegitimacy rates.

---

61. *Economic Report of the President,* 1972 (Washington, D. C., Government Printing Office, 1972), Table B-20.

62. L. Rainwater, *It's a Living* (forthcoming), for analysis of Gallup polls and related data on relative income.

In the case of white and nonwhite differences in illegitimacy the trend in economic status of the two populations over the years suggests a decline in the relative economic position of black compared to white incomes. Therefore if relative economic position in some way acts to determine illegitimacy rates, there is no reason to expect that the trend in the difference between white and nonwhite illegitimacy since 1950 should be other than what we have observed. Among teenagers, the differences have increased rather than decreased.

The same perspective can be used to consider differential rates within the white and the black population. As Table I-X shows, the rates within each population are much higher for the lower than the higher income groups. Within the white and nonwhite population and for the population as a whole, one measure of relative economic status suggested by the Gallop poll would calculate the percentage of families that lived below 60 percent of median family income in each year. This would measure the percent of families defined by the public (and themselves) as being poor. A measure using the percent with less than 50 percent of median family income is available since 1947.[63] Since 1947 the percent of families with less than half the median income has not changed; in each year it is about 20 percent of all families. The lowest fifth of all families consistently are found to share about 5 percent of all money income in a given year.[64] The income of the lowest fifth of families has continually fallen further behind the purchasing power of the average family. This is true within the white and nonwhite population. Therefore, the lowest fifth of whites and nonwhites in 1970 are further behind the median income than was the lowest fifth of whites and nonwhites in 1950 or earlier years. Thus, not only has the percentage of families defined as poor not changed, but their economic position relative to that of average families has become worse. If teenage illegitimacy rates are, in some way, linked to the relative economic position of the teenager's family or racial group, then the trend in relative incomes would suggest that both

63. President's Commission on Income Maintenance Programs, *Poverty amid Plenty* (Washington, D. C., Government Printing Office, 1969), Table 3-4.
64. *Ibid.*, Table 3-2.

white and nonwhite teenage rates should increase rather than decline.

To reduce permanently the racial difference in teenage illegitimacy we would argue that a large improvement in the economic position of blacks relative to that of average whites will be required. This movement must be perceived as real by the black population. This last point suggests that the black teenager's view of the future will have to change along with an economic shift if the expected decline in illegitimacy rates is to occur. Much the same applies to any change in the illegitimacy rates of low income whites that might be expected to follow from a more favorable economic position of that group's economic status relative to that of the average white.

In this chapter our main emphasis has been on noneconomic factors—changes in health conditions. Aside from health conditions, the noneconomic factors that are largely responsible for racial differences in teenage illegitimacy in 1940 as well as in 1971 can be grouped together under what may be called the "culture of fertility regulation." The degree to which young white or nonwhite unmarried persons have a strong or relatively weak culture of fertility regulation is related to historical and current social and economic arrangements.

The concept of a culture of fertility regulation refers to male and female behaviors that control illegitimate as well as legitimate childbearing. One component is the degree to which a population feels it can control fertility. A second component stems from the extent to which a population has access to and effective use of the available means through which fertility is regulated by the sexually active. A third component has to do with the number of children women want to bear. More subtle aspects of the culture of fertility regulation are measured by male and female orientations about themselves, each other, and toward children.[65]

In 1970 there was only a 3 percent difference between young

---

65. J. Scanzoni and M. McMurry, "Continuities in the Explanation of Fertility Control," *Journal of Marriage and the Family*, 34:312-322 (May, 1972).

white and black wives in the percent not using contraception.[66] Black wives aged twenty-four or under expect to have 2.4 children compared to 2.2 among white wives.[67] These small differences among married whites and blacks mask a host of more subtle differences between the two populations that affect the culture of fertility regulation outside marriage.

The causes of this racial difference are historical. The deliberate and effective reduction of fertility in the white population began around 1820;[68, 69] for nonwhites the spread of effective birth control practices occurred after 1940, more than a century later. Nonwhite women entering childbearing years in the 1980's will be the first generation whose mothers practiced contraception, though somewhat less effectively, at a level similar to that of whites. It takes time for a cultural pattern regarding birth control and careful control over legitimate and illegitimate childbearing to develop. Earlier age at entry to sexual unions, a higher proportion of the unmarried involved in nonmarital sex, and ineffective use of birth control indicate a weak culture of fertility regulation outside of marriage.

Illegitimacy rates are vulnerable to change from demographic and economic factors.[70] This should not obscure the point that differences among populations on the components of the culture of fertility regulation probably explain more of the differences among populations' illegitimacy rates at a given time than do differences on economic and demographic characteristics.

---

66. C. F. Westoff, "The Modernization of U. S. Contraceptive Practice." *Family Planning Perspectives*, 3: Table 2 (July, 1972).

67. U. S. Bureau of the Census. "Birth Expectations and Fertility: June 1972," *Current Population Reports*, Series P-20, No. 240 (September 1972), Table 1.

68. D. Heer, *Society and Population* (Englewood Cliffs, N. J., Prentice-Hall, Inc., 1968), p. 51.

69. A. J. Coale and N. W. Rivers, A Statistical Reconstruction of the Black Population of the United States 1880-1970; Estimates of True Numbers by Age and Sex, Birth Rates and Total Fertility. *Population Index* 39 (January, 1973), pp. 3-36.

70. P. Cutright, "Illegitimacy: Myths, Causes and Cures," *Family Planning Perspectives*, 3: Table 2 (January, 1971).

CONCLUSION

Racial differences in the culture of fertility regulation are one consequence of the history of social and economic subordination of the nonwhite by the white population. Discrimination not only increases the economic difference between whites and nonwhites, but it also perpetuates differences in the culture of fertility regulation.

The enormous declines in nonwhite marital fertility since 1960 have recently been followed by large declines in illegitimacy rates of unmarried nonwhites twenty and older.[71] These trends are caused by the adoption of effective means of fertility regulation, which is a sign that may predict some decline in nonwhite teenage illegitimacy in the years ahead. However, achievement of a long run goal of diminishing white and nonwhite differences in teenage illegitimacy and reducing the illegitimacy rates of lower income groups within each population will depend, not only on the spread of the culture of fertility regulation, but on a shift toward a more equal distribution of income as well. At present there is little reason to believe that the distribution of income within the white or nonwhite population will change.

---

71. P. Cutright, "Illegitimacy in the United States, 1920-1968," *op. cit.*, Table 2.

CHAPTER II

TEENAGE ILLEGITIMACY: THE PROSPECT FOR DELIBERATE CHANGE

Phillips Cutright

THIS CHAPTER PROVIDES an overview of economic, demographic, and social factors that affect the probable impact of deliberate efforts by organized groups to reduce teenage illegitimacy in the United States. After eliminating a number of policies and programs that might be considered as steps through which teenage illegitimacy could be reduced, we turn our attention to efforts to reduce illegitimacy through contraception. The probable success of contraception-only programs is assessed with intuitive and empirical evidence. The probable impact of contraceptive programs on teenage illegitimacy under a variety of hypothetical conditions is calculated with the aid of a simple mathematical model. Some attention is directed to the probable impact of abortion on illegitimacy.

SOME POLICIES AND PROGRAMS THAT NEED NOT BE CONSIDERED

The most common sociological explanation of illegitimacy sees the rate as a function of norms that affect the degree of stigma attached to the illegitimate birth and norms that are believed to govern the level of premarital sexual activity. There is no evidence that these norms actually do determine the rate, and some data indicate that they are not of overwhelming importance.[1] There seems to be little point in further discussion of this view

1. D. Johnson and P. Cutright, "Problems in the Analysis of Latin American Illegitimacy," in M. Armer and A. Grimshaw (eds.), *Comparative Social Research: Methodological Problems and Strategies* (New York, John Wiley & Sons, 1973). P. Cutright, *Illegitimacy: Measurement and Analysis* (Cambridge, Mass., Joint Center for Urban Studies of M.I.T. and Harvard Universities, 1970), Chapter 7. P. Cutright, "Illegitimacy: Myths, Causes and Cures," *Family Planning Perspectives*, 3:30-31 (January, 1971).

47

of illegitimacy, since no one has any practical ideas on how they would change the norms—and hence the illegitimacy rate.

Our analysis of the relationship of Aid to Families with Dependent Children (AFDC) benefits to illegitimacy allows us to reject a policy that would seek to control illegitimacy by reducing AFDC benefits.[2]

Efforts to force more responsibility on unwed mothers by, perhaps, making it more difficult to release the child for adoption are unlikely to have any impact. This option is not available to nonwhites, for example, but is available to whites. There is nothing in the comparison of white and nonwhite illegitimacy over time to indicate that the "sanction of sole responsibility" deters illegitimacy.

Analysis of historical trends and changes in illegitimacy rates in developed nations after World War II indicate that illegitimacy rates often move up or down with changing birth control practices by married couples, with shifts in the age at marriage, with changes in the age of legitimate childbearing, with the rate of economic growth and perhaps, with changes in the enrollment of women in higher education.[3] While interesting, such findings do not appear to have immediate policy implications, because changes in these macrodemographic and economic events do not always produce the desired change in illegitimacy; they do not move illegitimacy to acceptable low levels; and, it is unrealistic to believe that the rate of economic growth, childspacing patterns among married couples, or the age at marriage can or will

---

2. P. Cutright, "The Rise of Teenage Illegitimacy in the United States: 1940-1971," Chapter 1, this volume. P. Cutright, *Illegitimacy and Income Supplements*, Reports of the Joint Economic Committee, Subcommittee on Fiscal Policy, United States Congress (Washington D. C., U. S. Government Printing Office, 1973). P. Cutright, "Economic Events and Illegitimacy in Developed Countries, *Journal of Comparative Family Studies*, 2:33-53 (Spring, 1971.

3. P. Cutright, "Historical and Contemporary Trends in Illegitimacy," *Archives of Sexual Behavior*, No. 2, 2:97-118 (1972). E. Shorter, "Illegitimacy Sexual Revolution and Social Change in Modern Europe," *Journal of Interdisciplinary History*, 2:237-272 (1971). E. Shorter, J. Knodel, and E. van de Walle, "The Decline of Non-marital Fertility in Europe: 1880-1940," *Population Studies*, 25:375-393 (November, 1971). P. Cutright, "Illegitimacy: Myths, Causes and Cures," *op. cit.*, Table 2.

be changed by government activity, simply because a reduction in the illegitimacy rate is desired.

It is unlikely that school-based contraceptive education programs can be introduced on a nation-wide scale. Such programs would do nothing to reduce illegitimacy among women already in their childbearing years. Also, we examined such evidence as was available and concluded that these education programs do not increase control over illegitimacy among students that were exposed to them.[4]

Public programs aimed directly at one or more of the immediate causes of the illegitimacy rate can also be assessed. First, no one has the vaguest idea of how to decrease sexual activity that results in illegitimate births. Second, the proportion of out-of-wedlock conceived births that are legitimated by marriage cannot (and should not) be increased through public policy. Third, a deliberate reduction of public health programs to increase spontaneous abortion and involuntary sterility is unthinkable. This process of elimination leaves us with only two remaining causes —voluntary control over conception and voluntary control over gestation. We first consider the view that contraception-only programs can have a significant impact on illegitimacy and then consider the likely impact of adding abortion on request to public programs.

ARE ILLEGITIMATE BIRTHS WANTED BIRTHS?

Before any voluntary family planning program can effectively reduce illegitimacy it must enlist the cooperative efforts of sexually active unmarried women. If it were the case that most illegitimate births were deliberate, then the prospects for a successful program would indeed be dim. By asking married women whether their births were wanted or unwanted, national surveys now provide estimates of the numbers of legitimate children that might not have been born had their parents had access to a

---

4. P. Cutright, "Illegitimacy: Myths, Causes and Cures," *op. cit.*, pp. 38-39. F. Furstenberg, Jr., C. Masnick and S. Ricketts, "How Can Family Planning Programs Prevent Repeat Pregnancies?" *Family Planning Perspectives*, 4:54-60 (July, 1972).

perfect contraceptive.[5] There have been no similar national surveys of unmarried mothers. In considering the probable maximum effect of a program that would allow women to bear only wanted children, one cannot reject out-of-hand the claim that some unmarried women deliberately conceive through nonuse of contraception.

Data on the "wanted" status of illegitimate births is fragmentary. The only study in which a large number of mothers of illegitimate children from a known population were directly asked whether they wanted their children is that of Greenleigh and associates. Their interviews with Negro women on AFDC in Chicago[6] found that 90 percent of mothers with illegitimate children defined the births as unwanted. This figure may or may not be an accurate representation of unwanted illegitimate births for the total population of mothers. However, in view of the recent finding that 52 percent of all Negro wives not trying to become pregnant reported their last (legitimate) birth as unwanted, the 90 percent figure for indigent unmarried Negro women may not be excessive.[7]

Several additional (though less direct) sources can be used to provide measures of the proportion of illegitimate white and black children that are unwanted. Some 60 to 70 percent of white unwed mothers give up their child for adoption, a decision that may be used as a measure of the extent to which the woman wanted the child. Among nonwhites, the lack of an adoption market renders nonwhite adoption figures meaningless.[8]

The only effort to interview a large and representative sample of white and nonwhite unwed mothers is that reported by Bower-

5. L. Bumpass and C. Westoff, "The Perfect Contraceptive Population: Extent and Implications of Unwanted Fertility in the United States," *Science*, 169:1177-1182 (1970).

6. Greenleigh and Associates, *Facts, Fallacies and the Future: A Study of the Aid to Dependent Children Program of Cook County, Illinois* (New York, 1960).

7. N. Ryder, and C. Westoff, "Fertility Planning Status: United States, 1965," *Demography*, 6:435 (1969).

8. U. S. Children's Bureau; Child Welfare Statistics, *Supplement to Child Welfare Statistics—Adoptions* (Washington, D. C., U. S. Government Printing Office, 1966). Child Welfare League of America, "Children Without Parents," Summarized in *Transaction*, 7:13 (1970).

man, *et al.*[9] This study was limited to the North Carolina population of never-married women with an illegitimate birth during the early 1960's. The report is based on interviews with 387 white and 552 black never-married unwed mothers. About 67 percent of the designated sample of Negroes but less than half the designated white sample was interviewed. The authors believe that unwed mothers most likely to have the child adopted and those most secretive and shamed by the birth were more likely than others to have been missed. It is known that the white sample was biased since many upper status whites were not interviewed because the directors of maternity homes reneged on an earlier commitment to the project. What can this study tell us about the wanted status of illegitimate births?

About 9 percent of white and 12 percent of black unwed mothers who were interviewed had married the alleged father some eighteen months after the birth.[10] This might indicate that some fraction of births to these mothers were deliberate, since commitment by both the mother and father is implied by the subsequent marriage. A second indirect measure of the wanted status of the birth is found by examining responses to questions about their reactions during the period following the discovery that they were pregnant. About 3 percent said they were "proud" to find themselves pregnant, and an additional 3 to 4 percent of whites and Negroes gave other responses that might be interpreted as indicating they welcomed the pregnancy.[11] Thus, both of these indirect measures indicate that the proportion of unwed mothers who may have wanted an out-of-wedlock birth is 8 percent or less.

The 1971 survey reported by Zelnick and Kantner[12] suggests that perhaps 10 to 12 percent of black and 4 percent of white

9. C. Bowerman, D. Irish and H. Pope, *Unwed Motherhood: Personal and Social Consequences,* Chapel Hill, N. C., Institute for Research in Social Science, 1966.

10. *Ibid.,* p. 123.

11. *Ibid.,* pp. 123 and 176.

12. M. Zelnik and J. Kantner, "Sexuality, Contraception, and Pregnancy Among Young Unwed Females in the United States," in C. F. Westoff and R. Parke, Jr. (eds.), *Demographic and Social Consequences of Population Growth,* I. (Washington, D. C., U. S. Government Printing Office, 1972), Tables 10 and 15.

sexually active teenagers wanted to become pregnant. This figure is inflated, however, because nonuse by males was not considered as a cause of lack of contraceptive use.

Our concern with the male role in contraceptive protection of the unmarried teenage girl emphasizes the point that the blame for nonuse of contraception is usually placed on the woman rather than the couple. Thus, in the 1971 survey the girls not protected by contraception are asked why *they* did not contracept— and their responses are taken as measures of the effect of their ignorance of reproduction, their wanting to get pregnant and so forth. As late as 1971 teenage sexually active girls reported overwhelming reliance on male protection—in spite of nearly a decade of pill use, the introduction of the IUD, and nearly 100 percent awareness that female methods of contraception are available from the drugstore, private physicians, or clinics. An alternative answer to the question of why a girl does not contracept, then, is that her sexual partner does not contracept. When the male fails to protect the girl, the girl will be unprotected. The absence of female use of contraception by the unmarried teenager is part of a tradition that sees male use as appropriate, considerate, and responsible and female use as inappropriate and possibly immoral. One estimate of the importance of the male role in contraception, as this role affects girls who become unwed mothers, comes from the Bowerman study.[13]

Among the unwed mothers in the Bowerman study 86 percent of whites and 84 percent of Negroes who had used contraception reported that only condom or withdrawal methods were used, while an additional 11 percent of whites and 12 percent of Negroes reported combined male and female methods. Only about 3 percent of whites and less than 5 percent of black unwed mothers reporting use were using exclusively female methods. It is clear that these unmarried mothers were dependent on the male for protection. The resulting pregnancies can, therefore, hardly be seen as a deliberate result of the woman's nonuse of contraception; rather the pregnancies are the result of nonuse or ineffective use by men. The pattern of male contraceptive use re-

---

13. Bowerman, *et al., op. cit.,* p. 408.

sulting in illicit pregnancies provides no evidence that the woman wanted these pregnancies. Rather, these data support the idea that the status of being unmarried, lack of access to physicians, and the pseudomoral barrier (see text that follows for discussion) result in female dependence on males for protection.

Because it is unlikely that programs to increase male contraceptive use will work, programs to increase voluntary control over illicit conceptions must focus on unmarried women.[14] Also, effective contraception for women (pill, IUD, and diaphragm) is controlled by physicians. What steps, then, are necessary to increase the use of effective contraception by unmarried women, and what evidence exists that a contraception-only program can reduce illegitimacy rates?

PRESENT POLICIES AND PROGRAMS

Present government policy emphasizes provision of effective contraception to the low-income population.[15] Since effective contraception for women is controlled by physicians, it follows that if women are to become effective contraceptors they must be able to have the services of physicians willing to prescribe effective contraception for them. Subsidized contraception programs are based on the idea that two primary barriers to effective contraceptive use exist: location and finances. The success of the program is seen to depend on overcoming these two barriers.

I. Location and Financial Barriers

The location barrier exists when the woman cannot get to a physician who will supply her with effective contraception. This factor is a consideration for isolated rural women above and below the poverty line.

The location problem is related to the financial barrier, since money is a means of overcoming distance. However, there are other nuances to the location barrier that become clear when one

---

14. P. Cutright, "Illegitimacy: Myths, Causes and Cures." *op. cit.,* p. 39. Y. Matsumoto, A. Koizumi, and T. Nohara, "Condom Use in Japan," *Studies in Family Planning,* 3:251 (October, 1972) .

15. S. Scheyer, "DHEW's New Center: The National Commitment to Family Planning," *Family Planning Perspectives,* No. 1, 2:25 (1970) .

considers the problem that the urban poor have in obtaining effective contraception. In the absence of an adequate government program, the poor urban woman must search out a private physician who may or may not be willing to help her. It has been estimated that perhaps 10 percent of those poor women who need contraception get it from private physicians.[16] Since most of the urban poor depend on publicly financed hospitals and public health programs for medical care, family planners assumed that effective contraceptive use might be increased if they were given access to such service.[17] In turn, this meant that medical services would have to be subsidized.[18] Subsidized contraception programs are designed to overcome the financial and location barriers to effective contraception.

Recent estimates by Jaffe indicate that the percent of women in need of receiving subsidized services rose from 14 in 1968 to 20 in 1969 and possibly 30 in 1970.[19] For example in 1969 about 53 percent of the counties in the United States had no public or private programs.[20] Only 11 percent of the nation's 4,603 nonprofit general care hospitals offer family planning services.[21] Among counties with programs, idiosyncratic decisions by local authorities result in great differences in participation from one community to the next. For example, within Colorado, Denver County had 90 percent of its women in need enrolled in its program; nearby Pueblo County reported 27 percent enrolled, while El Paso County had only 11 percent in its programs. Forty-four

16. Office of Economic Opportunity, *Need for Subsidized Family Planning Services: United States, Each State and County, 1968.* (Washington, D. C., U. S. Government Printing Office, 1969) , p. 3.

17. F. Jaffe and S. Polgar, "Family Planning and Public Policy: Is the 'Culture of Poverty' the New Cop-Out?" *Journal of Marriage and the Family,* 30:228 (May, 1968) .

18. F. Jaffe and A. Guttmacher, "Family Planning Programs in the United States," *Demography,* 5 (1968) .

19. F. Jaffe, "Toward the Reduction of Unwanted Pregnancy: An Assessment of Current Public and Private Programs," *Science,* 174:119-127 (October 8, 1971) .

20. J. Dryfoos, F. Jaffe, D. Weintraub, J. Cobb and C. Bernsohn, "Eighteen Months Later: Family Planning Services in the United States, 1969," *Family Planning Perspectives,* 3: Table 2 (April, 1971) .

21. *Ibid.,* Table 9.

counties in Colorado had no programs.[22] Variation from place to place in the percent of eligible women enrolled is a function of local operation of the programs, not the motivation of the women. Although both location and financial barriers remain, there may be a third major barrier that acts to reduce contraceptive use by unmarried women.

II. The Pseudomoral Barrier

It is claimed that many young unmarried women do not use contraceptives because they have moral objections,[23] a condition which might be described as a pseudomoral* barrier inhibiting both male and female contraceptive use.[24] In time, a program to prevent illegitimate births must go beyond financial and location barriers and take into account the apparent fact that the major reason unmarried women do not use effective contraception is because they are unmarried. The same women who do not use contraception themselves (or insist that the male use it) while they are unmarried will, after marriage, contracept. The validity of this statement is found by the observation that the completed fertility of white and black ever-married mothers whose first birth was illegitimate is little different from that of mothers whose baby was conceived after marriage.[25]

American society has not established a norm that bars all un-

---

22. Office-Economic Opportunity. *Need for Subsidized Family Planning Services: United States, Each State and County, 1969.* (Washington, D. C., U. S. Government Printing Office, 1971) , Table 1.

23. M. Zelnik and J. Kantner, "United States: Exploratory Studies of Negro Family Formation—Factors Relating to Illegitimacy," *Studies in Family Planning,* 60:7 (1970) . This is a common theme in the literature distributed in crisis clinics, abortion referral groups, and college students concerned with out-of-wedlock pregnancy.

* The term "pseudomoral" seems appropriate because, if one wishes to take a moral stance regarding illicit coitus, the actual behavior indicates that traditional moral ideals have already been abandoned.

24. P. Cutright, "The Teenage Sexual Revolution and the Myth of an Abstinent Past," *Family Planning Perspectives,* 4:24-26 (January, 1972) .

25. P. Cutright, "Timing the First Birth: Does It Matter?" *Journal of Marriage and the Family,* Table 3 (November, 1973) . *See also* J. Kantner and M. Zelnick, "Contraception and Pregnancy: Experiences of Young Unmarried Women in the United States," *Family Planning Perspectives,* 5:34 (Winter, 1973) .

married persons from becoming contraceptive users. It only applies moral reproach to unmarried women. This makes for real problems under conditions where the shift toward female methods among married women increasingly has defined contraception as a female responsibility but where the unmarried woman is constrained to feel that her use of contraception is not socially acceptable. Unmarried women having coitus, but not using contraception, are thus victims of a pseudomoral barrier.

If illicit pregnancy rates are to decline, this pseudomoral barrier must be removed. Unfortunately, present economic restrictions on patients in government subsidized programs inhibit the potential of the program to lower the pseudomoral barrier, because the potential impact of the program itself as a legitimizing force is lost when it is restricted to the poor.

III. Economic Restrictions on Patients of Public Programs

If government-sponsored contraception programs are to have a significant impact on prevention of unwanted pregnancies among unmarried women, the programs must be made as open as possible. They should be accessible to all unmarried women, wherever they live or whatever their family income. This does not imply that upper-income unmarried women should receive free service—only that they should get what they come in to get, just like a poor woman. It is a mistake for the program to be limited to poverty area clinics and to city and county hospitals. Programs "for poor people only" limit their impact on the majority of the population, as well as risk rejection by the poor themselves. The assumption that only the poor need organized family planning services may be incorrect.

For example, studies in both the United States and England show that many physicians are unwilling to prescribe contraception for unmarried women—even when the women are about to be married and can pay for it.[26] In the United States, unmarried

---

26. S. Spivack, Family Planning in Medical Practice, in C. Kiser (ed.) : *Research in Family Planning* (Princeton, N. J., Princeton University Press, 1962) . A. Cartwright, "England and Wales: General Practitioners and Family Planning," *Studies in Family Planning*, 10:162 (1968) .

women visiting physicians in general practice (rather than physicians specializing in obstetrics and gynecology), older physicians, or Catholic physicians, are unlikely to get an effective method from the doctor. Also, many hospitals do not provide contraception, legal abortions, or sterilization services to patients at any income level.

Limiting government-sponsored family planning programs to the poor will not provide ready access to effective contraception for many nonpoor unmarried women. If teenagers above the 125 percent of poverty line are ineligible, this economic limit will exclude 86 percent of white, 43 percent of nonwhite, and 80 percent of all teenagers.[27] If one considers the economic status of teenage unwed mothers, then about 40 percent of all white, 20 percent of all nonwhite, and 28 percent of all teenage unwed mothers would be excluded from a preventive program because they are above the 125 percent poverty line.[28]

Outside of the Office of Economic Opportunity (OEO), government-sponsored family planning programs have not explicitly refused service to the nonpoor unmarried women. However, the services are scarce and are quite properly located in clinics within poverty areas and in hospitals serving the poor. The program is, one suspects, defined by the public as a program for the poor. Especially while they remain so few, this public image of government-funded programs almost guarantees that these clinics will continue to serve only the poor, by virtue of public attitudes about them as well as the location of the services. It is ironic, perhaps, that unless contraceptive programs expand to include the nonpoor, the potential effectiveness of the program to increase contraceptive use by poor unmarried women will also be minimized, because the program may not acquire the legitimating ef-

27. P. Cutright, Illegitimacy in the United States: 1920-1968," in C. F. Westoff and R. Parke, Jr. (eds.), *Social and Demographic Aspects of Population Growth*, I:375-438 (Washington, D. C., U. S. Government Printing Office, 1972), Appendix Table 6.

28. *Ibid.*, Table 29. A. Campbell, "The Role of Family Planning in the Reduction of Poverty," *Journal of Marriage and the Family*, 30: Tables A and B (May, 1968).

fect necessary to lower the pseudomoral barrier that now depresses contraceptive use among both poor and nonpoor unmarried women. Whatever the impact of widespread contraception program on legitimating contraceptive use by unmarried women, it is possible to gain some idea of the likely limits inherent in a contraception-only program by examining contraceptive effectiveness among married couples in the United States, the characteristics of the majority of unwed mothers, and the impact of existing contraception programs on illegitimacy.

THE LIMITS OF A CONTRACEPTION-ONLY PROGRAM
I. Contraceptive Failures Among Married Couples

One method of assessing the extent to which married couples have contraceptive failures is simply to ask them about each birth. If the wife says that she was not trying to get pregnant and that she and/or her husband did not want another child at any time, the birth is called a "number failure." This technique understates the actual number of unwanted legitimate pregnancies because most unwanted pregnancies terminated by spontaneous and induced abortion are not reported.

"Timing failures" may be superior to number failures as a measure of family planning mistakes by married couples. A timing failure is a birth reported by the married woman as having occurred before she wanted it to happen.

When both timing and number failures are considered, Ryder and Westoff[29] report that in the 1960-1965 period 72 percent of U. S. white mothers and 92 percent of U. S. black mothers (who said they had tried to plan their children) were, in fact, not able to avoid these types of birth planning failures.

It is worthwhile to consider the rate of contraceptive failure among married couples interviewed in the 1965 National Fertility Study. These failure rates show the proportion of women who became pregnant within a twelve-month period while using a given contraceptive method. Pill and IUD clearly provide superior protection with failure rates of 5 and 8 percent, respectively.

---

29. N. Ryder and C. Westoff, "Fertility Planning Status: United States," *op. cit.*

The diaphragm or condom are about equal, with failure rates of 18 or 19 percent. Withdrawal is superior to rhythm (23 versus 30 percent failure) and rhythm is inferior to all other methods except foam, which exhibits the highest failure rates of all (32 percent). These annual failure rates among contraceptive users—ranging from 5 to 32 percent—should, however, be contrasted to the pregnancy rate that would be found if no contraceptive methods had been used: 80 to 90 percent.[30]

Data from the same study show failure rates within twelve months by race and birth order. At each birth order, the black was more likely than the white wife to experience contraceptive failure. For example, the failure rates for first through fifth birth orders among whites were 34, 24, 18, 17, and 19. Among Negroes the comparable rates were much higher: 54, 51, 43, 40, and 40. Thus, effectiveness improves in both populations as birth order increases, but method and use failures still result in high rates of unwanted pregnancies among married couples trying to prevent pregnancies.[31]

This statistical appraisal of the effectiveness of recent family planning efforts by married women in the nation with a tradition of the world's highest level of contraceptive use is sobering. If contraceptive programs among unmarried women could promote only the level of fertility control comparable to that practiced by married white women, considerable numbers of illicit pregnancies and illegitimate births would still be expected.

II. The Magnitude of the Teenage Illicit Pregnancy Problem

During 1964-1966, the annual average number of teenage illegitimate births was 123,400. This number, however, does not represent the number of illicit pregnancies to be prevented by a contraception program. Rather, as indicated in Table II-I, illegitimate births are only part of the "iceberg" which represents the actual number of illicit pregnancies.

---

30. P. Cutright, "Illegitimacy: Myths, Causes and Cures," *op. cit.*, Table 3. N. Ryder and C. Westoff, *Reproduction in the United States,* 1965 (Princeton, N. J., Princeton University Press, 1971) , Chapter XI.

31. L. Westoff and C. Westoff, *From Now to Zero* (Boston, Little, Brown & Company, 1971) , Table 24.

TABLE II-I

ESTIMATED ANNUAL AVERAGE NUMBERS AND RATES OF PREGNANCIES
TO UNMARRIED TEENAGERS, BY PREGNANCY OUTCOME AND COLOR:
UNITED STATES, 1964-1966

Pregnancy Outcome	Number of Pregnancies (in Thousands)			Rates per 1,000 Unmarried 15-19		
	Total	White	Nonwhite	Total	White	Nonwhite
Illegitimate live birth ...	123.4	51.1	72.3	16.4	7.8	72.4
Legitimate live births ..	151.8	122.4	29.4	20.2	18.8	29.4
Subtotal births	275.2	173.5	101.7	36.6	26.6	101.8
Fetal loss to brides	33.3	22.5	10.8	4.4	3.4	10.8
Fetal loss to nonbrides ..	59.3	23.6	35.7	7.9	3.6	35.8
Total	367.8	219.6	148.2	48.9	33.6	148.5

Source: P. Cutright, "Illegitimacy in the United States: 1920-1968," *op. cit.*; Table 22, for births; Table 14 for spontaneous fetal loss of four weeks or later gestation only (184 per 1,000 legitimate live births for whites and 368 for nonwhites); Table 16 for estimated spontaneous and induced fetal loss per 1,000 illegitimate live births—462 for whites and 494 for nonwhites. Fetal loss reduced by 20 percent of estimates for all ages to apply to teenage mothers.

When we determine the percentage of illicit pregnancies (Table II-I), we find, for example, that illegitimate live births represent only about 23 percent of white and 49 percent of nonwhite illicit pregnancies. Legitimated births represent 56 percent of white and just 20 percent of nonwhite illicit pregnancies. Spontaneous and induced abortions account for about 21 percent of white and 31 percent of nonwhite illicit pregnancies.

It is reasonable to think that a sizable proportion of the legitimated births represent wanted births that need not be the primary concern of a contraceptive program. Evidence from the 1965 National Fertility Study indicated that 36 percent of white and 50 percent of Negro wives defined their first births as timing failures; they would have preferred to have it later in marriage.[32] The inclusion of postmarital conceptions in the Bumpass and Westoff calculation obviously leads to an underestimate of self-defined timing failures among pregnant brides.

If the data used to estimate pregnancy wastage among brides

32. L. Bumpass and C. Westoff, "The Perfect Contraceptive Population . . . ," *op. cit.*, Table 6.

and nonbrides is as conservative as we think it to be, the figures in Table II-I understate the number of illicit pregnancies to some unknown degree. In any case, one is talking about 368,000 pregnancies, rather than 123,000 illegitimate births, to be prevented.

In terms of the percent of the unmarried teenage female population experiencing illicit pregnancy each year, the rates in Table II-I indicate this number is about 3 percent for whites and 15 percent for nonwhites—5 percent of all unmarried women each year. This estimate clearly understates the percent of each population engaged in coital activity during the year, since many women having coitus do not become pregnant.

III. Characteristics of Unwed Mothers

1. POVERTY. Unwed mothers are much more likely than wed mothers to be poor. Studies of fertility control problems among married couples indicate that the low-income wife is twice as likely as other wives to report an unwanted birth.[33] Although it is undoubtedly true that some portion of this difference in effective birth planning is related to financial and location barriers that depress contraceptive effectiveness among the married poor, one must conclude that, controlling method, use effectiveness of contraception is lower among the poor than the nonpoor. The fact that unwed mothers are recruited so heavily from the poor population means that efforts to upgrade contraceptive use to high levels must be able to overcome this patient characteristic that militates against the success of such an effort. In the case of the unmarried, two other known characteristics also indicate further difficulties for a contraception program.

2. LOW BIRTH ORDER. The previous fertility of unwed mothers differs from that of wed mothers; nearly 73 percent of white and 54 percent of nonwhite unwed mothers in 1968 were having their first birth. About 63 percent of all illegitimate births were first births.[34] This finding is radically different from what one

---

33. *Ibid.*, Table 4.

34. U. S. Bureau of the Census, *Fertility Indicators* (1970), *Current Population Reports*, Series P-23, No. 36 (Washington, D. C., U. S. Government Printing Office, 1971), Table 28.

finds in studies of unwanted legitimate births; less than 5 percent are first births. Contraceptive programs to prevent the vast bulk of unwanted legitimate births can, properly, use postpartum care in maternity wards. But postpartum programs cannot possibly reach nearly two-thirds of potential unwed mothers. To date, most of the contraceptive programs that reach a substantial portion of the target population are postpartum programs. These programs can have only a limited impact on illegitimacy rates. This observation implies no criticism of postpartum programs, since the prevention of unwanted legitimate births is a problem affecting more women than the problem of preventing illegitimate births. In theory, at least, 20 percent of teenage illegitimate births could be prevented with a postpartum program. However, a contraception-only program that will affect the remaining 80 percent of teenage illegitimate births that are first births must go beyond postpartum care.[35]

The fact that some 80 percent of unwed teenage mothers are having a first birth indicates that many of these women have relatively slight sexual experience. Presumably, the effective practice of contraception is something that requires some experience, at least with most of the available methods. Most unwed mothers lack the experience that works in favor of the more mature and experienced married woman.

3. AGE. The third characteristic of unwed mothers that bodes ill for a contraceptive program is their youth. In 1968, for example, 45 percent of white and 61 percent of nonwhite teenage illegitimate births occurred to girls age seventeen or less.[36] Put another way, nearly 45 percent of white and 61 percent of nonwhite teenage illegitimate births resulted from pregnancies to girls age sixteen and under. Under the laws of most states minors cannot legally be treated by government programs without parental consent, nor can they legally receive the services of private physicians without parental consent.[37] Even if legal barriers were removed, the youthful age of this large segment of young unwed

35. National Center for Health Statistics, *Trends in Illegitimacy in the United States—1940-1965* (Washington, D. C., U. S. Government Printing Office) , Table 7.

36. National Center for Health Statistics, unpublished data.

37. H. F. Pilpel and N. F. Weschler, "Birth Control, Teen-agers and the Law: A New Look, 1971," *Family Planning Perspectives* 3:37-45 (July, 1971) .

mothers may work against effective practice of contraception, since they are less likely than older women to be able to cope with moral confusions surrounding sex and contraception.

A fourth characteristic—infrequent and irregular coitus—also depresses effective female contraception. This problem is discussed in a later section.

IV. The Impact of Existing Programs on Illegitimacy

If a birth control program is to depress illegitimacy, unmarried women must have access to the program and be willing to use it. Data from Orleans Parish, Louisiana (New Orleans) and Fulton County, Georgia (Atlanta) show that when a program does not bar unmarried women, these women will use it. For example, the marital status of patients is quite similar to that of the nonwhite population of women fifteen to forty-four; about half the patients and half the nonwhite population are not married and living with a spouse. Although these comparisons rely on 1960 Census and late 1960's patient characteristics, there is little reason to believe that the marital status of these populations changed greatly during the 1960's. One should note that the unmarried patients in both these programs are generally recruited into postpartum programs. Young never-pregnant unmarried women are not in the program. Further, because these postpartum programs have operated in hospitals used almost exclusively by Negroes, few whites are recruited. Thus, the high rate of acceptance of birth control services can only be demonstrated to exist for unmarried low-income nonwhite ever-pregnant women. It is likely that when the limitations governing the recruitment to these programs are lifted, whites will use the program as frequently as do nonwhites, and that never-pregnant women will also enter the program.[38]*

Because the decline in nonwhite illegitimacy after 1965 was

---

38. F. S. Jaffe, J. G. Dryfoos and M. Corey, "Organized Family Planning Programs in the United States: 1968-1972," *Family Planning Perspectives* 5:73-79 (Winter, 1973) , p. 79.

* Jaffe *et al., op. cit.* Note that recent data suggest a change to lower parity patients. A large scale study of patients in organized programs in 1971 found about 30 percent reporting zero parity. It is not known, however, whether these patients were married or unmarried.

limited to women twenty and older,[39] and because this decline occurred at the same time government support for public birth
control clinics was expanding, it is worthwhile to test the hypothesis that illegitimacy among older women declined because
the government program began to expand. This hypothesis can
be tested when appropriate birth and program data are available
to allow comparisons among populations with large and small
programs. If the program is causing a change in the illegitimacy
rate, then the rate of change in illegitimacy should differ according to the percent of women in need who are enrolled in the
program.

Table II-II examines percentage change in the numbers of second and higher order nonwhite births in various areas in Georgia
from 1962 through 1969.* First-order illegitimate births are omitted because the program in Fulton County is generally restricted
to postpartum work. We look only at nonwhite births because
when the state is broken into smaller areas, there are too few
white illegitimate births to allow reliable comparisons over the
years. Also, very few whites are in the program, and the program
could hardly be a cause of change in white illegitimacy.

In Table II-II three large urban areas arranged according
to the high or lower level of program utilization. Also, seven
small rural counties that had had active family planning for two
or more years prior to January 1, 1968 are compared to seven
matched control counties lacking such a birth control effort.[40]
Data are grouped into two-year periods to decrease sampling variation.

The first time period shows the percentage change in the num-

---

39. P. Cutright, "Illegitimacy in the United States: 1920-1968," *op. cit.*, Table 2.

* Over short periods of time, changes in the numbers of illegitimate births
should reflect changes in illegitimacy rates, unless drastic changes in the number
of unmarried women occur due to migration. In the following analysis we compare rural and urban areas within Georgia and the metropolitan areas in Tennessee. It is unlikely that net migration effects will bias our interpretation of
these data.

40. R. Rochat, C. Tyler, Jr. and A. Schoenbucher, *The Effect of Family Planning
Services in Georgia on Fertility in Selected Rural Counties.* Atlanta, Health Services
and Mental Health Administration, 1970 (unpublished) .

TABLE II-II

FAMILY PLANNING PROGRAMS AND PERCENTAGE CHANGE IN TWO
YEAR AVERAGE NUMBERS OF SECOND AND LATER ILLEGITIMATE
BIRTHS: GEORGIA NONWHITES, 1962-1969

| | | | Percent Change in Number of Second and Later Illegitimate Births | | |
| | | Percent in Need Served by Program, 1968 | | 1962-63 1964-65 | 1964-65 1966-67 | 1966-67 1968-69 |
Area					
Fulton Co. (Atlanta)	41*		− 3	−21	−13
Muscogee (Columbus)	18*	18‡	7	− 9	−22
Chatham (Savannah)	12*	6‡	− 2	− 8	−12
Rural study	32†		−12	−20	−35
Rural control	5†		− 5	−31	−26
State	12*	9‡	1	−17	−11

* Office of Economic Opportunity, *Need for Subsidized Family Planning Services: United States, Each State and County, 1968* (Washington, D. C. Government Printing Office, 1969), Table 1.

† End of 1968. Roger W. Rochat, Carl W. Tyler, Jr., and Albert K. Schoenbucher, "The Effect of Family Planning Services in Georgia on Fertility in Selected Rural Counties" (Atlanta, Georgia, Health Services and Mental Health Administration, mimeo, 1970).

‡ Georgia State Department of Health for active patients, November, 1968.

bers of second and higher order illegitimate births between 1962-1963 and 1964-1965. Since large scale programs did not exist during this time anywhere in the state, the changes shown indicate some change (especially in the rural study counties) in the absence of program efforts. In the next time period the largest percentage decline (−31 percent) occurred in rural control counties. The declines in the entire state of −17 percent are comparable to the declines in Fulton County and the rural study counties. Thus, it is difficult to ascribe the Fulton County and rural study counties decline in higher order births from 1964-1965 to 1966-1967 to the effects of the program. Still, our program data are for 1968, and the rise in the numbers of patients was concentrated in the two years prior to this time, so one might not expect births prior to 1968 to be greatly affected by the program.

The final column of the table, however, gives no support to the hypothesis that the 1966-1967 to 1968-1969 decline in numbers of higher order births was caused by the program. Fulton

County experienced a 13 percent decline, while the other two urban areas (with much weaker programs) experienced roughly equal or larger declines. In the rural areas, the counties with virtually no programs continued to experience declining illegitimacy, while the rural study counties also participated in this downward trend. If we compute the percentage decline in illegitimate births in the contrasting rural areas between 1964 and 1969 we have a downward shift of 55 percent in the study counties and 57 percent in the control counties. In short, we find no evidence that the programs have had a direct impact on higher order illegitimate births in Georgia.

If, as we have indicated, the prospect for controlling illegitimacy through the introduction of a contraception program is less hopeful for the teenagers than for the older woman with one or more births, the results of the experience in Georgia would indicate little prospect for deliberate change in teenage illegitimacy through the introduction of subsidized clinic or postpartum services.

A similar analysis of change in the number of illegitimate births by age and color was possible for areas with varying levels of program development in the State of Tennessee. These data are shown in Table II-III.

Davidson County (Nashville) has the largest percent in need in its program—triple the participation figures in the remaining three metropolitan counties. Nonmetropolitan counties had no programs to speak of; only 1 percent of the women in need in these areas were in a program.

The Davidson County program was one of the first (1964) OEO programs in the nation. It did not rely on postpartum recruitment but established a network of neighborhood clinics. Because OEO did not allow service to unmarried women, only married women were served in the first year or so. However, by 1966 unmarried women were being served with funds from other sources. About half the Davidson County patients are white and half black. Therefore, we include white as well as nonwhite births.

Among whites, Davidson County (with the only large program in the state) shows the largest gains between 1965 and 1969 in

TABLE II-III

PERCENTAGE CHANGE IN NUMBERS OF ILLEGITIMATE BIRTHS, BY
COLOR, AREA, AND AGE OF MOTHER: TENNESSEE, 1965-1969

Color and Age	Area	Percent in Need Enrolled	Change Periods 1965 to 1966-7 (%)	1966-7 to 1968-9 (%)	1965 to 1968-9 (%)	Number of Illegitimate Births, 1965
White						
Under 20	Davidson	32	21	11	48	86
	Other metro	12	33	3	37	212
	Nonmetro	1	4	8	11	523
	State	7	13	8	22	821
20-29	Davidson	32	−13	22	5	130
	Other metro	12	−10	18	6	293
	Nonmetro	1	−1	5	4	585
	State	7	−5	16	10	1,008
30+	Davidson	32	−37	47	−7	27
	Other metro	12	−5	−21	−26	66
	Nonmetro	1	−14	−1	−13	192
	State	7	−14	−2	−16	285
Nonwhite						
Under 20	Davidson	32	−5	6	0	307
	Other metro	12	5	9	15	1,480
	Nonmetro	1	4	5	9	768
	State	7	3	8	12	2,555
20-29	Davidson	32	−22	9	−15	281
	Other metro	12	−10	−10	−19	1,496
	Nonmetro	1	−7	−1	−9	683
	State	7	−11	−6	−16	2,460
30+	Davidson	32	−37	−2	−38	91
	Other metro	12	−14	−20	−31	509
	Nonmetro	1	−16	−21	−34	264
	State	7	−17	−19	−32	864

Source: Percent of population in need that were enrolled in 1968 from Office of
Economic Opportunity, *Need for Subsidized Family Planning Services;* United States,
Each State and County, 1968 (Washington, D. C., Government Printing Office,
1969), Table 1. The statistic is for all age groups combined. Birth data, courtesy of
Tennessee State Department of Public Health.

Note: Davidson County (Nashville) is separated from other metropolitan counties. The three other metropolitan counties are Hamilton (Chattanoga), Knox
(Knoxville) and Shelby (Memphis). Nonmetropolitan counties include the balance
of the state.

teenage illegitimacy—about double the state average. Among
whites aged twenty to twenty-nine Davidson County experiences
a rise about equal to other metropolitan areas in the state. White
illegitimacy to women thirty and older declined by 26 percent for

the other metropolitan areas; in Davidson County the decline was only 7 percent. The far right-hand column shows the numbers of illegitimate 1965 births that form the base for these percentages. Because there are so few births to Davidson County whites thirty and older, it is likely that comparison of changes in number of births to these women in Davidson County and elsewhere have little significance. Both younger white age groups, however, have large populations and more births. In these younger groups we find no evidence that the program reduced white illegitimacy. Areas with weak programs or no programs at all experienced smaller increases or larger declines than are found in Davidson County.

Among nonwhites under twenty, the number of illegitimate births remained stable in Davidson County, but increased by 10 to 15 percent in other areas of Tennessee. If this difference is an effect of the program, one should expect still larger impact among nonwhites twenty and older, since the program should be more likely to serve them than the teenage population. Comparisons of percentage changes for nonwhites twenty to twenty-nine and thirty or older between Davidson County and the remaining areas does not allow such a conclusion. Older nonwhite women in areas with little program effort show declines in illegitimate births similar to those declines in Davidson County. We find no evidence that the program is a cause of the decline in illegitimate births among older nonwhites.

These negative conclusions for both Tennessee and Georgia suggest that the number of unmarried women helped is so small that illegitimate births in these populations have not been significantly altered by program inputs.

1. WHY THE PROGRAMS HAVE NOT WORKED. One reason the programs are not depressing illegitimate births is because many women are not in the program. Although over a third of the Georgia nonwhite rural study county patients and nearly half of the Fulton County patients were unmarried, only 41 and 36 percent, respectively, of all indigent women in these two areas were in the program; a large majority of unmarried women in need were not patients. Further, using the percent in need as a mea-

TABLE II-IV

GROSS CUMULATIVE UNWANTED PREGNANCY RATES PER 100 CLINIC
PATIENT ACCEPTORS WITHIN 12 MONTHS, BY AGE OF PATIENT
AND INITIAL METHOD CHOSEN: ATLANTA, BUFFALO
AND BROOKLYN CLINICS

Age of Patient	Initial Method	
	IUD	Orals
Under 20 years	13	27
20-24	8	11
25-29	5	12
30 or more	3	9
Atlanta—all ages	10	24
Brooklyn—all ages	6	13
Buffalo—all ages	5	8

Source: Christopher Tietze and Sarah Lewit, "The IUD and the Pill: Extended
Use-effectiveness," *Family Planning Perspectives*, 3 (April, 1971), Tables 3 and 5.

sure of patient service overestimates coverage of potential unwed
mothers because all nonpoor women are excluded.

A second reason the program does not depress the rate could
be that patients are not much better protected from the risk of
pregnancy than are women who are not patients.[41]*

The women treated in Fulton County constituted at least one-
fourth of the unmarried nonwhite women at risk in that County, by our estimate, and this group should encompass a large
enough segment of the unmarried population to push the illegitimacy rate downward. The program could only depress illegitimate births if it prevented pregnancy. Table II-IV indicates that
many patients, especially the younger age groups, in the Fulton
County (Atlanta) program became pregnant within twelve
months. Looking first at the lower panel of Table II-IV we see
that in Atlanta's program, 10 percent of IUD and 24 percent of

41. F. Jaffe, "Estimating the Need for Subsidized Family Planning Services,"
Family Planning Perspectives, 3: Table 2 (January, 1971).

* Jaffe notes that about half of the women entering the program in Orleans
Parish from 1967 through 1970 had used contraceptives before. Nearly 25 percent
of all new patients had used the pill. Still some 75 percent of the new patients received contraceptive services that should provide protection superior to what
they had before they came to the clinic and former users of the pill may also
have been helped by the clinic staff.

Pill patients were pregnant within twelve months. These failure rates are double the rates for patients in Buffalo and Brooklyn and may indicate failure in the Atlanta program to provide adequate patient care after the initial contact. Also of interest is that in these programs, Pill failure rates are about double IUD failure rates, thus indicating the importance of method.

In the upper panel of the Table II-IV, we have failure rates from all these programs combined, by the age of the patient. Some 27 percent of married and unmarried Pill patients under twenty years of age were pregnant within twelve months while 13 percent of similar young IUD patients were pregnant. Failure rates decline with increasing age. Failure rates after eighteen months were even higher; over 40 percent of young Pill patients were pregnant. This pattern of age and method effects on contraceptive effectiveness may help to explain why illegitimacy in Georgia and Tennessee was not reduced by public programs.

2. THE LIKELY IMPACT OF CONTRACEPTION PROGRAMS. A more systematic assessment of the likely impact of varying levels of patient participation in a program on reduction of illicit pregnancy is given in Table II-V. In this table we also show three different failure rates in the population of sexually active unmarried women before they do or do not become patients. We vary the percent of sexually active women in the program from 10 to 100 percent and have alternate annual contraceptive failure rates of 10 and 20 per 100 patients in the program.

Table II-V shows that a contraception program with a failure rate of 20 percent could reduce illicit pregnancies by as much as 60 percent, so long as 100 percent of women were in the program and the failure rate had been 50 percent prior to the beginning of the program. While a failure rate of 50 percent may be appropriate for the American population of nonwhite married indigent women,[42] it is too high for the population of sexually active unmarried women, because the coital activity of the unmarried is well below that of married women over a year's time. In Table II-I we estimated that 3.3 percent of all white and 14.8 percent of all nonwhite unmarried girls age fifteen to nineteen

42. A. Westoff and C. Westoff, *op. cit.*, Table 24.

TABLE II-V

PERCENTAGE REDUCTION IN NUMBERS OF ILLICIT TEENAGE
PREGNANCIES UNDER ALTERNATIVE FAILURE RATES
BEFORE AND AFTER A PROGRAM: BY PERCENT OF
SEXUALLY ACTIVE UNMARRIED WOMEN
IN THE PROGRAM

Contraceptive Failure Rate Before Program (%)	Percent of Sexually Active Women in the Program	Percentage Reduction of Illicit Pregnancies	
		10% Patient Failure Rate	20% Patient Failure Rate
50	10	−8	−6
	40	−32	−24
	70	−56	−42
	100	−80	−60
30*	10	−7	−4
	40	−27	−13
	70	−46	−23
	100	−67	−33
20†	10	−5	0
	40	−20	0
	70	−35	0
	100	−50	0

* Most likely failure rate among unmarried sexually active nonwhite teenage women eligible for a subsidized program.
† Likely failure rate for white sexually active teenagers.

experienced pregnancy each year of the 1964-1966 period. What do these estimated pregnancy rates imply for a preprogram contraceptive failure rate among unmarried teenagers, if we use the 1971 Zelnik and Kantner data on sexual activity?[43]

Zelnik and Kantner report that 23 percent of whites and 54 percent of single nonwhites aged fifteen to nineteen had had intercourse at some time. To use these data to estimate contraceptive failure rates we must adjust for these not having intercourse in the previous twelve months. The authors report that of the teenagers who had ever had intercourse 41 percent of the blacks and 37 percent of the whites had not had coitus in the previous month. Another one-third of each group of the ever sexually active had had sex once or twice, while about 25 percent of the

43. M. Zelnik and J. Kantner, "Sexuality, Contraception, and Pregnancy Among Unwed Females in the United States," *op. cit.*, Tables 1 and 7.

nonwhites and 34 percent of the whites reported three or more coital acts in the previous month. Part of the higher white level may be related to their more recent entry to the ranks of the sexually active.[44]

For 1971, therefore, we estimate 20 percent of white and 46 percent of all nonwhite unmarried teenagers would have one or more coital acts. Among whites the pregnancy data in Table I-I implies that about 17 percent of those with one or more coital acts during a year would experience pregnancy; among nonwhites the percent pregnant would be thirty-two of those with coitus. These figures may be estimates of the contraceptive failure rates (using the term to apply to nonuse as well as misuse) in the two populations. For nonwhites the 30 percent preprogram failure rate shown in Table II-IV would seem appropriate, while the 20 percent rate would seem appropriate for white teenagers. This should not blind the reader to the obvious fact that the failure rates are higher among the poor than the nonpoor, and, since it is the poor who are actually eligible for the program, the conclusions drawn from Table II-IV should be specified by economic class as well as color.

The number of coital acts unprotected by contraception randomly distributed over the cycle required to produce a 17 and 32 percent failure rate in the two populations (assuming all women are fecund) is about 6 and 12, respectively.[45] Adjusting for subfecundity (by 25 percent in the unmarried teenage population) raises the number of unprotected coital acts to about 8 and 16 for whites and nonwhites respectively.

Returning now to Table II-V and examining the estimated nonwhite failure rate of 30 percent, we see that a program that could reduce this rate to 10 percent could, theoretically, reduce illicit pregnancies by 67 percent—if 100 percent of women were in the program. If the patient failure rate could be moved to only 20 percent, the program could—even with 100 percent of the women in it—reduce illicit pregnancies by only 33 percent. The estimated preprogram failure rate of 20 percent among

44. F. Furstenburg, *et al., op. cit.*
45. A. Westoff and C. Westoff, *op. cit.,* Table 2.

whites *requires* a patient failure rate below 20 percent if any results are to be observed, even with 100 percent in the program.
However, if we follow through some implications of the distribution of coital activity among unmarried women for a realistic
level of program utilization, we would be more likely to expect
that 40 to 50 percent (rather than 100 percent) would be in a
program offering services that now exist. Some reasons to support
this view follow.

COITAL ACTIVITY AND UTILIZATION OF PROGRAM SERVICES

A failure rate of 30 percent with the implied *average* number
of unprotected coital acts of sixteen, also reminds us that the
median number of coital acts per woman will be less than the
mean. Half of all women exposed to risk will have less than the
median, and half will have more than the median number of
coital acts per year. Since we know only a little about the nature
of the distribution around the mean for one month, we can only
speculate on the implications of a distribution in which some
40 percent had no coitus in the previous month, a third had
coitus just one or two times, while very few experienced coitus
at normal marital levels.[46]

First, the fact that more than half of sexually active unmarried teenagers do not experience regular and frequent intercourse over an extended period of time should depress the self-
perceived need for protection. For, unlike married women, many
unmarried women who will be sexually active at some time during a year are unable to look ahead and see a future of frequent
and regular intercourse. However, the group of sexually active
women most likely to get pregnant are those having frequent intercourse. This group should be more likely than the less active
to perceive the need for contraception and to come into the clinics to get it.

At present both the Pill and IUD are defined by most women
as methods to be used during long-run periods of exposure to

---

46. M. Zelnik, and J. Kantner, "Sexuality, Contraception, and Pregnancy Among
Young Unwed Females in the United States," *op. cit.*, Table 7.

risk. For many sexually active unmarried women their actual sexual behavior does not fit this definition, and we would not expect them to accept this type of contraception. This should, in theory, be true of poor and nonpoor, younger and older, low and higher parity women. Until something similar to the morning after pill is available, this segment of sexually active unmarried women are unlikely to have an acceptable female method of contraception from either public or private sources. In the absence of such a breakthrough in technology (and in use when it comes to pass), the above comments on the distribution of coital acts among sexually active unmarried women suggests that a successful program using currently available methods is likely to attract 40 rather than 100 percent of teenage women at risk of pregnancy. Table II-V indicates that a program open to *all* economic classes could realistically expect to reduce nonwhite illicit pregnancies by 13 to 27 percent. Among whites perhaps 20 percent could be prevented. Because the existing program does not reach the nonpoor population, its effects on the total number of illicit pregnancies would be even less.

This 40 percent guess-estimate of the percentage participating in a program may be on the high side because the majority of potential teenage unwed mothers in any year are not only involved in a sexual activity pattern that depresses their perceived need for self-protection, but most of them have not yet experienced pregnancy, they are poor economically, and they are terribly ignorant of the facts of reproduction.[47] To each of the characteristics that depress the level of effective contraceptive use among the unmarried as compared to the married we must add a multiplier effect to account for the status of being unmarried. That is, each of the above characteristics has a greater impact on depressing the effective contraceptive practice among the unmarried teenager than among married women.[48]

We conclude that if unwanted illicit pregnancies and illegiti-

---

47. *Ibid.,* Tables 3 and 4.
48. P. Cutright, "Timing the First Birth; Does It Matter?" *op. cit.* J. Kantner and M. Zelnik, "Contraception and Pregnancy: Experiences of Young Unmarried Women in the United States," *op. cit.,* p. 43.

mate births are to be greatly reduced through public programs, the programs will have to change. The single thought that has dominated the thinking of policy makers in the past has been to get women into the program, but we have demonstrated that this will not be enough. The program will have to change in other ways. The major barrier to increased impact is the contraceptive failure rate. The programs can only prescribe those contraceptives which exist and, even with stronger efforts to follow up and switch patients who have discontinued one method, the problems inherent in contraception-only programs will remain.[49] For some years to come, available contraceptive methods will leave large numbers of patients with unwanted pregnancies.

An alternative to the goal of preventing unwanted pregnancy is one of preventing unwanted births. That is, public programs could include abortion as a backstop method for contraceptive failure. Inclusion of abortion would not help reduce unwanted pregnancies, but it might reduce illegitimate births. The following section discusses the probable impact of abortion programs on illegitimacy.

PROBABLE EFFECTS OF ABORTION-ON-REQUEST ON ILLEGITIMACY

Although it is often said that nonwhites are less likely than whites to use abortion as a means of controlling fertility,[50] empirical evidence does not support this view.[51] Table II-VI shows the ratio of legal abortions per 1,000 live births by patient char-

49. R. Potter, "Inadequacy of a One-Method Family Planning Program." *Studies in Family Planning*, pp. 1-6 (January, 1971). R. Potter and J. Sakoda, "A Computer Model of Family Building Based on Expected Values," *Demography*, 3:450-461 (1966).

50. P. Gebhard, W. Pomeroy, C. Martin and C. Christensen, *Pregnancy, Birth and Abortion* (New York, John Wiley & Sons, 1966), Chapter 6. M. Zelnik and J. Kantner, "United States: Exploratory Studies of Negro Family Formation—Factors Relating to Illegitimacy," *op. cit.*, p. 8.

51. G. Greenberg, and D. Horvitz, "Estimates of Induced Abortion in Urban North Carolina," *Demography*, 7:19-30 (February, 1970). J. Pakter and F. Nelson, "Abortion in New York City: The First Nine Months," *Family Planning Perspectives*, 3:5-11 (July, 1971) C. Tietze, "Two Years' Experience with a Liberal Abortion Law: Its Impact on Fertility Trends in New York City," *Family Planning Perspectives*, 5:36-41 (Winter 1973).

TABLE II-VI

ESTIMATED LEGALLY INDUCED ABORTIONS PER 1,000 LIVE BIRTHS:
NEW YORK CITY RESIDENTS, JULY 1970-MARCH 1971

Patient Characteristics	*Legal Abortions Per 1,000 Live Births*
Poor (municipal hospitals)	775
Nonwhite	594
First births	590*
Aged 19 or less	527
White	422
All women	448

*First births estimated by assuming that one-third of all live births were first births.

Source: Pakter and Nelson, *op. cit.*, pp. 6-7.

Note: The abortion ratio increased from 448 to 650 for all women in the 1971-1972 period. See C. Tietze, "Two Years' Experience with a Liberal Abortion Law: Its Impact on Fertility Trends in New York City," *op. cit.*, Table 4.

acteristics in New York City. There were an estimated 594 legal abortions for every 1,000 nonwhite births; among whites the abortion ratio was 422. Whatever the truth of the old argument about illegal abortion use by nonwhites and whites, Table II-VI proves that nonwhites will be more likely than whites to abort a pregnancy when abortion is legalized.

Table II-VI also shows that the same women we have suggested are least likely to be effective contraceptors are more likely than other women to use abortion when it is legal. Patients in hospitals serving the poor have a legal abortion ratio of 775; the legal abortion ratio for first births was 590; among women nineteen years and under the ratio was 527. All these ratios are far above the ratio for all New York City residents, which was just 448 in 1970 and early 1971. Thus, the poor, the nonwhite, the never-before-pregnant, and the very young are more likely than other women to abort. The reason for this is simple: these are the same women least skilled in contraceptive practice and thus the most likely to experience unwanted pregnancy.

Detailed data on illegitimate births in New York City during the first year of the legal abortion era are now available. Tietze comments that for the first time since illegitimacy statistics were tabulated in New York (1954), the number of illegitimate births has declined.[52] Between 1960 and 1968 the average annual percentage increase in the number of illegitimate births in New York City was 11 percent.[53] In contrast to this pattern of rising illegitimacy, there was a decline of 12 percent between 1970 and 1971. Because the ratio of abortions to live births is increasing, it is likely that further declines in illegitimate births will occur. Since the numbers of unmarried women age fifteen to forty-four has increased, while the number of illegitimate births has declined, it seems clear that the illegitimacy rate has declined. This decline in the illegitimacy rate appears to be a function of the abortion rather than the contraception program in New York City. From 1960 through 1968, for example, the number of white and nonwhite illegitimate births increased more rapidly than elsewhere in the nation. These increases occurred in spite of the fact that there were virtually no contraceptive services available in 1960, while 44 percent of the population in need were estimated to be in a program in 1968.[54] Thus, while it may be true that illegitimacy would have increased even more rapidly in the absence of a contraceptive program, we conclude that the contraceptive program is not responsible for the recent decline in illegitimacy. Rather, the decline is due to the abortion program. It is too early to say what the long-run impact of abortion on request will be on illegitimacy in New York City, but the probable impact can be judged with data from Eastern European nations and Japan.

Table II-VII shows illegitimacy rates in the first year (or before) and then in years following the introduction of legal abortion on request. In Hungary the number of legal abortions rose rapidly *after* 1954, stabilized during the early 1960's, and then rose again after 1962. The illegitimacy rate declined from a high of 23.8 in 1954 to a low of 10.1 in 1965.

---

52. C. Tietze, *op. cit.,* p. 39.

53. H. Cohen, "Coping With Poverty," in L. Fitch and A. Walsh (eds.) , *Agenda for a City: Issues Confronting New York* (New York, Sage Publications, Inc., 1970) , pp. 127-128.

54. Office of Economic Opportunity, *Need For Subsidized Planning Services: United States, Each State and County, 1968. op. cit.,* Table 1.

TABLE II-VII

ILLEGITIMACY RATES PER 1,000 UNMARRIED WOMEN AGED 15-44 IN
NATIONS BEFORE AND AFTER LEGALIZATION OF ABORTION
ON REQUEST

| | | Country | | |
Year	Hungary	Czechoslovakia	Poland	Japan
1947	16.1	na	na	11.9
1950	20.0	na	na	6.9
1952	19.3	na	na	na
1954	23.8	na	na	na
1956	18.8	17.3	19.3	3.1*
1958	14.1	15.1	19.0	na
1960	12.5	12.3	15.6	3.0
1962	10.9	10.9	13.6	na
1964	10.3	12.3	11.6	na
1965	10.1	11.9	11.4	1.6

na = Not available.
Source: P. Cutright, *Illegitimacy: Measurement and Analysis, op. cit.,* Chapter 4.
S. Hartley, "The Decline of Illegitimacy in Japan," *op. cit.*
    * 1955.

In Czechoslovakia a significant number of legal abortions were first performed in 1958, and the numbers have remained fairly stable since 1959. The illegitimacy rate declined from 17.3 in 1956 to 11.9 in 1965.

In Poland the number of legal abortions rose from only 19,000 in 1956 to 45,000 in 1958, and then peaked at around 150,000 in 1960. As in the case of Hungary and Czechoslovakia, the rise in the number of legal abortions in Poland is paralleled by a declining illegitimacy rate.

In Japan abortion was legalized for economic reasons in 1948, and 1952 brought further liberalization of the law. The legal abortion ratio was 209 in 1950 and rose to 690 by 1956. Although other conditions in Japan before and after World War II suggest that some decline in Japanese rates would have occurred had abortion not been legalized, both Hartley and I attribute some of the observed decline to the independent effects of legalization of abortion.[55]

For these four populations we conclude that one effect of le-

---

55. P. Cutright, *Illegitimacy: Measurement and Analysis, op. cit.,* Chapter 4.
S. Hartley, "The Decline of Illegitimacy in Japan," *Social Problems,* 18:119-127 (1970) .

galization of abortion was a net increase in the induced abortion rate to unmarried women. Also, it took several years before the full effect on legal abortion was realized, and it may be the case that the European illegitimacy rates continued to decline after 1965. Thus, to judge the effects of New York City's abortion program on illegitimacy after only one or two years is premature. From the trends in Table II-VII we suspect that abortion will increase among the unmarried. If New Yorkers follow the trends indicated for Hungary, they will reduce their illegitimacy rate by some 50 percent in six or eight years. There is no evidence from any population that such a decline in an illegitimacy rate can be achieved with a contraception-only program.

Recent analysis of the impact of California's steps toward more open access to legal abortion on illegitimacy support the New York City reports. Sklar and Berkov[56] report increasing use of legal abortion by white and black unmarried women from 1969 through 1972. Legal abortion ratios per 1,000 illegitimate live births in 1971-1972 were 2,326 and 1,105 for white and nonwhite unmarried, compared to 98 and 253 per 1,000 legitimate births for white and nonwhite married women. The 1970-1971 legal abortion rates per 1,000 unmarried white and black women aged fifteen to forty-four were 17 and 38, respectively, with the legal abortion rates for unmarried girls aged fifteen to nineteen being 28 and 55, respectively.

The long run upturn in California's illegitimacy rates was reversed by a sharp decline in the rate between 1970 and 1971. The illegitimacy rate in 1972 was still lower than that of 1971. The age and marital status detail in the California data suggest that the impact of legalization of abortion on illegitimacy the first year or so after the procedure becomes widely available is greater among older than among teenage unmarried women.

PUBLIC OPINION AND BIRTH CONTROL SERVICES FOR THE UNMARRIED TEENAGER

If it were true that most of the American public opposed contraception or abortion services, it might be useless to discuss the

56. June Sklar and Beth Berkov, "The Role of Legal Abortion in Fertility Decline: The California Experience" (Institute of International Studies, University of California, Berkeley, 1973).

merits of such a program. We now turn to recent polls that have measured public attitudes on these issues.

A June 1972 Gallop poll of 1,574 adults aged eighteen and older asked whether respondents agreed or disagreed that sexually active teenagers should have "professional birth control information, services, and counseling."[57] The first column in Table II-VIII shows the percentage of different types of adults who agreed with the above question. Overall 73 percent of adults agreed. There is a tendency for younger persons, Protestants, whites, and persons with high school or college educations to be more favorable than older persons, Catholics, blacks, or persons with less than a high school education. Still, the majority of the less well-educated and over two-thirds of Catholics approve of birth control for teenagers.

A second question asked whether the respondent agreed that the abortion decision should be a matter between the woman and her doctor. Nearly two-thirds of all Americans agreed with this statement. College educated persons, whites, and Protestants were most favorable. There was little difference among older or younger respondents or between men and women. Again, even in the less favorable groups the majority of respondents were in favor of elective abortion. The responses on this question closely follow other surveys which have asked whether adults favored changing state laws so abortion would be a matter between the woman and her physician.[58]

The high level of agreement with the concept of elective abortion does not mean that the majority of the population approve of abortion. When asked in 1972, we find that 40 percent of the population still disapproves of abortion for unmarried women.[59] However, this is not a relevant datum if one is assessing the feasibility of including abortion in a birth control program. Rather, given the Supreme Court decision of January 1973, the

---

57. R. Pomeroy and L. C. Landman, "Public Opinion Trends: Elective Abortion and Birth Control Services to Teenagers," *Family Planning Perspectives*, 4:44-55 (October, 1972).

58. *Boston Globe*, p. 5 (March 24, 1971).

59. R. Pomeroy, *et al., op. cit.*, Table 6.

TABLE II-VIII

PERCENTAGE OF AMERICAN ADULTS FAVORING BIRTH CONTROL
FOR SEXUALLY ACTIVE TEENAGERS AND THE PERCENTAGE
AGREEING THAT ABORTION SHOULD BE A MATTER
SOLELY FOR A WOMAN AND HER DOCTOR
TO DECIDE: 1972

Characteristics of Respondents	Percentage for Teenage Birth Control Services	Percentage Favoring Elective Abortion
Total	73	64
Sex		
Male	73	63
Female	72	64
Age		
18-29	81	65
30-39	80	62
40-49	76	65
50+	61	63
Religion		
Protestant	73	65
Catholic	68	56
Race		
White	73	65
Black	63	52
Education		
Not high school graduate	58	50
High school graduate	77	70
College	87	74

Source: R. Pomeroy and L. C. Landman, "Public Opinion Trends: Elective Abortion and Birth Control Services to Teenagers." *Family Planning Perspectives,* 4:44-55 (October, 1972). Data are from national Gallup Poll of June, 1972.

Respondents were asked: "To what extent do you agree or disagree with the following statement: Professional birth control information, services, and counseling should be made available to unmarried teenagers who are sexually active," and "The decision to have an abortion should be made solely by a woman and her doctor."

problem now rests in changing actual behavior in local hospitals and clinics.

The Court decision had, it appears, wide public approval. If the current efforts in local communities to implement that decision are successful, illegitimacy rates should decline over the next few years, as abortion use increases. On the other hand, if the minority now working to overturn the Court decision by means of a constitutional amendment are successful, the bulk of legal abortions will revert to illegal abortions. Tietze[60] notes that about 70 percent of the legal abortions represented in the 1971-1972 New York City resident abortion ratio of 650 legal abortions per 1,000 live births were formerly performed illegally.

CONCLUSIONS

If teenage illegitimacy rates are to decline in the near future because of deliberate actions by government, such a decline may be achieved by greatly expanding the contraception program and by including abortion on request as part of the public and private birth control services. Contraception-only programs have not yet demonstrated their capacity to prevent a significant number of unwanted illicit pregnancies in any large population. In contrast, there is substantial evidence that abortion on request can reduce first as well as higher illegitimate births and cut the illegitimacy rate by 30 to 50 percent in less than a decade.

While the case of abortion-on-demand as a method of reducing illegitimate births seems to be rather well documented and the case for contraception programs is not, we need not become too enthusiastic for abortion at the expense of contraception. First, some unmarried girls will use contraception if it is available but will not abort if pregnant. Second, there seems little reason why failure rates in contraception programs need be as high as they are. Perhaps less dependence on the pill and improved care of patients will result in lower patient failure rates. Third, new contraceptive methods are on the way. In particular, the newer types of IUD's which can be used by never-pregnant women have much lower expulsion rates and much greater effectiveness while in place than do the IUD's currently used for parous women.[61] Fourth, the effect of marital status and poverty on depressing effective contraception practice among older women appears to be lessening—witness the huge declines in marital fertility and illegitimacy among older nonwhite women. It would be premature to abandon the effort to increase the use of effective contraception by unmarried women, simply because the task is difficult.

---

60. C. Tietze, *op. cit.*, p. 41.

61. S. B. Schearer, "Tomorrow's Contraception," in C. F. Westoff, (ed.), *Toward the End of Growth* (Englewood Cliffs, N. J., Prentice-Hall, Inc., 1973), p. 47-56.

CHAPTER III

OBSTETRICAL AND MEDICAL PROBLEMS OF TEENAGE PREGNANCY

Robert C. Stepto, Louis Keith, and Donald Keith

I INTRODUCTION

PREGNANCY AMONG TEENAGE GIRLS is a phenomenon of our times. Until recently its occurrence was not particularly frequent in the United States, but rapidly changing attitudes, coupled with the so-called "sexual revolution," have changed this. No cultural, racial, or socioeconomic group has managed to prevent pregnancy among its adolescent women. Slowly but steadily, a body of knowledge has appeared demonstrating that the phenomenon of teenage pregnancy may be associated with numerous problems which are related, at least in part, to the age of the parturient. Ballard and Gold[1] have called teenage pregnancy "the adolescent trap," compounded from such factors as peer group pressure, parental deprivation, poor health and psychologic problems, drug abuse, and juvenile delinquency.

The allover incidence of teenage pregnancy has been increasing steadily despite a generally declining birth rate in the general population. Few signs of leveling off or reversal have been noted. In 1971, more than 200,000 women under the age of eighteen were parturients.[2] In the State of Illinois, modest declines in the age-specific resident live birth rate for women age fifteen to nineteen years have been contrasted by an almost twofold increase in the same rate among girls aged ten to fourteen years (Table III-I) when the decade years of 1950, 1960, and 1970 are considered.

Problems related to teenage pregnancy will undoubtedly occu-

1. W. M. Ballard and E. M. Gold, "Medical and health aspects of reproduction in the adolescent," *Clinical Obstetrics and Gynecology*, 14:338 (1971).

2. M. Howard, "Comprehensive community programs for the pregnant teen-ager," *Clinical Obstetrics and Gynecology*, 14:473 (1971).

TABLE III-I

AGE-SPECIFIC LIVE BIRTH RATES BY FIVE-YEAR AGE GROUPS
(LIVE BIRTHS PER 1,000 IN AGE GROUPS) *

Race and Age (years)	Illinois			Chicago			Downstate		
	1950	1960	1970	1950	1960	1970	1950	1960	1970
All races									
10 to 14	0.6	0.7	1.3	0.9	1.5	2.9	0.4	0.3	0.6
15 to 19	65.3	82.8	68.1	61.4	96.7	100.8	67.7	75.6	54.8
White									
10 to 14	0.2	0.2	0.3	0.2	0.3	0.4	0.3	0.2	0.3
15 to 19	56.3	69.9	50.7	40.3	63.9	57.4	65.0	72.3	49.0
Other									
10 to 14	4.4	4.7	5.9	4.4	5.0	5.8	4.5	3.7	6.1
15 to 19	166.5	194.7	162.7	173.9	205.1	164.0	144.9	161.1	158.6

* Illinois Department of Public Health.

py greater proportions of the physicians' time in the next decade if the birth rate among older women continues in its present trend. Ideally, the management of large numbers of pregnant teenagers should be purely logistical. Unfortunately, this is not the case. Teenage pregnancies are a potential risk to the mother and child.[1] The first paper on the complications of teenage pregnancy appeared in 1922.[3] In the past decade there have been numerous articles on all aspects of teenage pregnancy. Pregnant teenagers are more likely to have complications of hypertension, toxemia, increased prematurity rate, higher perinatal mortality, anemia, prolonged labor, and higher rate of vaginal infections.[4-11] Classical textbooks of obstetrics generally mention teenage pregnancy only tangentially as it is related to specific conditions and problems.[4, 12]

3. J. W. Harris, "Pregnancy and labor in young primiparae," *Bulletin of the Johns Hopkins Hospital*, 333:12 (1922).

4. D. Jovanovic, "Pathology of pregnancy and labor in adolescent patients," *Journal of Reproductive Medicine*, 9:61 (1972).

5. M. H. Hassan and F. H. Falls, "The young primipara—A clinical study," *American Journal of Obstetrics and Gynecology*, 88:256 (1964).

6. A. A. Marchetti and J. S. Menaker, "Pregnancy and the adolescent," *American Journal of Obstetrics and Gynecology*, 59:1013 (1950).

7. S. R. Poliakoff, "Pregnancy in the young primigravida," *American Journal of Obstetrics and Gynecology*, 76:746 (1958).

8. A. C. Posner and M. Pulver, "An analysis of labor in young girls," *American Journal of Obstetrics and Gynecology*, 20:357 (1935).

This chapter will present an overview of the literature concerning the problems related to teenage pregnancy and an evaluation including some general principles of management for these pregnancies.

II THE SCOPE OF THE PROBLEM

Nature of the Teenager

The period of adolescence is difficult to define. It means different things to different observers. The teens, however, are clearly the years between thirteen and twenty. These years are a transitional period in developmental processes, having as their supposed goal the preparation of the individual to take his or her place in the family and the community. They are also characterized by biological drives which press for outlets while psychological development frequently lags behind physical development. Individuals are often unable to control and direct these opposing forces in a socially satisfactory or constructive manner.[13–15] At the same time compensating social restrictions are disappearing for young persons; opportunities for sexual activities have increased dramatically. Society, with its emphasis on fun and total exposure to sexual stimulation via the mass media, has forced the teenage female into situations that she is frequently incapable of handling.[13]

Table III-II presents a tabulation of some factors governing adolescent sexual activity and their sequelae.* The psychologic impact of pregnancy in a young girl may be a great deal more detrimental than the effects or complications, however grave in

---

9. J. B. Coates, "Obstetrics in the very young adolescent," *American Journal of Obstetrics and Gynecology,* 108:68 (1970).

10. P. M. Sarrel and L. V. Klerman, "The young unwed mother," *American Journal of Obstetrics and Gynecology,* 105:575 (1969).

11. J. Scher and W. H. Utian, "Teen-age pregnancy—An interracial study," *Journal of Obstetrics and Gynaecology at the British Commonwealth,* 77:259 (1970).

12. N. J. Eastman and L. M. Hellman, *Williams Obstetrics* (New York, Appleton-Century-Crofts, Inc., 1966.

13. W. G. Cobliner, "Teen-age out-of-wedlock pregnancy." *Bulletin of the New York Academy of Medicine,* 46:438 (1970).

14. H. Deutsch, *Selected Problems of Adolescence.* Psychoanalytic Study Child, Monograph No. 3 (New York, International Universities Press, Inc., 1967).

15. H. Deutsch, "The contemporary adolescent girl," *Seminars in Psychiatry,* 1:99 (1969).

TABLE III-II

FACTORS GOVERNING ADOLESCENT HETEROSEXUAL BEHAVIOR

Motives for or circumstances of sexual exposure
Curiosity, loneliness, need for affection, passivity (girls), preservation or enhancement of (sexual) self-image, rebellion, spirit of adventure, impulsivity, "disproving" homosexual tendencies, boredom, sexual needs, peer group pressure, conscious or unconscious desire for a child.
Awareness of associated risks
Misinformation, ignorance, incomplete information, diffusion of information (correct or incorrect) in peer group.
Intention for protection
Relation to partner, level of maturity, feeling of responsibility, reality orientation.
Access to protection
Available community resources, community attitudes.
Usage of protection
Personal experience, available practical instruction.

nature, of biologic immaturity.[16] Pregnancy is frequently psychologically traumatic and, in some cases, a disaster to the person who has not fully developed.[17] Poor obstetrical performance, on the other hand, is most likely (but not completely) related to the physical immaturity of the mother.[18]

Definition of Maturation Point

The average age of maturation has fallen considerably over the past seventy years. Tanner[19-21] observed that the decline in age of maturation in the United States has leveled off in the past fifteen years, after dropping from about 14.25 years in 1900 to about 12.5 years in 1955.[16] The average age of menarche is now

16. W. J. McGanity, *et al.*, "Relation of nutrition to pregnancy in adolescence," *Clinical Obstetrics and Gynecology*, 14:367 (1971).

17. J. D. Teichner and J. Jacobs, "Adolescents who attempt suicide: Preliminary findings," *American Journal of Psychiatry*, 122:1248 (1966).

18. D. G. Gill, R. Illsley and L. H. Koplik, "Pregnancy in teen-age girls," *Social Science and Medicine*, 3:549 (1970).

19. J. M. Tanner, *Growth at Adolescence*, Second edition (London, Blackwell Scientific Publications, 1962).

20. J. M. Tanner, *Growth and Endocrinology of Adolescence*, Endocrine and *Genetic Diseases of Childhood* (Philadelphia and London, W. B. Saunders Company, 1969).

21. J. M. Tanner, "The development of the female reproductive system during adolescence," *Clinical Obstetrics and Gynecology*, 3:135 (1960).

12.5 to thirteen years of age.[19, 22] A similar decline in age of menarche occurred during the same time span in Norway, Germany, Finland, Sweden, Denmark, and Great Britain.[19] Adolescent mothers are at the greatest risk if pregnancy occurs before cessation of linear growth. About four years after menarche, or at about seventeen years of age, most American teenagers have completed linear growth and have achieved gynecologic maturity. Correspondingly, mortality and nationality data indicate that the course and outcome of pregnancies in women seventeen to twenty years of age resemble those of young mature women, twenty to twenty-four years of age.

Age of the Adolescent Mother

While the literature frequently deals with patients of specific ages, the average age of adolescent mothers in the United States is about sixteen years.[4, 10, 23] The extremes include a low of ten years and conclude with the end of the nineteenth year. The percentage of teenage parturients in a given obstetric population varies with the nature and location of the sample. Specific ages of the total teenage population also vary in different locations. In the twelve hospitals which cooperated in the Collaborative Perinatal Study of the National Institute of Neurological Disease and Stroke (hereinafter referred to as the Niswander-Gordon study), the percentage of registrants in individual hospitals under fifteen years of age ranged from 0.1 to 3.3 percent, with an average of 0.9 percent.[24] When registrants between the ages of fifteen and nineteen years were considered, the range was from a low of 4.8 percent to a high of 29 percent with an average of 22.2 percent.[24]

Overview

There are diverse and conflicting opinions regarding the ob-

---

22. F. P. Heald, "Growth and development," *Clinical Obstetrics and Gynecology,* 14:327 (1971).

23. B. V. Lewis and P. J. Nash, "Pregnancy in patients under 16 years," *British Medical Journal,* 2:733 (1967).

24. K. R. Niswander and M. Gordon, *The Women and Their Pregnancies* (Philadelphia, W. B. Saunders Company, 1972).

stetrical performance of the teenage parturient.[10, 16, 18, 25-33] It is often difficult to draw substantive conclusions from the literature because of the nature of the study groups reported. These groups vary widely regarding chronologic and gynecologic age, racial, or ethnic background, socioeconomic strata and in the diagnostic or therapeutic routines used and the criteria against which they were measured.

The most frequently mentioned complications in recent literature on pregnancy among teenagers are (not in order): premature labor, low birth weight, increased neonatal mortality, iron-deficiency anemia, toxemia, prolonged labor, fetopelvic disproportion, vaginal infection, and vaginal lacerations.[1, 9, 16, 29] Table III-III presents a comparison of the incidences of some of the problems that can complicate the course and outcome of pregnancy among the very young (fourteen years or less) compared with patients above this age. While the numbers available for comparison in each group are not comparable, certain trends are noted.

The incidence and severity of complications of teenage pregnancy vary with the mother's race and socioeconomic situation. Indeed, life expectancy for an individual can be correlated with his or her social class.[10] The poor are prone to early and untimely

25. R. Aznar and A. E. Bennett, "Pregnancy in the adolescent girl," *American Journal of Obstetrics and Gynecology*, 81:934 (1961).

26. V. Jorgensen, "Clinical report on Pennsylvania hospitals' adolescent obstetric clinic," *American Journal of Obstetrics and Gynecology*, 112:816 (1972).

27. R. E. Lane and M. Brown, "Teen-age maternal mortality in Chicago (1956-1968)," *Illinois Medical Journal*, 139:241 (1971).

28. L. Klein, "Nonregistered obstetrics patients," *American Journal of Obstetrics and Gynecology*, 110:795 (1971).

29. I. W. Gabrielson, *et al.*, "Suicide attempts in a population pregnant as teenagers," *American Journal of Public Health*, 60:2289 (1970).

30. H. J. Osofsky, *The Pregnant Teen-Ager: A Medical, Educational and Social Analysis* (Springfield, Charles C Thomas, 1968).

31. M. S. Van de Marke and A. C. Wright, "Hemoglobin and folate levels of pregnant teen-agers," *American Diet Association Journal*, 61:511 (1972).

32. W. A. Daniel, J. R. Mounger and J. C. Perlsins, "Obstetric and fetal complication in folate deficient adolescent girls," *American Journal of Obstetrics and Gynecology*, 111:233 (1972).

33. J. L. Rauh, L. B. Johnson and R. L. Burket, "The management of adolescent pregnancy and prevention of repeat pregnancies," *HSMA Health Reports*, 86:66 (1971).

TABLE III-III

COMPARISON OF COMPLICATIONS IN PATIENTS LESS THAN
14 YEARS OF AGE WITH CONTROLS[9]

| | Women Less Than 14 Years of Age | | Women Over 14 Years of Age | |
	No.	Percent	No.	Percent
Prenatal care	71	51.8	1,309	44.1
Acute toxemia	20	14.6	234	7.9
Heart disease	4	2.9	26	0.9
Uterine dysfunction	54	39.4	922	31.1
Contracted pelvis	21	15.3	334	11.3
One-day fever	25	18.3	249	8.4
Postpartum hemorrhage	0	00.0	94	3.2

demise for a variety of reasons. Obstetric patients are no exception. While mortality rates for infants and mothers have improved in the past years, there has been a disproportionate improvement among white patients and favored socioeconomic groups when compared to black patients and those at the lower end of the social spectrum.

If one accepts the premise that, among the primary goals of most obstetricians is the continued health of the mother before, during, and after gestation, pregnancy in the exceedingly young patient frequently fails to achieve this objective.[1] The outcome of a pregnancy cannot be measured in the quality of maternal health alone. It is equally important to consider the fate of the infant, the area of greatest risk associated with adolescent pregnancy. The continuing excessive loss of human life in the form of pregnancy wastage can be detected by even a casual observer through the examination of infant and perinatal mortality and morbidity rates of teenage mothers. Tragically, most of this wastage has preventable factors which can be detected, treated, and corrected either preconceptually and/or prenatally.[34-36]

34. E. M. Gold and W. M. Ballard, "The role of family planning in prevention of pregnancy wastage," *Clinical Obstetrics and Gynecology*, 13:145 (1970).

35. J. P. Semmens, "Implications of teen-age pregnancy," *Obstetrics and Gynecology*, 26:77 (1965).

36. W. T. Tompkins, "National efforts to reduce perinatal mortality and morbidity," *Clinical Obstetrics and Gynecology*, 13:44 (1970).

The implications are clear. Prenatal care, preventive medicine, and careful screening for special conditions may reduce the incidence and severity of complications of teenage pregnancy.[16, 30, 37] Interestingly, as the incidence of complications rises, so does the incidence of suicide among teenage pregnant patients,[16, 30, 38] as documented by Evans,[39] Gabrielson and associates[29] and others.[11, 40, 41] The risk of self-harm is a real one and the myth that suicide does not occur during pregnancy must be regarded exactly as that.

Capsule Comments from the Literature

Several studies demonstrate the complex intertwining of out-of-wedlock pregnancy, socioeconomic background, age, and race. Patker *et al.*[42] found the incidence of hypertension and toxemia to be 50 percent greater among unmarried patients. Indeed, almost all complications of pregnancy were more prevalent among unmarried women. The puerperal maternal death rate was more than four times as high for unmarried women (21.3 per 10,000 live births) as for the married sample (5.0 per 10,000 live births). When deaths resulting from illegal abortions were excluded, the mortality rate for unmarried mothers was still almost twice that of married mothers.[42] Many of the differences between married and unmarried women were correlated to ethnic background and socioeconomic state.[42]

---

37. J. P. Semmens and W. M. Lamers, *Teen-age Pregnancy. Including Management of Emotional and Constitutional Problems* (Springfield, Charles C Thomas, 1968).

38. Article: "Suicide risk in teen-age pregnancy," *British Medical Journal,* 2:602 (1971).

39. J. G. Evans, "Deliberate self-poisoning in the Oxford area," *British Journal of Preventative and Social Medicine,* 21:97-107 (July, 1967).

40. T. F. Pugh, B. K. Jerath, W. M. Schmidt and R. B. Reed, "Rates of mental disease related to childbearing," *New England Journal of Medicine* 268:1224 (1963).

41. F. A. Whitlock and J. F. Edwards, "Pregnancy and attempted suicide," *Comprehensive Psychiatry,* 9:1 (1968).

42. J. Pakter, H. J. Rosner, H. Jacobziner and F. Greenstein, "Out-of-wedlock births in New York City," II, "Medical Aspects," *American Journal of Public Health,* 51:846 (1961).

Stine[43] compared neonatal and prematurity rates on the basis of the race and age of the mothers. The incidence of prematurity was 14.2 percent in nonwhite mothers but only 7.6 percent in white mothers. The neonatal death rate of 29.5 percent per 1,000 live births among the nonwhites dropped to a 17.4 percent among the whites. Age also had a correlation to prematurity. The seventeen to nineteen year group showed a 13.9 percent prematurity rate. This increased to 18.1 percent in mothers under seventeen. These young patients had a neonatal mortality rate of 35.8 percent per 1,000 live births as compared to 27.5 percent per 1,000 live births for the seventeen- to nineteen-year-old mothers and 23.2 percent per 1,000 live births for all mothers regardless of age. When Stine combined age and race the results became even more dramatic. Mothers, who were white, ages seventeen to nineteen, had an incidence of prematurity of 8.5 percent. For those who were nonwhite and the same age the rate rose to 17.3 percent. Mothers who were white and under seventeen had 11.1 percent prematurity. The nonwhite mothers of the same age had 20.3 percent prematurity. Additional comments in this area have been made by Battaglia *et al.*[44]

Zackler and co-workers[45] studied the outcome of pregnancy in 2,403 girls receiving prenatal care at the Chicago Board of Health clinics. This was compared to the outcome of pregnancy in 4,400 girls in the same age group who had not received prenatal care at the Chicago Board of Health. In all parameters studied, the patients who had been in a well-organized health care program fared better. The general conclusions are evident and they are consistent. Low maternal age by itself is related to an increased incidence of complications and fetal wastage. If the

---

43. O. C. Stine, R. V. Rider and E. Sweenez, "School leaving due to pregnancy in an urban adolescent population," *American Journal of Public Health*, 54:1 (1964).

44. F. C. Battaglia, T. M. Frazier and A. E. Hellegers, "Birth weight, gestational age, and pregnancy outcome, with special reference to high birth weight, low gestational age," *Pediatrics*, 37:417 (1966).

45. J. Zackler, S. L. Andelman and F. Bauer, "The young adolescent as an obstetric risk," *American Journal of Obstetrics and Gynecology*, 103:305 (1969).

young mother is also from a poverty situation, is unmarried, and happens to be nonwhite, the degree of risk becomes extremely high for mother and child.

III MEDICAL COMPLICATIONS

Iron Deficiency Anemia and Folate Deficiency

Gravid patients frequently function in a state of mild anemia. They are also susceptible to folic acid deficiency. The causes and the dietary requirements are discussed in detail in Chapter IV.

Drug Abuse

Drug abuse among teenagers is a complex problem. It is compounded by an inability to define where use becomes abuse. The effects of psychedelic or hallucinogenic drugs, sedatives, tranquilizers, stimulants, and narcotics on mother and fetus still remain in dispute.[46–51]

From an obstetric point of view, most pregnant drug-dependent patients who come to delivery do not present diagnostic or therapeutic challenges. Some indications exist that these patients have a higher incidence of complications such as toxemia, premature separation of the placenta, or postpartum hemorrhage. Most obstetricians in the average hospital can treat those conditions. If the medical complications common to drug-dependent persons are superimposed on a pregnant patient, however, diagnostic and therapeutic challenges may occur. Infectious hepatitis,

46. L. Bender and D. V. Siva Sankar, "Chromosome damage not found in leucocytes of children treated with LSD-25," *Science (NY)*, 159:749 (1968).

47. M. M. Cohen, K. Hirschhorn and W. A. Frosch, "In vivo and in vitro chromosomal damage induced by LSD-25," *New England Journal of Medicine*, 277:1043 (1967).

48. M. Hultin, J. Lindsten, L. Lidberg and H. Ekelund, "Studies on mitotic and meiotic chromosomes in subjects exposed to LSD," *Annales de Genetique*, 11:201 (1968).

49. S. Irwin and J. Egozcue, "Chromosomal abnormalities in leucocytes from LSD-25 users," *Science (NY)*, 157:313 (1967).

50. D. J. Lyon, "Developing a program for pregnant teen-agers through the cooperation of school, health department, and federal agencies," *American Journal of Public Health*, 58:2225 (1968).

51. B. J. Polland, L. Wagon and J. Calvin, "Teen-agers, illicit drugs and pregnancy," *Canadian Medical Association Journal*, 107:955 (1972).

malnutrition, syphilis, thromboembolic phenomena, repeated and recurrent infections, anemia, and possible drug withdrawal or drug intoxication from heroin or other drugs are all complications experienced by the drug-dependent gravida.[4, 16]

The admissions of 104 drug-dependent patients to the obstetric service of the Cook County Hospital were reviewed for the thirty-nine-month period from January 1, 1961 to March 31, 1972.[52] Nine teenage patients accounted for 8.9 percent of the group. Six of the nine patients delivered; one patient had an incomplete abortion followed by a dilatation and curettage; another patient was admitted to rule out ectopic pregnancy (she was found to have pelvic inflammatory disease); and the last patient had false labor, was sent home with advice, and never returned. Among the six who delivered, Table III-IV lists their course from admission.

The prematurity rate of 66 percent was higher than for the whole sample (41.7%. Both of these rates are more than three times the general prematurity rate of the hospital 14%). The percentage of ruptured membranes prior to admission was equal in teenage and older addicted patients (50%). Two-thirds of the teenagers had no prenatal care. This is more than twice the figure for the general obstetric population of the hospital. The incidence of prematurity, lack of prenatal care, and rupture of the membranes prior to the onset of labor corresponds in general to the reports in the literature.

Therapy of the drug-dependent pregnant patient depends in large part on whether the patient requests withdrawal during pregnancy or becomes an addicted obstetric patient. The major advantage of using the antepartum period to accomplish withdrawal is the opportunity to institute prenatal care which is otherwise often lacking. With adequate prenatal care, there is a *chance* of reducing the risk associated with pregnancy in this special group of patients.

---

52. L. Keith, D. Clark, R. Pildes and G. Vargas, "Drug-dependent obstetric patients: A study of 104 admissions to the Cook County Hospital," *Journal of Obstetric Gynecology, Neonatal Nursing* (1974) in press.

TABLE III-IV

TEENAGE DRUG ADDICTED PREGNANT PATIENTS AT
COOK COUNTY HOSPITAL 1969-1971

Patient	Gravidity	Parity	Gestational Age (Weeks)	Prenatal Care	Ruptured Bag of Water	Drug Use in Previous 24 Hrs.	Birth Weight	Postpartum Maintenance	Complication
VB	3	2	26	+	+	+	2 lb. 15 oz.	+	
DB	4	1	28	–	–	N.S.*	2 lb. 12 oz.	+	Preeclampsia
BH	1	0	40	–	–	–	7 lb. 13 oz.	–	
JE	1	0	24	–	+	N.S.	2 lb. 6 oz.	N.S.	
BW	1	0	30	–	+	+	4 lb. 7 oz.	+	Endometriosis
NH	2	1	40	+	–	+	5 lb. 7 oz.	+	Acute appendicitis 3 days postpartum

* Not stated.

Venereal Disease

Statistics from all over the world support the existence of a pandemic of venereal disease greater than any previously known. In the United States, the incidence of reported cases of syphilis and gonorrhea has risen in the past decade (Table III-V). In some communities, patients under twenty years of age account for almost half of the reported cases of venereal disease. Repeated infections are common, as is a laissez-faire attitude toward treatment.

Accurate statistics regarding the incidence of venereal disease

TABLE III-V

INCIDENCE OF SYPHILIS AND GONORRHEA IN THE U. S. A.*

Age	Year	Male	Rates† Female	Total
		PRIMARY AND SECONDARY SYPHILIS		
0-14	1956	.1	.2	.2
	1960	.1	.4	.3
	—			
	1969	.3	.5	.4
	1970	.2	.6	.4
	1971	.3	.8	.5
15-19	1956	10.1	11.3	10.7
	1960	20.4	19.2	19.8
	—			
	1969	18.1	19.7	18.9
	1970	18.8	19.8	19.3
	1971	18.9	20.7	19.8
		GONORRHEA		
0-14	1956	2.9	11.5	7.1
	1960	5.4	12.1	8.7
	—			
	1969	7.7	13.6	10.6
	1970	9.1	17.1	13.0
	1971	9.3	19.9	14.5
15-19	1956	462.9	372.0	415.7
	1960	480.9	347.1	412.7
	—			
	1969	898.5	531.7	713.5
	1970	960.1	605.5	782.2
	1971	1012.7	761.9	887.3

* Venereal Disease Fact Sheet 1972, U.S.P.H.S.

† Rates per 100,000 population by age group and sex, United States—calendar years 1956, 1960 and 1969-1971.

among pregnant teenagers are not available. A 5 to 7 percent asymptomatic gonorrhea detection rate among all pregnant patients has been reported in several large areas. At the Cook County Hospital in Chicago, the rate of asymptomatic gonorrhea in the general obstetric population is 6.25 percent. In the Niswander-Gordon collaborative study, 0.31 percent of white gravidas and 3.2 percent of black gravidas had a positive serologic test for syphilis (STS).[24] No figures were available for rates of gonorrhea in this population.

A. Gonorrhea

Gonorrhea is a disease which defies efforts toward eradication. Factors making control difficult are the extremely short incubation period and the fact that little or no immunity is produced by the infection. Repeated infections are common, and many carriers remain asymptomatic. Fully 90 percent of the women harboring the organism fall in this class.[53, 54] Five to 10 percent of men are similarly affected.

PATHOGENICITY. The gonococcus generally enters the body via the mucosa of the genitourinary tract in most cases,[53, 54] and the anal canal[55] or the posterior pharynx in some instances. Penetration occurs most frequently via the urethra, cervix, Bartholin gland ducts, and periureteral ducts. Infection leads to an acute inflammatory response resulting in a purulent yellow-white discharge.

Passage of the gonococci into lymphatic channels occurs soon after initial infection. Lymphatic spread of the gonococcus results in infection of the uterus and fallopian tubes. Occasionally pus escaping into the peritoneal cavity results in peritonitis. Anorectal involvement is seen in women and often leads to perianal and ischiorectal abscesses. If the infection becomes blood borne, other sequelae may occur.

CLINICAL INFECTION. In women, acute urethral or endocervical

53. L. G. Keith and C. Rosenberg, "Venereal disease: A timely reminder," *Chicago Medicine*, 72:797 (1969).

54. L. Keith, "The female urethra," Chapter 31, *Davis' Gynecology and Obstetrics*, J. J. Rovinsky (Ed.), III:1, 1972.

55. J. Bang, "Demonstration of gonoccocci in rectal culture," *Acta Dermato-Venereologica*, 34:4 (1954).

gonorrhea is generally difficult to detect. Diagnosis is based on bacteriologic evidence or on a history of contact with an infected man. Spread of the infection leads to involvement of the fallopian tubes and uterus. Frequently, salpingitis recurs in repeated episodes marked by pain and fever. The physician cannot be certain whether these recurrent episodes reflect reinfection or reactivation of organisms not destroyed by prior treatment.

COMPLICATIONS OF GONORRHEA. The commonest extragenital complication of gonorrhea is arthritis. Even so, it occurs in less than 3 percent of infected persons. The ratio of women to men is two to one. The onset frequently occurs shortly after the menses, and 25 percent of cases occur in the immediate postpartum period. Meningitis is a less common but more severe complication of gonorrhea and gonococcal endocarditis is an even rarer complication. Gonococcal conjunctivitis may result in corneal perforation. Pharyngitis with abscess may result from the practice of fellatio or blood-borne infection. Other uncommon complications of gonorrhea include uveitis, myocarditis, pericarditis, glomerulonephritis, perihepatitis, osteomyelitis, liver abscess, and pneumonia.

DIAGNOSIS. The most reliable method of diagnosis in women is culture. The cervix is most frequently involved, yielding positive results in up to 85 percent of cases. In about 10 percent of female patients the only positive culture occurs in the rectum. Other sites of positive culture may be the vagina and urethra. Use of selective culture media is essential for the proper growth of these organisms.[56]

THERAPY. The treatment of gonorrhea, once considered a simple and unquestioned procedure, has changed in recent years. Penicillin still remains the drug of choice despite the marked escalation in the dosages required to achieve a cure. For patients who cannot take penicillin, alternate drugs are available.

B. Syphilis

Despite reports to the contrary, virulent forms of the causative organism, *Treponema pallidum,* have not been grown *in vitro.*

---

56. J. D. Thayer and J. E. Martin, Jr., "A selective medium for the cultivation of N. gonorrhea and N. meningitidis," *Public Health Reports,* 79:49 (1964) .

The organism will remain viable in whole blood for twenty-four hours but not for forty-eight hours when stored at 4°C. The organism is immediately killed at 41.5 to 42°C. It is immobilized *in vitro* by various arsenicals, bismuth, and mercury and is killed by penicillin.

CLINICAL INFECTION. Syphilis is generally transmitted by direct contact with a lesion. The organism may enter by penetration through the intact mucosa or may enter the skin directly via small breaks. The STS during the incubation period of ten to sixty days may be negative. Secondary lesions appear within two to twelve weeks after primary infection. They are highly infectious. Late lesions may begin several years after primary infection. Not every untreated patient will go on to develop these lesions. Fifty percent of untreated cases pass into the tertiary stage. Except for gumma formation, which is probably hyperimmune in etiology, the damage done to the body during late syphilis is produced by an obliterative arteritis of the small arteries and arterioles.

Immunity to syphilis is a subject of considerable controversy. Most authorities agree that resistance to reinfection begins about three weeks after appearance of the primary lesion. If adequate treatment is begun early, the host is fully susceptible to reinfection. The persistence of latent infection causes resistance to be maintained. Presence of immobilizing antibodies in the circulation as indicated by positive TPI tests is a contributing factor to acquired resistance.

DIAGNOSIS. Laboratory diagnosis of syphilis requires the detection of *T. pallidum*. This may be done directly by darkfield examination of material obtained from a primary or secondary lesion. Fluorescent labeled antibody tests confirm the presence of treponema in the blood. Secondary information concerning infection is derived through the use of STS. Biologic false positive reactions may result from such diseases as malaria, infectious mononucleosis, systemic lupus erythematosis, and leprosy. Other patients may react falsely because of certain drugs they may be taking.

Syphilis during pregnancy requires special considerations. Infection of the fetus takes place via the placenta but the treponema is not passed to the fetus prior to the fourth month of gestation. Proper antepartum care requires an STS. Therapy before sixteen weeks of gestation will effect a cure *in utero* but may not prevent various stigmata of the disease.

Syphilis usually produces stillbirth rather than abortion. A woman who is adequately treated should be followed with quantitative serologic tests. A mother may become reinfected during a pregnancy, even after treatment. This is a good reason for continued quantitative testing. When the fetus is infected with the treponema and is not stillborn, congenital syphilis results.

THERAPY. The treatment has become fairly standardized since the widespread availability of penicillin. Continued use of fever therapy or arsenical or bismuth therapy no longer has a place in the modern medical armamentarium. As opposed to the treatment of gonorrhea, all forms of penicillin except oral are acceptable for treatment. Erythromycin is the drug of choice for pregnant women who are sensitive to penicillin, as tetracycline may produce staining of the teeth in the child. When there is a history of previous treatment in a pregnant woman with a positive STS, one must question carefully the type and amount of treatment already given, since an adequate course of penicillin treatment is enough unless reinfection or relapse occurs. A rising titer of reagin or TPI antibodies is indicative of active infection while a constant low titer probably is a residual of former infection and does not indicate active disease.

Vaginal Infection

The occurrence of vaginitis in pregnant women is common and occurs at all ages. Some studies elevate this condition to the status of a complication. Others simply mention it in passing. Treatment of all forms of vaginitis during pregnancy may be frustrating due to the tendency to recurrence but efforts at treatment for the patient and her partner are worthwhile. England *et al.*[57] have demonstrated that the cervices of a group of preg-

---

57. D. England, F. Bartizal, L. Keith, C. Fields and E. Brown, "The presence of corynebacterium, lactobacillus, trichomonas species and yeast in the external os of pregnant women," *Chicago Medical School Quarterly*, 31:5 (1972).

nant women harbored a variety of microorganisms, with yeast, lactobacillus, and corynebacteria predominating. Trichomonas species were noted in smaller numbers. When special anaerobic culture techniques are used, organisms of pathogenic potential can be grown from the normal cervix of nonpregnant women.[58] These organisms were most frequently cultured from abscesses in patients admitted to the Department of Obstetrics and Gynecology at the Cook County Hospital with severe infections of the generative tract.[59] Thus, treatment of vaginitis and cervicitis appears indicated in pregnant women.

A. Trichomonas Vaginalis

T. vaginalis vaginitis accounts for 50 percent of all cases of pathologic leukorrhea. This disease is present in 25 percent of all obstetric and gynecologic patients, though the incidence may go higher in some high-risk populations.

T. vaginalis is a flagellated protozoan that survives and multiplies at a vaginal pH of five to six. Its sources are both endogenous and exogenous, with the main endogenous source supposedly being the colon; however, some authorities doubt that *T. vaginalis* vaginitis results from fecal contamination because the organism lives in the intestinal tract for only a very short time. Other endogenous sources include the bladder, Bartholin's glands, Skene's ducts, and the urethra. The most common exogenous source is the urethral and the seminal fluid of the male which causes infection at time of coitus. Almost all transmission of this disease occurs via sexual intercourse.

Predisposing factors to *T. vaginalis* vaginitis include: (1) hyperestrinism (e.g. more acute infections in pregnancy and worse infections immediately after menses); (2) vaginal hypoacidity (e.g. from menstrual blood, cervical mucorrhea, *Haemophilus*

---

58. S. L. Gorbach, K. B. Menda, H. Thadepalli and L. Keith, "Anaerobic microflora of the cervix in healthy women," *American Journal of Obstetrics and Gynecology* 117:1053 (1973).

59. H. Thadepalli, S. L. Gorbach and L. Keith, "Anaerobic infections of the female genital tract: Bacteriologic and therapeutic aspects," *American Journal of Obstetrics and Gynecology* 117:1034 (1973).

vaginalis vaginitis), and (3) vaginal floral change with predominance of diphtheroids, streptococci, and staphylococci.

The disease exists in three forms. One form is the asymptomatic variant (mentioned here for completeness) in which the vaginal pH ranges between 3.8 and 4.2 with Doderline bacilli predominating in the flora. The other forms are the acute symptomatic and chronic symptomatic variants.

Acute symptomatic *T. vaginalis* vaginitis occurs in an alkaline vagina (i.e. the usual vaginal pH in this stage is between 5.2 and 5.5) or in the presence of a symbiosis between *T. vaginalis* and *Streptococcus subacidus*. With this form of the vaginitis, lactobacilli are absent from the flora. The vagina may appear mildly or diffusely reddened as well as moderately edematous. Numerous punctate red spots may be found on the face of the cervix and wall of the vagina yielding the so-called flea-bitten or strawberry mucosa. The discharge is heavy, yellow or green, often frothy with an odor described varying as faint and unpleasant, heavy, or fetid. The discharge may be creamy, purulent, fluid, or watery. The frothiness, if present, is from trichomonad fermentation and is highly characteristic.

With chronic symptomatic *T. vaginalis* vaginitis, no lactobacilli are present and there are no gross vulvar or vaginal changes. In about three-fourths of these cases, the discharge is gray. A greenish tint, if present (here or in the acute symptomatic form), is highly suggestive of the disease. Urinary tract invasion may be present.

In all the symptomatic forms, the findings include pruritis, vulval and/or vaginal soreness, and dyspareunia. Chafing is a pathognomonic sign. If *T. vaginalis* has produced a urinary tract infection, then dysuria and frequency will also be present.

One of the major ways to diagnose *T. vaginalis* vaginitis is via a wet mount containing one drop of discharge and one drop of warm isotonic saline. A positive result occurs when the motile organism, larger than a leukocyte and having three to five flagella at the anterior end as well as an undulating cell membrane, is observed. Another method substitutes Trichomonas diluent for isotonic saline. This stains pus and epithelial cells a light pink and leaves *T. vaginalis* unstained.

Another diagnostic technique is culture, which has similar accuracy to the wet mount and is therefore rarely warranted. The medium of choice is either simplified trypticase serum of Kupferberg or Wittington-Feinberg medium.

The pap smear may also be used diagnostically, even though it is much less satisfactory than either wet mount or culture. Finally, colposcopy can yield a diagnosis of *T. vaginalis* vaginitis. The presence of a 0.1-mm diameter red point surrounded by a white areola (0.5 mm in total diameter) is pathognomonic for this disease, although absence of this finding does not mean absence of disease. Furthermore, the presence of double crested capillaries has been correlated with the presence of *T. vaginalis.*

In treating *T. vaginalis* infection, the object is not only good immediate results but also the avoidance of recurrence. The major principles of therapy are: (1) instruction of the patient in good perineal hygiene (i.e. daily vulvar and perianal tissue washing with soap plus wiping the anus away from the vagina and the use of tampons instead of napkins); (2) proper douche technique, and (3) organism location and destruction. The theory behind the idea of good hygiene and proper douches is to keep the vaginal flora normal once the organisms have been killed.

The most successful treatment uses 250 mg of metronidazole (Flagyl®) orally thrice a day for ten days or four times a day for five days. In severe cases, 500 mg suppositories may be given intravaginally simultaneously. If the husband or consort is the suspected source, he should take 250 mg of Flagyl orally twice a day for ten days or four times a day for five days. With persistent cases, a repeat course of therapy can be given, but thirty days should elapse between courses. Flagyl is contraindicated in persons with blood dyscrasias or central nervous system disturbances because theoretically it can cause bone marrow depression. Oral therapy during pregnancy does not have FDA approval and vaginal suppositories are preferred.

B. Candida (Monilia) Albicans

The chief etiologic agent of this type of vaginitis is *C. albicans* which grow best at a pH of 5.5 to 6.8. Candidal organisms are indigenous to man. Fewer than 50 percent of patients who harbor this organism show clinical disease; it is not the only species among the Candida that can be pathogenic. *C. tropicalis* is also found (i.e. 28% of the time compared with 67% for *C. albicans*). In fact, *C. tropicalis* is more likely to be associated with chronicity and recurrence than is *C. albicans*. It is important to emphasize that Candida are found as part of the normal vaginal flora in 20 percent to 30 percent of women and in the feces of normal persons and hence the rectum. Other sources include the male foreskin, the male genitocrural area, and the prepuce of the clitoris. Transmission may be by conjugal means or by rectal contamination.

Predisposing factors to Candida infections include (1) pregnancy, with the severity of infection increasing with increasing gestational length (because of increased vaginal glycogen); (2) the time just prior to menstruation, again because of hormonal factors; (3) oral contraceptives with the sequential products having an effect less than that of the combinations because in the former, progestrogens are taken only during the last five days (i.e. estrogens induce glycogen deposition primarily in the intermediate cells, while progestogens cause the shedding of these cells); (4) antibiotics, especially the tetracyclines (i.e. producing increased candidal growth, reduced bacterial competition, decreased concentration of bacterial antifungal substances, or direct stimulation of Candida by the antibiotic—all questionable); (5) corticosteroid use (which produces an increased *in vitro* susceptibility with systemic application, though no aggravation of disease if applied topically and no effect on Candida *in vitro*); and (6) diabetes mellitus which can cause obstinate candidiasis. With these predisposing factors, it comes as no surprise that the disease occurs primarily between menarche and menopause.

Usually, candidiasis produces a reddened vaginal mucosa with white or yellow loosely adherent patches on the walls. There is a copious, curdy white discharge that may adhere to the external cervix and can be removed with an applicator. There may or may not be involvement of the vulva, interlabial, and intercrural folds (i.e. reddening). Less commonly, there is only a diffuse reddening of the vagina. In this case, a homogeneous white mucoid or mucopurulent discharge is present. The mean vaginal pH is 4.5 (i.e. range 4.0 to 4.7). The discharge is odorless. Besides the leukorrhea, which is not classical for this disease, the patient has an intense pruritis. There is usually irritation and dyspareunia as well and perhaps burning after urination. It would appear that the key to clinical candidiasis are host factors controlling susceptibility and not chance contamination by *C. albicans.*

The most efficient method for rapid identification of Candida is the potassium hydroxide preparation in which vaginal material is intermixed with 10 to 20 percent potassium hydroxide, causing immediate dissolution of erythrocytes and pus cells as well as transparency of the vaginal epithelial cells. The mycelia and Candida stand out well. The presence of pseudohyphae is pathognomonic.

Culture is diagnostic. Brown to black colonies appear five days after the inoculation of the discharge on Nickerson's medium kept at room temperature. The characteristic hyphae and buds are seen on a slide made from a small part of one of these colonies dissolved in 10 percent potassium hydroxide. This method, however, does not provide species differentiation.

Therapy uses nystatin (Mycostatin®) as vaginal tablets along with a locally applied cream of nystatin, neomycin, gramicidin, and triamcinolone acetate (Mycolog®), for one month daily including the menses. The regimen to be followed in resistant cases is 500,000 units of nystatin three to six times a day orally.

Other modes of therapy include (1) 100,000 units of vaginal nystatin twice a day for seven to fourteen days and nightly for the next two to three weeks; (2) candicidin (Candeptin®) vaginal tablets or ointment which have a similar efficacy, though a claim of greater potency, to nystatin—same regimen as for 1, and (3) chlordantoin (Sporostacin®) which has a decreased efficacy vis-à-vis either vaginal nystatin or candicidin as well as an increased incidence of local reactions—same regimen as for 1.

In pregnancy, the main idea is to control the symptoms via the use of intravaginal agents several times weekly since eradication may be impossible.

C. Haemophilus Vaginalis

H. vaginalis vaginitis used to be classified as a nonspecific vaginitis. Gardner and Dukes[60] proved Koch's postulates with this organism and believe that it accounts for most cases of nonspecific vaginitis, although other authors dispute this point.

H. vaginalis is a true surface parasite living on epithelial glycogen. It has an autogenous reservoir in the female urethra but the organism's concentration is small and cannot contribute to reinfection because of constant irrigation by the urinary stream. An exogenous source is the male urethra where this bacteria can be present asymptomatically. Transmission is almost always via intercourse.

The main predisposing factor to disease is hyperestrinism; hence, this disease occurs primarily in the reproductive years. When postmenopausal women carry this bacteria, the results are usually asymptomatic. An associated *H. vaginalis* infection appears in one-fourth of the cases of *T. vaginalis* vaginitis.

With *H. vaginalis* vaginitis, the vulva appears normal or slightly reddened, while the vaginal mucosa is either normal or contains small punctate hemorrhages. The vaginal pH is between 5.0 and 5.5 (range 4.0 to 6.0), and *H. vaginalis* predominates, the Doderline bacilli being eliminated by the first week. The discharge consisting primarily of bacteria and affected epithelium, usually soils undergarments and is gray-white, thin and frothy, smooth and homogeneous, or curdy. It has an offensive odor. Besides the leukorrhea, the patient may complain of a pruritis or vulvar burning or dyspareunia. Rarely is she asymptomatic.

The diagnosis of *H. vaginalis* vaginitis can be made from (1) a wet mount (presence of a clue cell: a large vaginal epithelial

---

60. H. L. Gardner and C. D. Dukes, *"Haemophilus vaginalis, vaginitis,"* **American** *Journal of Obstetrics and Gynecology,* 69:962 (1955).

cell with granular cytoplasm, indefinite cell membrane, and a covering of *H. vaginalis* on its surfaces; few if any leukocytes are present), (2) a gram stain, (3) a culture (with rabbit blood agar plates incubated in a candle jar and thioglycollate broth; oblique lighting should be used to detect the resultant colonies). Of these methods, the gram stain is the most accurate. *T. vaginalis* or *C. albicans* may be present simultaneously with *H. vaginalis*. In fact, a rough rule on differential diagnosis of vaginitis is that if the vaginal pH is greater than five, 95 percent of the women have either *T. vaginalis* or *H. vaginalis*. If the pH is less than five, eliminate *T. vaginalis* from consideration. Pruritis along with a flora predominant in lactobacilli should make one suspicious of a candidal problem.

For therapy, oxytetracycline (Terramycin®) or Terramycin-Polymyxin-B vaginal suppositories, one for each of ten days have been found efficacious but a high frequency of *C. albicans* super-infections follow this regimen. Thus, either vaginal nystatin should be given concomitantly with the above drugs or hexetidine (Steresil®) should be used in their place. Procaine penicillin, 300,000 units intramuscularly for two days, has been used but most strains of *H. vaginalis* are highly penicillin resistant. Other local and likewise less effective therapeutic regimens include: triple sulfa (Sultrin®) cream and tablets, sulfisoxazole (Gantrisin®) cream, sulfadiazine (Gynben®) vaginal suppositories and cream, or nitrofurazone (Furacin®) twice daily for ten days. Systemic antibiotics have also been tried: (1) 500 mg of ampicillin every six hours for five days—the most effective systemic agent but many strains are totally resistant; (2) 250 mg of oral tetracyclines every six hours for five days—partially effective but some strains are totally resistant, and (3) oral sulfonamides —unsuccessful. With all the forms of therapy, if the contact is not treated, recurrences are frequent. The male can be treated with systemic ampicillin (same regimen as above) or with 250 mg of Terrastratin®, every six hours for five days. With any of the above treatments, neither douching nor coitus should be permitted.

IV OBSTETRIC PROBLEMS

Lack of Prenatal Care

The importance of prenatal care is stressed repeatedly in literature. There is an inverse relationship between the quality of prenatal care and the incidence of complication before, during, and after delivery.[5] Toxemia, excessive weight gain, prematurity, prenatal mortality, high morbidity rates for mothers and children, anemia, mental retardation, and increased rates of suicide are some of the complications resulting from a lack of prenatal care.[1, 4, 9, 28]

The reasons for failure to seek adequate prenatal care are elusive, complex, and apparently highly interrelated. Psychological factors include pride, resistance, motivation, and ignorance.[1, 30] It is difficult to assess the effect of pride on a person's behavior. The gravid teenager, when seeking help, finds the routine geared mainly for others. In the private office it is geared mainly to the middle class. In the public clinic there frequently exists an impersonal, mechanical "get them in—get them out" attitude for the treatment of sick people.[1, 28, 30] Since the pregnant teenager is not sick and does not relate easily to the middle class matron, the young mother is often "turned off" in her efforts to seek medical help. The formal, impersonal traditional clinic atmosphere is aggravated by a kaleidoscope of changing faces of the dedicated and well-meaning house staff which deter all but the most determined patient. Resistance is related to the feeling expressed by many women that they have no control over the fact that they are pregnant. There is resistance, rebellion, and denial of the fact that they are pregnant. A small number of women in this group also exhibit a subconscious death wish. Motivation for prenatal care is the most logical area to build while tearing down ignorance regarding this care. When ignorance of the benefits to the mother and child is removed, motivation to seek prenatal care is subconsciously built up. This educational process must begin years before a woman has her first child; it should, in fact, begin in the primary school.[1]

TABLE III-VI

COMPARISON OF OBSTETRIC RESULTS IN PATIENTS WITH AND
WITHOUT PRENATAL CARE[28]

Complication	Registered Patient* Percent	Nonregistered Patient† Percent
Maternal deaths per 10,000 live births‡	9.3	33.1
Perinatal deaths in infants per 1,000 live births		
(Overall for study period was 44.1/1,000 live births)	27.3	131.9
Premature births	15.3	23.4

* Received prenatal care.
† Did not receive prenatal care.
‡ Patients with pregnancies of less than 20 weeks eliminated except one due to death from septic abortion.

Osofsky[30] suggests several sociological factors which act as barriers to adequate prenatal care including ethnic background and socioeconomic class. The patient's socioeconomic class possibly affects her attitude toward specific medical symptoms. The higher the class of patient, the more likely she is to consult a physician for specific symptoms. There may be a lack of knowledge on the part of the patient regarding the importance of specific symptoms which frequently results in delay in seeking medical care. A girl's definition of what is good health and what is illness affects her desire to seek medical care. Since pregnancy is not illness why go to the doctor? The doctor-patient relationship may be a barrier to a woman seeking out prenatal consultation. Osofsky believes that the medical team perceives, diagnoses, and treats lower socioeconomic class patients differently.

TABLE III-VII

IMPEDIMENTS TO CARE IN 978 NONREGISTERED PATIENTS[28]

Impediments	Percent
Lack baby sitters	21
Time required (clinic and transportation)	44
Transportation	16
Employment	13
Family responsibility	21
Ineligible nonresident	25
Ineligible income	12

TABLE III-VIII

PERCENT INADEQUATE OR ABSENT PRENATAL CARE, 1970*

	All Patients	White				Other			
		All Ages	20 Yrs	20-34 Yrs	35 Yrs	All Ages	20 Yrs	20-34 Yrs	35 Yrs
Chicago									
All patients	23.2	17.5	32.8	15.0	17.0	29.7	36.7	26.3	29.0
First births	21.8	17.2	30.9	12.1	12.6	27.3	33.4	18.2	20.6
Illegitimate first births	37.5	48.7	50.6	46.5	36.8	34.3	36.2	27.6	18.8
Illinois									
All patients	13.4	9.8	20.1	8.0	10.5	27.3	34.8	23.7	26.4
First births	14.0	11.0	19.2	7.4	9.5	25.8	31.6	17.0	20.0
Illegitimate first births	35.8	39.6	39.9	39.0	42.1	33.1	34.7	27.3	22.2

* Illinois Department of Public Health.

A study of the effect of prenatal care was made by Klein.[28] He compared the performance of 978 patients who received no ante-partum care to 1,000 patients who received prenatal care of at least one visit. Table III-VI shows a comparison of the results. The women who received no prenatal care fared much worse than those who did. Table III-VII lists various reasons given by the 978 women who failed to seek care for not doing so. Of the women who did not seek prenatal care, 23 percent had valid hospital cards and were eligible for health services at the time of pregnancy.

Failure to seek adequate prenatal care is a major concern to providers of health care. In Chicago, where prenatal care is provided by the Board of Health and where a high risk program exists, significant percentages of teenage parturients have inadequate or absent prenatal care. Similar statements can be made for the state of Illinois. Table III-VIII lists these percentages for 1970. Zackler *et al.*[45] studied the effect of prenatal care in a large series of patients in Chicago. They found (1) the hebdomadal death rate 92 percent higher and neonatal death rate 94 percent higher in adolescent patients who did not receive prenatal care; (2) a lower prematurity rate (13.3%) in patients receiving prenatal care than in those who did not receive prenatal care (16.6%), and (3) a decreased rate of birth injuries associated with asphyxia in patients receiving prenatal care (10.6%) than in those not receiving prenatal care (26.4%). The problem is complex and involves provision of adequate facilities and factors which motivate the patient to use the prenatal care available. Much work remains to be done in this area.

Low Birth Weight

A disproportionate number of babies born of young mothers are underweight at birth. As the age of the mother increases the ratio of low birth weight infants decreases.[16] Table III-IX shows a distribution of live births under 2,500 g correlated to the age and race of the mother.[61] Table III-X shows differences between the birth weight of offspring of white mothers compared to non-

TABLE III-IX

PERCENT OF LIVE BIRTHS 2,500 G BY AGE AND COLOR, 1965[61]

Age of Mother	Birth Weight 2,500 g or Less	Color White	Nonwhite
Total	8.3	7.2	13.8
Under 15	18.7	13.0	21.3
15-19	10.5	8.5	16.4

TABLE III-X

MEDIAN BIRTH WEIGHTS BY AGE AND COLOR, 1965[61]

Age of Mother	Median Weight (g)* White and Nonwhite	White	Nonwhite
Under 15	3,020	3,180	2,930
15-19	3,210	3,270	3,040

* Computed to the nearest 10 g.

TABLE III-XI

LOW BIRTH WEIGHT AND MEAN BIRTH WEIGHT BY AGE AND RACE[24]

	White	Black
Birth Weights 2,500 g		
All patients	71.37	134.18
10-15 years	97.40	173.40
16-17 years	79.29	157.79
18-19 years	66.61	149.28
Mean Birth Weights		
All patients	3,272	3,039
10-15 years	3,193	2,939
16-17 years	3,211	2,941
18-19 years	3,237	2,976

white mothers in similar age groups.[61] The Niswander-Gordon collaborative study[24] supplements the HEW statistics.[61] The occurrence of low birth weight infants was higher among blacks than among whites, and the mean birth weights among blacks was uni-

61. U. S. Department of Health, Education, and Welfare, Public Health Service, *Vital Statistics of the United States, 1965,* Volume I-Natality (Washington, D. C., U. S. Government Printing Office, 1967).

formly less than among whites (Table III-XI). Only at the age of eighteen and nineteen did the rate of birth of infants 2,500 g approach that of the total population. On the other hand, the mean birth weights by specific age did not show great variation. A close correlation, however, exists between the 1965 HEW mean weights for infants born to patients under fifteen years of age[61] and those reported in the Niswander-Gordon study.[24]

Contracted Pelvis

Pelvic architecture is a major factor in the determination of the length of labor and manner of delivery. Ballard and Gold[1] believe that the dividing line between pelvic adequacy and disproportion occurs between the ages of fourteen and fifteen. If the adolescent pregnancy occurs after the age of fifteen and the mother escapes the complications of toxemia, anemia, and premature labor, she may enjoy a rather benign obstetric course. Hassan and Falls,[5] Battaglia *et al.*[62] and Hulka and Schaaf[63] concur with this. Some authors believe that if a patient's pelvis is contracted it has been so since puberty. If this is an indication for a cesarean section at a later age, it is also an indication at puberty. Thus, pelvic contracture as an indication for cesarean section is no more prevalent for the teenager than for older patients.

Friedman[64] has discussed the problem of bony dystocia and abnormal progress in labor *in extenso*. In any early study of term nulliparous labors, it was found that among patients with radiographically demonstrated bony disproportion, primary uterine dysfunction was the rule and secondary arrest of dilatation was a common feature. A later and more extensive investigation found three major classes of progression in labor: (1) those which approximated the normal curve; (2) those with an abnor-

62. F. C. Battaglia, T. M. Frazier and A. E. Hellegers, "Obstetric and pediatric complications of juvenile pregnancy," *Pediatrics,* 39:902 (1963) .

63. J. F. Hulka and J. T. Schaaf, "Obstetrics in adolescents: A controlled study of deliveries by mothers 15 years of age and under," *Obstetrics and Gynecology,* 23:678 (1964) .

64. E. A. Friedman, *Labor. Clinical Evaluation and Management.* New York, Appleton-Century-Crofts, Inc., 1967.

mally prolonged deceleration phase and/or prolonged second stage only, and (3) those with secondary arrest of dilatation in the active phase or arrest of descent. The outcome of these labors was marked by a significantly higher cesarean section rate in group 2, which ultimately approached 100 percent in group 3. There was a higher midforceps rate than normal in group 1; this was more than doubled in group 2.

If indeed the incidence of contracted pelvis at the time of parturition is age-related, then it is clear that the potential outcome for mother and fetus in terms of either a cesarean section or a midforceps delivery is co-related.

Abortion

Abortion has always been used as one solution to unwanted pregnancy. Until recently, restrictive abortion laws have made this operation illegal and inaccessible except to the most affluent members of society. As a result of the 1973 Supreme Court decision, abortion can no longer be considered "someone else's problem and someone else's job." The general availability or lack of availability of abortions, the methods employed to perform them, and the possible resulting complications are real problems within the total sphere of unwanted adolescent pregnancies.

A request for abortion from a teenager is, in reality, a cry for help. The plea is for the solution of an immediate problem, but it carries with it an implied request for support in the future. Abortion without counseling, birth control information, and medical follow-up is a prescription for another abortion. The primary line of prevention appears to lie in the areas of human behavior and family life education. The secondary defenses are in contraceptive knowledge and usage. Abortion is a poor third alternative backup. Ignorance and nonuse or nonavailability of the first and second defensive barriers have forced many adolescent women to resort to abortion as a primary method of contraception.[1]

Legal abortion will be used by the many women who resorted to illegal abortions in the past. It will also attract those who previously would have carried their pregnancy to term and placed

TABLE III-XII

AGE-SPECIFIC LEGAL ABORTION RATIOS*
SELECTED STATES,† 1971[65]

State	15	15-19
Alaska	3,429	349
Arkansas	110	29
California	1,966	615
Colorado	1,031	195
Delaware	1,397	200
Georgia	119	19
Hawaii	1,654	446
Kansas	2,770	491
Maryland	1,299	250
New York	2,864	2,011
(City)	(3,745)	(3,442)
(Upstate)	(2,157)	(812)
North Carolina	275	62
Oregon	2,842	428
South Carolina	188	16
Virginia	415	72
Washington	1,735	520
Total	1,208	581

* Calculated as the number of legal abortions for women of a given age group per 1,000 live births to women of the same age group.
† All states with data available.

the child for adoption.[1] The number of adolescents availing themselves of legal elective abortions will increase dramatically. In a report from the Center for Disease Control this prediction is justified.[65] For those under fifteen years of age in states with liberal abortion laws, the number of abortions per 1,000 live births is higher than any other age group (1,208); in those fifteen to nineteen years of age, it is 581 (Table III-XII).

In 1971, patients under fifteen years of age accounted for less than 1 percent of all abortions in all states with data available. However, patients aged fifteen to nineteen years accounted for almost 30 percent. As abortion has become available to the population, the greatest increases in age-specific legal abortion ratios was seen in teenage patients (Fig. III-1).

65. Abortion Surveillance 1971, Center for Disease Control, United States Public Health Service.

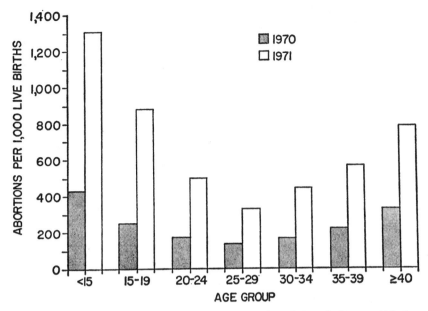

Figure III-1. Age Specific Legal Abortion Ratios, Selected States (Alaska, Colorado, Delaware, Georgia, Hawaii, New York, Oregon, South Carolina), 1970-71.

In a study of 16,000 Illinois teenagers desiring contraceptives,[66] the overwhelming majority (99.9%) of those who were pregnant at the time, or who had been pregnant, did not desire the pregnancy. In adolescence, many girls do not use contraceptives because of ignorance or fear that the parents might learn of their sexual activity. The increased availability of effective contraceptive methods has not caused increased teenage sexual activity. Rather, changing mores and liberalized social contacts between the sexes have resulted in sexual experience at earlier ages. The sexually active teenager urgently requires help to delay pregnancy until a more opportune time which allows for the maintenance of her health.

The American Academy of Pediatrics concurs with the above

66. S. Wilson, L. Keith, J. Wells and R. C. Stepto, "A preliminary survey of 16,000 teenagers entering a contraceptive program," *Chicago Medical School Quarterly*, 32:26 (1973).

statements in principle. Their executive board and house of delegates have recognized the magnitude of the problem of teenage pregnancy and the problems of the professionals who are responsible for the care of young patients.[67] Though the Academy neither sanctions nor condemns abortion to terminate unwanted pregnancies in teenagers, it does suggest that physicians considering this course of action provide appropriate counseling and support for the patients and other involved persons, including the young fathers. The Academy feels that abortion must never be allowed to replace adequate preventive care or contraceptive measures. The physicians or counsellor who deals with the adolescent girl should explore all possible alternatives without the addition of his or her own coercive, punitive, or prejudicial attitudes. If abortion is elected, the physician must determine the appropriate procedure for the individual patient. Whoever deals with the essentially defenseless teenage patient should safeguard her physical and emotional welfare and protect her right to privacy and confidentiality.

Fetal Mortality

The incidence of perinatal death among the pregnancies of teenage parturients is effected by external factors. Among them are out-of-wedlock pregnancy, inadequate nutrition, poor or absent prenatal care, repeated pregnancy, and the race of the patient.

Out-of-wedlock pregnancy is associated with high rates of perinatal mortality among other complications. Gill *et al.*,[18] in an examination of social class, marital status, and timing of pregnancy among teenage girls, have found striking differences in perinatal death rates while comparing birth weight, age of mother at confinement, time of conception and marital status. Tables III-XIII and III-XIV present their results. Zackler *et al.*[45] found that the hebdomadal and neonatal death rates were almost doubled in patients not receiving prenatal care in Chicago.

Women under twenty who have repeated pregnancies (those with high parity) have higher perinatal death rates, but the gra-

67. American Academy of Pediatrics Committee on Youth, "Teen-age pregnancy and the problem of abortion," *Pediatrics*, 49:303 (1972).

TABLE III-XIII

PERINATAL MORTALITY BY PREGNANCY CATEGORY,
BIRTH WEIGHT AND AGE AT CONFINEMENT[18]

| | Perinatal Deaths Per 1,000 Births | | | | |
| | By Birth Weight | | By Age at Confinement | | |
Pregnancy Category	5½ lbs. or Less	More Than 5½ lbs.	18	18 and 19	All Ages
Postnuptial conception	250.0	2.43	41.6	22.4	24.4
Prenuptial conception	301.2	12.6	43.9	31.8	36.7
Illegitimate pregnancy (City residents)	304.3	14.1	42.5	42.5	42.5
Illegitimate pregnancy (Mother and baby home)	333.3	X*	X*	15.0	8.3

* X = No deaths.

dients of risk are hard to determine because of the practice of reporting natality and mortality data by five year groupings. This practice tends to conceal subtle differences. In the study by Niswander and Gordon[24] in 1972, the neonatal death rates are shown in five-year groups but in two-year groups for two periods in the

TABLE III-XIV

PERINATAL MORTALITY BY PREGNANCY CATEGORY,
BIRTH WEIGHT AND ANTENATAL CARE[18]

	All Births Perinatal Mortality per 1,000 Births
Postnuptial conception	
Antenatal care	24.4
No antenatal care*	0
Prenuptial conception	
Antenatal care	36.9
No antenatal care*	0
Illegitimate pregnancy (City residents) †	
Antenatal care	23.0
No antenatal care	277.7
Illegitimate pregnancy (Mother and baby home) ‡	
Antenatal care	8.3
No antenatal care*	0

* The small number of cases precluded calculation of a perinatal death rate.

† These figures include general unscreened population.

‡ These figures include selected population admitted to home only if rigid health requirements are met.

TABLE III-XV

NEONATAL DEATHS BY AGE BY PARITY[24]

Age (Years)	0	1	Rate Parity 2	3-4	5 or More	Total*
White						
10-15	6.67	0†	—	—	—	6.41
16-17	11.21	17.09	0†	0†	—	11.75
18-19	10.96	22.03	7.69	0†	—	13.26
Black						
10-15	17.63	20.00	0†	0†	0†	17.65
16-17	20.13	19.28	14.49	0†	—	19.76
18-19	11.55	22.92	36.11	28.57	0†	18.16

* Excludes unknown parity.

† Rate based on less than 20 cases.

teenage years. Table III-XV illustrates the fact that parity influences the neonatal death rate subtly.[24]

Race has a strong influence on the incidence of fetal mortality. HEW has published data showing that (1) the death rate for infants born to mothers, either black or white, who were under the age of fifteen, is higher than for those born to older mothers, and (2) the death rate of black infants is higher than that of white infants (Table III-XVI).[61] This was confirmed in 1972.[24] Figure III-2 shows a higher perinatal death rate among black women for all but a few years in the normal childbearing span.

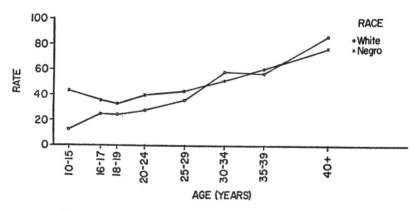

Figure III-2. Perinatal Deaths by Age of Gravida by Race.

TABLE III-XVI

MORTALITY OF WHITE AND NONWHITE INFANTS BY AGE OF
MOTHER AND AGE AT DEATH BY RACE[a]

Rate per 100 Live Births

Age of Mother	Neonatal (Under 28 Days)			Postneonatal (28 Days to 11 Months)			Infant (Under 1 Year)		
	Total	White	Nonwhite	Total	White	Nonwhite	Total	White	Nonwhite
Total	18.4	16.9	26.7	6.7	5.3	14.7	25.1	22.2	41.4
Under 15	41.2	32.1	46.5	17.6	15.5	18.8	58.7	47.5	65.3
15-19	22.7	20.4	30.9	10.1	7.7	18.6	32.8	28.1	49.5

Additional work remains to be done to determine what factors push the death rate so high in blacks. Is it race, coupled with low socioeconomic status, poor nutrition, and inadequate prenatal care, or is it illegitimacy and multiple pregnancy which tip the scale? The answers to these questions are still unsolved.

Out-of-Wedlock Pregnancy

Out-of-wedlock pregnancy is singled out as a factor responsible for numerous complications of pregnancy at all ages. Such pregnancies result from numerous social, emotional, and physical factors which contribute to the behavior patterns of youth.[1, 68, 69] Cobliner[13] calls it a phenomenon of many dimensions, having to do with maternal race, socioeconomic class, age, nutritional situation, and more importantly, a host of outside psychological factors which can influence the teenager in some manner.

The frequency of out-of-wedlock births has risen from 3.6 percent of the total live births in 1938 to 9.7 percent in 1968. In the years 1940 to 1965 there was a 63.2 percent increase in the incidence of such births nationally.[70] Statistics from the state of Illinois reveal striking changes in out-of-wedlock pregnancy rates in all racial groups at each specific age (Table III-XVII).

Gill et al. [18] investigated variations in teenage reproductive performance as related to marital status. They found an increased incidence of preeclampsia and toxemia among the out-of-wedlock pregnancies. The girls in the study who were not married tended to register for prenatal care at a later stage in the pregnancy. Little variation occurred in the length of labor, the methods of delivery, and the outcome in the puerperium. There was an increased incidence of low birth weight among the older teenagers who bore out-of-wedlock children. The perinatal mortality increased from 24.4 percent for postnuptual conceptions to 42.5

---

68. A. H. Parmelee, Jr., "Prematurity and illegitimacy," *American Journal of Obstetrics and Gynecology*, 81:81 (1961) .

69. S. Shaprio, E. R. Schlesinger and R. E. L. Nesbitt, Jr., "Infant, perinatal, maternal, and childhood mortality in the United States," *American Public Health Association*, Vital and Health Statistics Monographs, 1968.

70. C. V. Von Der Ahe, "Problems in the management of illegitimate pregnancy," *American Journal of Obstetrics and Gynecology*, 86:607 (1963) .

OUT-OF-WEDLOCK LIVE BIRTHS IN ILLINOIS—1950, 1960, 1970*

Out-of-Wedlock Live Births per 1,000 Live Births by Race for Selected Age Groups: Illinois—1950, 1960, 1970

Age	All Races 1950	All Races 1960	All Races 1970	White 1950	White 1960	White 1970	Black 1950	Black 1960	Black 1970
14	725.8	780.6	940.2	632.7	455.8	754.0	786.7	911.2	991.3
15	514.0	549.2	827.8	311.4	260.1	542.9	745.0	773.5	969.6
16	286.9	327.3	615.3	141.1	159.4	350.4	541.4	625.6	877.8
17	176.1	197.4	449.7	103.8	101.4	234.1	390.6	465.0	764.6
18	113.9	135.8	330.5	68.8	70.8	186.8	302.2	357.6	621.5
19	74.9	104.7	248.2	44.1	49.4	133.4	282.9	328.4	523.0

Out-of-Wedlock Live Births per 1,000 Female Population at Census by Race for Selected Age Groups: Illinois—1950, 1960, 1970

Age	All Races 1950	All Races 1960	All Races 1970	White 1950	White 1960	White 1970	Black 1950	Black 1960	Black 1970
14	1.69	2.70	5.08	0.63	0.51	1.06	13.32	21.23	24.91
15	4.23	6.37	14.21	1.49	1.47	3.70	35.17	48.25	67.93
16	7.35	10.98	24.51	2.50	3.80	8.25	61.31	76.30	111.49
17	9.67	13.45	28.74	4.65	5.61	10.46	65.44	88.61	131.23
18	10.48	16.71	31.88	5.55	7.54	14.44	67.19	94.40	134.90
19	9.99	20.45	32.43	5.37	8.73	14.53	61.41	112.01	130.43

Resident Live Births by Race, Legitimacy Status, and Age of Mother: Illinois—1950, 1960, 1970

Age of Mother	1950 White Total	White Illegitimacy	Other Total	Other Illegitimacy	1960 White Total	White Illegitimacy	Other Total	Other Illegitimacy	1970 White Total	White Illegitimacy	Other Total	Other Illegitimacy
All ages	169,179	2,668	19,962	4,170	200,483	4,141	38,277	10,210	162,649	9,463	42,554	18,192
10-14	60	41	103	85	78	37	224	208	143	112	561	557
15	228	71	200	149	346	90	446	345	606	329	1,217	1,180
16	822	116	471	255	1,556	248	876	549	2,012	705	2,030	1,782
17	2,157	224	727	284	3,817	387	1,370	637	3,797	889	2,600	1,988
18	4,116	283	986	298	6,369	451	1,865	667	6,306	1,178	3,115	1,936
19	6,614	292	1,288	300	9,526	471	2,354	773	8,713	1,162	3,642	1,905

* Illinois Department of Public Health.

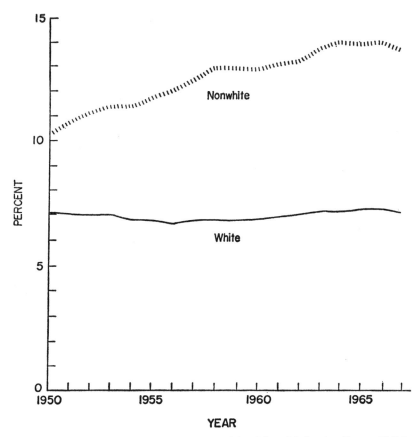

Figure III-3. Percent of Low Birth Weight Live Births by Race, U.S.A., 1950-1967.[75]

percent for out-of-wedlock births.[18] Both abortion and marriage occasionally intervene to reduce the number of out-of-wedlock births. These solutions are frequently imperfect, but have been viewed as the lesser of available evils.[1]

Prematurity

Like toxemia, and probably related to it, prematurity rates are highest in the youngest patients.[1, 5, 63, 71–73] Wallace[74] states that prematurity is the highest cause of perinatal mortality in ward or

71. A. D. Claman and H. M. Bell, "Pregnancy in the very young teen-ager," *American Journal of Obstetrics and Gynecology*, 90:350 (1964).

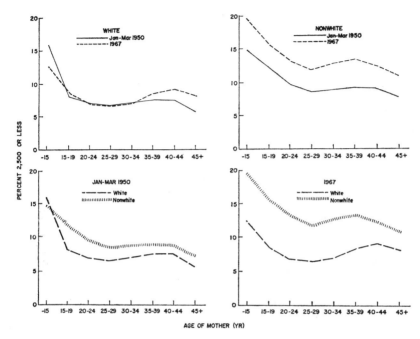

Figure III-4. Percent Live Births with Low Birth Weight by Age of Mother, January-March, 1950-1967.[75]

charity services for the indigent and is second in incidence in private patient services surpassed only by Rh incompatibility. Chase and Byrnes,[75] present evidence that prematurity in the non-white obstetric patient is on the increase. Figure III-3 shows the results of their studies from 1950 to 1965. Figure III-4 shows the addition of the variable of maternal age to the incidence of prematurity. The teenage mother, especially the nonwhite mother, is clearly at higher risk than the general population.

The findings of Wallace,[74] as well as Chase and Byrnes[75] re-

72. S. L. Israel and T. B. Woutersz, "Teen-age obstetrics: A cooperative study," *American Journal of Obstetrics and Gynecology*, 85:659 (1963).

73. J. F. Jewett, "Cesarean section, followed by generalized peritonitis and sepsis," *New England Journal of Medicine*, 266:204 (1962).

74. H. M. Wallace, "Teen-age pregnancy," *American Journal of Obstetrics and Gynecology*, 92:1125 (1965).

75. H. C. Chase and M. A. Byrnes, "Trends in 'prematurity.' United States, 1950-1967," *American Journal of Public Health*, 60:1967 (1970).

TABLE III-XVIII

BIRTH WEIGHTS <2,501 G BY AGE AND RACE[24]

Age	White	Black
10-15 . . . . .97.40		173.40
16-17 . . . . .79.29		157.79
18-19 . . . . .66.61		149.28

garding the influence of race on prematurity have been confirmed by Niswander and Gordon.[24] Table III-XVIII reveals an increasing risk associated with low age. Figure III-5 presents results for patients at all ages. The difference in the incidence of prematurity as related to maternal age is graphic. The exact cause of high rates of prematurity is unknown. Factors other than age or race alone must exert a synergistic influence on the incidence. Multiple birth, parity, improper spacing of pregnancy, social class, economic status, lack of prenatal care, and poor nutrition are some of the factors which may contribute to these high rates.

Type of Delivery

The method of delivery and conduct of the labor bear a direct relationship to the outcome of any confinement. Fortunately, these are two areas in which the physician has the opportunity for almost total direction and control. Proper conduct of labor

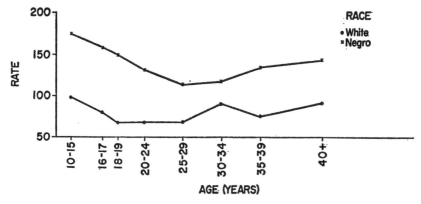

Figure III-5. Birthweights under 2501 gm by Age, by Race.[24]

TABLE III-XIX

METHOD OF DELIVERY AND DURATION OF LABOR[37]

			Labor	
			Less	More
	Total Number		Than	Than
	of Cases		3 Hrs.	21 Hrs.
Method of Delivery	*Number*	*Percent*	*Percent*	*Percent*
Spontaneous or low forceps	22,074	91.9	12.7	2.8
(under age 15)	(74)	(77.8)	(16.2)	(8.1)
Midforceps	700	2.9	6.1	14.3
(under age 15)	(13)	(13.7)	(8.0)	(0)
Cesarean section	372	1.6	9.4	14.0
(under age 15)	(3)	(3.2)	(33.3)	(0)
Breech—spontaneous or assisted	591	2.4	13.0	2.5
(under age 15)	(5)	(5.3)	(0)	(20.0)
Breech extraction	181	0.73	13.2	2.7
(under age 15)	(0)	—	—	—
Version and extraction	9	0.03	66.6	0
(under age 15)	(0)	—	—	—

and safe delivery contribute to decreased incidences of perinatal mortality, infant mortality, and maternal morbidity.

Semmens and Lamers[37] noted that the vast majority of their 24,000 teenage patients had either normal spontaneous delivery or delivery with low forceps; 77.8 percent of the patients under fifteen and 91.9 percent of those fifteen to nineteen years of age contributed to these figures. Utian[76] found 98 percent spontaneous deliveries or deliveries with low forceps in his series. Sarrel and Klerman observed a 75.6 percent rate of spontaneous or low forceps delivery.[10] Jovanovic reported similar findings.[4]

Semmens and Lamers' study population may have been somewhat atypical, as it came from Navy dependent daughters or wives enjoying a relatively stable home life. Medical care was totally without cost. Peer group pressure to make use of the facilities was most likely present. Table III-XIX presents a summary of their results: 418 fetal deaths were recorded among these patients (76% of the total). One-third of the fetal deaths occurred before or during labor, and two-thirds were neonatal. The

76. W. H. Utian, "Obstetrical implications of pregnancy in primigravidae aged 16 years or less," *British Medical Journal*, 2:734 (1967).

overall perinatal mortality associated with spontaneous or low forceps delivery was 1.89 percent. The highest perinatal death rates (16.5% and 33.3% respectively) were linked to breech extraction and version and extraction. Manipulative procedures for breech delivery were carried out among the fifteen- to nineteen-year-olds only. Five breech deliveries (5.3%) for mothers under fifteen years of age, were delivered spontaneously with or without assistance. Cesarean sections were performed on 375. All but three were in the fifteen- to nineteen-year-old group.

Two distinct trends regarding duration of teenage labor were found: an increase in precipitate labor and a tendency to permit more mothers to experience labor in excess of twenty hours. Labor lasting less than three hours was observed for 16 percent of the patients under fifteen years of age and beyond twenty-one hours in 8.1 percent. In both areas the incidence was twice the acceptable norm. Precipitate and prolonged labor among the fifteen- to nineteen-year-old patients for this group was within the normal limits.

It is difficult to compare published studies on duration of labor because a clear cut definition of prolonged labor in primiparas is lacking. Various observers report different duration of labor for teenage patients.[3, 5-7, 25] Some authors believe normal labor in young primiparas lasts up to thirty hours;[6, 77, 78] for others twenty-four hours is normal,[26, 79, 80] and for some[81, 82] eighteen to twenty hours marks the upper limit of labor under normal circumstances for the primipara.

-----

77. K. Bocnner, "Pregnancies in juveniles," *American Journal of Obstetrics and Gynecology*, 83:269 (1962).

78. E. F. Dodge and W. E. Brown, "Effect of age upon obstetric complication in primigravida," *Southern Medical Journal*, 43:1060, 1950.

79. E. A. Friedman, "Primigravid labor," *Obstetrics and Gynecology*, 6:567 (1955).

80. J. H. Morrison, "The adolescent primigravida," *Obstetrics and Gynecology*, 2:297 (1953).

81. J. F. J. Clark, *et al.*, "Pregnancy in the very young patient," *Journal of the National Medical Association*, 54:352 (1962).

82. J. P. Greenhill, *Obstetrics* (Philadelphia and London, W. B. Saunders Company, 1960).

Fetal Malformation

Fetal malformation occurs in about 2.5 percent of total births in the general population. There is no agreement among major investigators on expected rates of malformation. To detect trends in rare conditions, tens of thousands, or perhaps hundreds of thousands of cases must be observed.[1, 5, 25, 62] Butler *et al.*,[83] however, have shown that when anencephaly, spina bifida, and meningomyelocele are considered individually and related to maternal age, the baby of the adolescent mother is at equal or greater risk than those of older mothers.

Cesarean Sections

Even though the most frequent indications for cesarean sections in adolescents are cephalopelvic disproportion or abnormal presentation, true comparisons with the general population are difficult to make because of the differences in hospital policies relating to primary cesarean sections. An additional barrier to drawing valid conclusions is the discrepancy noted among reported series. Some are concerned with patients under fourteen; some include patients up to sixteen, etc.

Table III-XX lists some of the published studies. The control population in all reports was much larger than the sample groups. Even though the rate of cesarean section in the teenager may appear relatively low, the percentage of difference from the total population should be considered.[1] In four of the five studies shown in Table III-XX, the percentage of cesarean sections among teenagers was less than that of the control population. In the remaining study the percentage was substantially greater. A statistical evaluation of all data in the table was undertaken to determine if, in fact, the rate of incidence of cesarean section among adolescents was different from that of the general population.

A paired T test was conducted. The results showed that the differences were not significant at the 95 percent confidence level.

---

83. N. R. Butler, E. D. Alberman and W. H. Schatt, *The Congenital Malformations, Perinatal Problems* (Edinburgh and London, E & E Livingston, Ltd., 1969).

TABLE III-XX

TEENAGE CESAREAN SECTION RATE

Investigator	Number of Patients in Control Population	Percent Cesarean Section	Number of Teenage Patients	Percent Cesarean Section	Absolute Percent Difference (y)
Jovanovic[4]	9,536	5.1	1,033	3.2	−1.9
Jorgensen[26]	Unknown	8	350	14.4	+6.4
Coates[9]	2,968	5.4	137*	4.4	−1.0
Lewis[23]	8,366	6.5	102	3.9	−2.6

* 14 years or less.

Testing the hypothesis that the rates of incidence were not different, i.e. Mo-0, it was found that

$$t - \frac{\bar{y} - Mo}{\sqrt{S^2/N}} = .20966$$

for the 4 degrees of freedom in this table, and for a 95 percent confidence value, the theoretical t value is 2.132.* Since .20966 < 2.132, it must be concluded that the observed differences in rates of cesarean sections among teenagers are not significant and the hypothesis is therefore validated.

An exception to this is found in the Aznar-Bennetts study, where the low primary cesarean section rate of 1.8 percent for adolescents was compared to the rate of 1.4 percent for the hospital as a whole and found to be 28 percent higher (absolute) for the latter.[25]

Toxemia, Preeclampsia and Hypertension

These three complications lead all others in incidence. Although they could be reviewed separately, they are so interrelated as to exert an almost synergistic effect on the young mother. The single most consistently noted complication related to high risk

---

* Mo = true mean difference between adolescent and control groups.
  $\bar{y}$ = absolute mean of observed difference between each adolescent and associated control group.
  S^2 = variance of differences.
  N = number of studies evaluated.
  N-1 = degrees of freedom.

TABLE III-XXI

COMPARISONS OF RATES OF TOXEMIA, TEENAGE MOTHERS,
AND CONTROL GROUPS*

| | Teenage Population | | Control Population | |
| | Toxemia Preeclampsia | Unclassified Toxemia | Toxemia Preeclampsia | Unclassified Toxemia |
Study	(Percent)	(Percent)	(Percent)	(Percent)
Jovanovic[4] 7.3			5.1	
Coates[9] 14.6			7.9	
Battaglia[62]				
Age under 13 ..... 29.2			11.2	
Age 15-19 .... 21.1				
Marchetti[6]				
Age 13 42				
Age 16 .... 16.1			6	
Lewis[23]				
Age 16 20				
Utian[76] 21	15 (Total 35)		12	5 (Total 17)
Rauh[33] 25			7	

* Teenagers receiving comprehensive prenatal care.

observed among teenage patients is toxemia. The younger the mothers, the higher the rate of toxemia. In addition, preeclampsia and eclampsia are observed more frequently among adolescents.[1, 5, 15, 23, 25, 64, 74, 75, 84-86] Table III-XXI compares some of the reported rates of toxemia, eclampsia and hypertension. A line by line comparison is not possible because of variations among the sample populations but the table shows the higher incidence of these complications in teenagers.

The relationship of toxemia to inadequate nutrition deserves consideration. The average teenage girl's diet falls short of the optimal or even minimally recommended daily values. Physicians involved in the care of the gravid teenager must convey the importance of developing and maintaining a proper diet and the

84. J. F. Clark, "Toxemia is major complication in teen pregnancy," *Ob-Gyn News*, 5:35, June 15, 1970.

85. D. Y. Hsia, *Human Developmental Genetics* (Chicago, Medical Year Book Publishers, Inc., 1968).

86. Population Reference Bureau, Inc., *Population Profile: The Teen-age Mother* (Washington, D. C., June 3, 1962).

avoidance of excessive intake of sodium during pregnancy. Semmens and Lamers recommend a weight graph as depicted in Figure III-6.[37] This graph enables the patient to visualize the entire weight gain by trimester. For maximum effect the patient should have her own copy, bring it to each weigh-in and have the

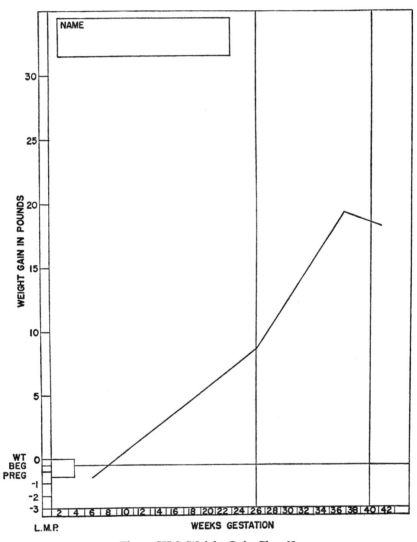

Figure III-6. Weight Gain Chart[37]

results recorded thereon. Uniform rates of weight gain is to be stressed, with less of the gain during the first two trimesters to compensate for the increased gain of the fetus in the last trimester.

These authors also make a strong case for the correlation of weight gain with the incidence of toxemia and hypertension. As weight went up in their large sample population, so did the incidence of toxemia. This was especially true in the fifteen- to nineteen-year-olds. As many patients are overweight at conception, weight gain during pregnancy is only one facet of the problem. These patients are three times more susceptible to toxemia.

Maternal Mortality

The incidence of maternal mortality has declined in the United States in the past fifty years. While pregnancy and delivery was more than twice as safe for women in 1970 than in 1950 and more than twenty times as safe as in 1930, the U. S. rate is still higher than in other advanced countries.[1]

While several large selected studies reveal no maternal deaths,[37, 75, 87] teenage maternal deaths do occur. Lane and Brown,[27] in their study of teenage maternal mortality in Chicago, postulate that socioeconomic factors play a significant if not dominant role in the cause of these deaths. Most of the deceased were single, 60.8 percent, and nonwhite, 69.5 percent. They make a strong case that 65.2 percent of these deaths were from preventable causes. A special Subcommittee on Maternal Mortality of the Chicago Board of Health agreed that this percentage of deaths was preventable. In general, delayed diagnosis and delayed treatment were common faults in those cases where the preventable factors were in the hands of professionals.

V PRINCIPLES OF MANAGEMENT

Vital statistics from all areas of the United States continue to report an increasing number of teenage girls who marry before the age of eighteen. It is estimated that fully one-third of the

---

87. J. Schneider, "Identification of high risk pregnancy," *Ob-Gyn Digest* (July, 1970, p. 31) .

high school teen marriages are after conception.[37] There is a need for a multidisciplinary approach to the care of pregnant teenagers. Teenagers who are in a semistable or stable marital situation and take advantage of planned prenatal care do not suffer the same consequences as reported in the bulk of obstetric literature. The obstetric experience of teenage mothers from lower socioeconomic levels should not be used as the basis for formulating concepts of the obstetric capacity of teenage mothers-to-be in other situations.

Physiologically the teenager is as capable as any so-called mature obstetric patient as she approaches term. Thus, she is entitled to the same consideration as any other woman in labor when she develops desultory labor, inertia, cephalopelvic disproportion, or abnormal lie. The dictum of vaginal delivery at any cost may sacrifice the life of the fetus. This may cause a significant physical and emotional trauma to the teenage mother which can jeopardize her future fertility.

To manage teenage pregnancy effectively, the professional must understand the risks and problems involved. Frequent prenatal visits are the key to success. A complete physical examination is indicated with particular emphasis on family history of diabetes, essential hypertension, cardiology, renal problems, and anemias. In blacks, a sickle cell screening is mandatory. Improvement in poor dietary habits and reassuring the young mother that teenagers in a well disciplined prenatal program fare as well as or better than any other group in pregnancy is paramount.

A composite of the young patient at greatest obstetric risk would have the following characteristics: she would be nonwhite, unwed, from the lower end of the socioeconomic spectrum; she would be either poorly nourished or undernourished and either under- or overweight; and finally, she would be anemic and well into the second or third trimester. Agewise, she would present any combination of the younger teen years, often having had a prior pregnancy with an interval of less than two years. Associated factors may include a school dropout, a broken or unstable family life, and having one or more of the following health problems: tuberculosis, venereal disease, nonspecific vaginitis, cervical cyto-

logic changes. She also might be on drugs and in need of extensive guidance medically, socially, legally, and financially.

In an adult-centered program, adolescent mothers will not get
optimal care. They are still struggling for mastery, control, and
independence at the same time they are struggling to accept responsibility for their own sexuality. A program centered on adult
needs does not maximize preventive care and use peer group in-
teraction to lower obstetric risk and decrease management problems.[27] Health education is indicated to improve successful family life and pave the way for responsible parenthood. The medical profession too needs education in order to narrow the gaps
and meet teenagers on some common ground for the benefit of
all.[1]

CHAPTER IV

NUTRITION AND PREGNANCY IN ADOLESCENCE

Janet C. King and Howard N. Jacobson

TEENAGERS ARE NOTORIOUS for their bizarre dietary habits and are reported to have the least favorable diets of all age groups.[1] Breakfast is skipped frequently and lunch and dinner may be replaced by snacks if the teenager's social activities do not allow time for meals. Adolescent girls frequently have poorer diets than boys. This consistent finding is attributable to a complex of cultural and psychological norms. Modern society emphasizes slimness as a dominant value, and the adolescent girl often regards a slender figure as the best way to achieve acceptance by her peer group and by society in general.

While the adolescent girl may be subjecting herself to a poor quality diet,[2] she is also experiencing a surge in physical development which is more pronounced than that during any other single period in life. Practically every muscle and skeletal dimension in her body increases during this spurt of growth. Also, sexual function matures and physiologic changes take place. The adolescent girl whose nutritional reserves have been depleted by poor dietary habits and increased nutritional demands for growth and development will be ill-prepared for reproduction.

The focus of the present chapter will be on the nutritional requirements, dietary intakes, and eating behavior of adolescents. The dietary habits of pregnant teenagers have been studied by only a few investigators,[3-5] but it appears that the pregnant teenagers select diets similar to their nonpregnant peers. Even though

---

1. A. F. Morgan, *"Nutritional Status . . . U. S. A., Calif Agr Exptl Sta Bull* 769, October, 1959.

2. H. A. Kaminetzky, A. Langer, H. Baker, O. Frank, A. D. Thomson, A. Opper, F. C. Behrle and B. Glista, "The effect of nutrition in teenage gravidas on pregnancy and the status of the neonate," *American Journal of Obstetrics and Gynecology,* 115:639 (1973).

the comments in this chapter on dietary habits are based on data from nonpregnant teenagers, what evidence there is suggests that the same comments apply to pregnant teenagers.

DIETARY RECOMMENDATIONS AND INTAKES

The Food and Nutrition Board of the National Research Council (NRC) has developed formulations of daily nutrient intakes that are judged to be adequate for the maintenance of good nutrition in healthy people in the population of the United States.[6] These formulations are designated as recommended dietary allowances (RDA), and are most useful for planning food intakes and for evaluating diets consumed by population groups.*

During adolescence increased amounts of food are needed for growth and development. The nutritional requirements of the adolescent are conditioned primarily by the occurrence of the pubertal spurt of growth. They are the greatest when growth peaks and they taper off as growth slows down. Because the pubertal acceleration in growth generally occurs in girls (10½ to thirteen years) before it occurs in boys (12½ to fifteen years),[7]

3. J. C. King, S. H. Cohenour, D. H. Calloway and H. N. Jacobson, "Assessment of nutritional status of teenage pregnant girls. I. Nutrient intake and pregnancy," *American Journal of Clinical Nutrition* 25:916 (1972).

4. W. J. McGanity, H. M. Little, A. Fogelman, L. Jennings, E. Calhoun and E. B. Dawson, "Pregnancy in the adolescent. I. Preliminary summary of health status," *American Journal of Obstetrics and Gynecology,* 103:773 (1969).

5. F. Smith, M. J. O'Connell and J. Zackler, "Food habits of pregnant teenagers and their potential relation to pregnancy outcome." *Public Health Report,* 84:213 (1968).

6. *Recommended Dietary Allowances,* 8th ed., National Academy of Sciences—National Research Council. Washington, D. C. (1974).

* These formulations do not represent minimal nutrient requirements. Such requirements would represent the basic physiological need for a nutrient to prevent deficiency symptoms or support a well-defined physiologic or biochemical response. (R. L. Pike and M. L. Brown, *Nutrition: An Integrated Approach* [New York, John Wiley & Sons, Inc., 1967]). Many dietary requirements have not been determined because the tools to evaluate human requirements are not available and because the criterion of physiologic response has not been ascertained. Formulation entails adding to the estimated requirement a margin of safety sufficient to cover variations among individuals. Therefore, dietary standards are generally called allowances to denote the lack of precision inherent in formulating them.

7. P. S. Timiras, *Developmental Physiology and Aging* (New York, Macmillan Company, 1972).

separate recommended allowances are proposed for girls and boys after nine years of age.

Timing and character of physical growth, as well as sexual maturation, differ greatly among individuals, but in general, the adolescent does not complete linear growth until four years postmenarche.[8] Adolescents who become pregnant within four years postmenarche are considered to be biological risks because they are structurally and physiologically immature. If these girls are still growing, they will have greater nutrient requirements than adult women. When growth is completed, usually at seventeen years of age, the adolescent is considered physiologically mature.

Pregnancy also is a period of rapid growth and development of fetal and maternal tissue. The average pregnant woman accumulates from 10 to 12.5 kg (24 to 27.5 pounds) of tissue and fluid during gestation representing about 20 percent of her prepregnancy weight. Most of the maternal and fetal tissues and fluids are synthesized during the last twenty weeks of pregnancy.[9]

Since most of the nutrient allowances for pregnant adolescents have not been firmly established, the additional allowances for an adult pregnancy are added to the NRC[6] allowance suggested for nonpregnant teenagers fifteen to eighteen years of age to estimate their needs (see Table IV-I). Such an additive approximation may overestimate the total requirements for pregnancy.*

---

8. Committee on Maternal Nutrition, Food and Nutrition Board, National Research Council, *Maternal Nutrition and the Course of Pregnancy* (Washington, D. C., National Academy of Sciences, 1970).

9. F. E. Hytten and I. Leitch, *The Physiology of Human Pregnancy*. 2nd ed. (Oxford, Blackwell Scientific Publications, 1971).

* For example, metabolic alterations may promote the retention of essential nutrients by decreasing nutrient catabolism or by increasing the efficiency of nutrient absorption. Animal studies (G. H. Beaton, "Nutritional and Physiological Adaptations in Pregnancy," *Fed Proc* 20, Suppl. No. 7, 1961, p. 196) suggest that the growth hormone acts to decrease protein catabolism and human studies (C. A. Finch, "Iron-deficiency anemia," *American Journal of Clinical Nutrition,* 22:512 [1969]) have shown that the efficiency of iron absorption increases progressively during pregnancy. The increased levels of circulating estrogen in pregnant teenagers may close their epiphyseal plates and terminate their growth. If this occurs nutritional allowances for both maternal and fetal growth would be unnecessary. Also, the additional energy required during pregnancy may be offset by a reduction in maternal physical activity.

This additive estimate is probably the best approximation available of their needs. Nutrient requirements of the physiologically mature pregnant adolescent are similar to the requirements of pregnant adults.

1. Energy

ADOLESCENCE. Predicting energy requirements for adolescents is especially difficult. Wide variations among individuals are normally observed in growth rates, body builds, and levels of physical activity. Of all total energy requirement predictors, age appears to be the least reliable. Body weight is perhaps the most reliable since it generally reflects both growth rate and body build.[10] Height is also a good predictor of total energy needs and, as an index, has the advantage over weight of being influenced less by diet. Thus, height can be used more effectively to predict the needs of the heavy or slight child.

Girls tend to reach puberty sooner and pass through it faster than boys, resulting in an increase in energy requirements at an earlier age and a much more rapid decrease in energy requirements after puberty.

Generally the increased energy requirements are accompanied by an increase in appetite. The adolescent girl overly concerned with achieving slimness may not respond to appetite signals. In one study[11] the average energy intake of girls nine to eleven years of age was found to be 2,000 calories a day; for girls twelve to seventeen years of age, it was 2,100 calories. The nine to eleven year old girls consumed 400 calories less than the levels recommended in 1973 by the Food and Nutrition Board of the NRC.[6] An adequate energy intake is critical for support of growth and development during adolescence, and the adolescent girl who has severely deprived herself of energy during this period may well have a decreased ability to adapt to stress such as infection or pregnancy.

10. B. Wait, R. Blair and L. J. Roberts, "Energy intake of well-nourished children and adolescents," *American Journal of Clinical Nutrition*, 22:1383 (1969).

11. U. S. Department of Agriculture, Agricultural Research Service, *Food Intake and Nutritive Value of Diets of Men, Women, and Children in the United States, Spring, 1965: A Preliminary Report*, ARS 62-18, U. S. Government Printing Office, Washington, D. C., p. 97.

PREGNANCY. The additional energy required during pregnancy may be traced to three sources: the deposition of fetal and maternal tissue, the additional metabolism the new tissues incur, and the increased energy required to move the additional body weight when engaging in physical activity. During the first quarter (ten weeks) of pregnancy, the amount of tissue deposited has been estimated to be only 0.64 g protein and 5.85 g fat,[9] so the additional oxygen required to maintain and move these tissues is small. However, during the remaining thirty weeks energy needs are relatively constant, as large amounts of maternal stores are deposited during the two middle quarters, and formation of fetal tissue is maximal during the last quarter. The data from Hytten and Leitch suggest that the metabolizable energy-needs average about 330 kilocalories daily during the last three-quarters of pregnancy.[9] If this increment is added to the recommendation for nonpregnant teenagers (see Table IV-I), the estimated needs for the pregnant teenager become 2,730 kcal, or 47 kcal per kg for a 58-kg girl. The estimate from the NRC allowances (see table) is 45 kcal per kg for the pregnant teenager.

Blackburn and Calloway[12] studied the basal metabolic rate (BMR) and energy cost of work in a group of pregnant teenagers. During pregnancy the BMR was 1.11 kcal per minute. At six to ten weeks postpartum the BMR was lowered to 0.98 kcal per minute as expected. Contrary to expectations, however, when the values were corrected for body weight, the differences in BMR between the two periods almost disappeared. These data suggest that the increase in body mass during pregnancy accounts for most of the increase in BMR.

These researchers also measured the energy expenditure of activities thought to be unrelated to body weight, such as quiet sitting, sitting and knitting, quiet standing, sitting and combing hair, washing dishes, and cooking at a stove, and found that the energy expenditure was lower in the postpartum period by about the same amount as the BMR was lowered.[12] Energy expenditures

12. M. L. Blackburn and D. H. Calloway, "Energy expenditure and pregnant adolescents" in *Protein Requirements of Pregnant Teenagers* (Final report to National Institutes of Health, Division of Research Grants, Grant no. H D 05246, 1973).

TABLE IV-I

ESTIMATES OF DIETARY NEEDS FOR PREGNANT TEENAGERS

Nutrient	Recommended Intake for Nonpregnant Teenagers 15-18*	Recommended Increment for Adult Pregnancy	Recommended Intake for Pregnant Teenagers
Energy, kcal per kg†	40	5	45
Protein, g/kg	0.9	0.4	1.3
Calcium, g	1.2	0.4	1.6
Phosphorus, g	1.2	0.4	1.6
Iron, mg	18	0	18‡
Magnesium, mg	300	150	450
Iodine, μg	115	25	140
Zinc, mg	15	5	20
Vitamin A, IU	4,000	1,000	5,000
Vitamin D, IU	400	0	400
Vitamin E, IU	11	3	14
Ascorbic acid, mg	45	15	60
Niacin, mg equiv	14	2	16
Riboflavin, mg	1.4	0.3	1.7
Thiamin, mg	1.1	0.3	1.4
Folacin, mg	0.4	0.4	0.8
Vitamin B₆, mg	2.0	0.5	2.5
Vitamin B₁₂, μg	3	1	4

* The value recommended for teenagers 15 to 18 years of age. (See footnote 6.)

† Intake for pregnant teenagers is 10.9 MJ (millijoules), for nonpregnant teenagers, 10.0 MJ and for pregnant adults, 9.2 MJ.

‡ Supplemental iron is recommended for pregnant teenagers.

for tasks thought to be affected by body weight, such as treadmill work, sweeping, and bedmaking, were not significantly different during or after pregnancy when adjusted for body weight. Consequently, body mass appears to be the dominant factor, and energy needs appear to be directly related to the increase in BMR and the cost of weight movement which accompanies increases in body mass. Since the body mass of a woman increases about 20 percent during pregnancy, jobs that involve a lot of movement must require as much as 20 percent more energy.

The diaries of daily activities from twelve pregnant teenagers showed that they spent 40 percent of their time sleeping or lying in bed with a magazine, 40 percent in quiet seated activities, 4 percent eating, 5 percent doing their hair or other similar activity, and 9 percent in other light activities.[12] This accounted for all of the time for seven of the twelve girls and 98 percent of the time for the whole group. The energy expenditure for the seven sedentary girls was 38 kcal per kg. The most active girl expended 50 kcal per kg. Energy expenditure for women who have other small children or who work or attend school would be expected to be higher. In any case since energy expenditure is so variable, the best assurance of adequate intake is a satisfactory weight gain.

SUMMARY. The NRC estimate of energy needs for the pregnant adolescent is about 45 kcal per kg (see Table IV-I). Data from Hytten and Leitch[9] suggest that it may be a little higher, 47 kcal per kg. Activity records suggest that pregnant adolescents tend to be very sedentary but, if they do attend school, work, or participate in some moderate exercise daily, their energy needs may be as much as 50 kcal per kg.[12] To allow for individual variation in activity and for possible maternal growth, if the adolescent is still in the growth phase, it is probably wise to recommend 300 additional calories daily during the last three quarters of pregnancy. A satisfactory weight gain will confirm the adequacy of amounts.

2. Protein

ADOLESCENCE. Protein requirements, like energy and other nutrient needs, follow the growth pattern. Nitrogen retention, and hence protein deposition,* is the greatest during the period of accelerated growth that precedes menarche in adolescent girls.[13] As growth decelerates, nitrogen retention diminishes. The factors responsible for the magnitude of nitrogen retention during the adolescent growth spurt are unknown but the additional nitrogen need is thought to be proportional to the additional energy need.

Several researchers have surveyed the protein intake of adolescent girls.[8] Protein seldom accounted for less than 10 percent of the caloric intake and it often represented 12 to 14 percent or more. In these studies the recorded average protein intakes ex-

---

* Protein is generally about 16 percent nitrogen.

13. F. P. Heald, M. Daugela, and P. Brunschuyler, "Physiology of adolescence (continued) ," *New England Journal of Medicine,* 268:243 (1963) .

ceeded the 44 to 54 g protein recommended in 1973 by the NRC.[6] The eleven-year-old girls consumed about 75 g protein per day; at twelve to thirteen years of age they consumed about 80 g; then intakes returned to about 75 g daily. This preference of adolescent girls for protein foods and a low caloric value may limit normal growth and development. If the energy supplied by the diet is so low that protein must be used for fuel, utilization of protein for building new tissue will be diminished. Adolescents should be encouraged to select diets containing enough energy, i.e. about 54 kcal per kg, so that protein utilization for tissue deposition is maximum.

PREGNANCY. Protein is required for normal growth and maintenance of the fetus and for growth of accessory maternal tissues in pregnancy. Animal studies[14] show that birth weight is reduced if the mother's protein intake falls below a critical level. Total lack of protein causes reproductive failure.

Even though the need for protein during pregnancy is well documented, the actual increment required is still undetermined. In the past all recommendations have been based on the amount of protein deposited in maternal and fetal tissue.*

The amount of nitrogen a woman stores during pregnancy can be measured by the nitrogen balance technique. In a series of studies,[15] the amount of nitrogen stored by pregnant women in 273 balance periods was reported to be 1.6 g a day, or 10 g protein. Small components of nitrogen loss, such as sweat, hair, nails, vaginal secretions, toothbrushing, exhaled ammonia, and plate waste were not measured in these balance studies. If these losses total 0.5 g daily, the nitrogen storage rate is about 1.1 g daily or 6.9 protein. This is about 1.5 g protein more each day than is ac-

14. M. M. Nelson, and H. M. Evans, "Relation of dietary protein levels to reproduction in the rat," *Journal of Nutrition,* 51:71 (1953) .

* Dry protein stores were estimated to be 925 g (148 g nitrogen) (see footnote 9) , and daily deposition was calculated to averages of about 5.4 g during the later half of pregnancy when tissue accumulation is proceeding rapidly. From these estimates in 1968 the NRC recommended that an additional allowance of 10 g of protein in the diets of all pregnant women, regardless of age, should provide for this accretion.

15. D. H. Calloway, "Nitrogen Balance During Pregnancy," M. Winick, ed., *Nutrition and Fetal Development* vol. II (New York, John Wiley & Sons, Inc.) .

counted for by previous estimates of dry protein stores in fetal and maternal tissue.

These balance studies indicated that during the first twenty weeks of pregnancy the nitrogen storage rate was slightly less, about 1.3 g a day or 0.8 g a day after adjustment for unmeasured nitrogen losses. The findings show that nitrogen retention to be appreciably larger than these calculated amounts and does not differ as much during the quarters of pregnancy as was formerly thought.

King *et al.*[16] measured the nitrogen retention in a group of pregnant teenagers living in a metabolic research unit during the third trimester of their pregnancy. When these fifteen- to nineteen-year-olds were fed the 1968 NRC protein recommendation, 65 g per day, they retained 1.4 g nitrogen (8.17 g protein) daily. As nitrogen was increased from 9.3 to 20.0 g a day (58 to 125 g protein) while energy varied little (about 43 kcal per kg), nitrogen retention increased linearly according to the equation: Nitrogen retention (g per day) = 0.3 (nitrogen intake) − 1.73. These findings suggest that the 1968 NRC RDA protein does not permit maximum protein storage during the third trimester in young primiparas.

Data from pregnant women living at home during balance studies[15] showed that as food intake increases both protein and energy increase. Because energy spares protein, increases in energy will have a positive effect on nitrogen storage and, therefore, increases in protein storage.*

SUMMARY. To allow maximal protein retention pregnant adolescents should probably consume at least 75 g protein a day if energy intake is 2,700 kcal. For a 58-kg girl 75 g protein is equivalent to 1.3 protein per kg.

3. Calcium

ADOLESCENCE. Calcium requirements are difficult to estimate because requirements predicted by balance studies merely reflect

---

16. J. C. King, D. H. Calloway and S. Margen, "Nitrogen retention, total ^{40}K and weight gain in teenage pregnant girls," *Journal of Nutrition*, 103:772 (1973).

* The relationship of these two factors to nitrogen retention is described by the equation: Nitrogen (N) retention (g/day) = 2.31 + [0.57 · 10^{-3} (kcal)] + .204 (N intake).

the level of calcium in the adolescent's diet during periods of rapid growth. Furthermore, calcium is absorbed more efficiently at lower than at higher levels of intake. Retention at low levels of intake is 90 percent whereas at high levels it falls to 27 percent, and chemical and histologic bone examinations fail to show any differences between the low-intake and high-intake groups.[13]

Results of balance studies show that during the premenarchal period and the growth spurt calcium absorption and retention is increased.[8] When calcium intakes range from 1.0 to 1.6 g a day and vitamin D intakes are about 400 IU a day, a mean retention of 400 mg of calcium a day is supported.[17] This level of daily calcium retention for several years during the period of rapid growth appears to be necessary for adequate skeletal mineralization.

Evidence of calcium deficiency is rare in the United States even though the calcium intake is frequently less than the NRC allowance. Longitudinal data show that premenarchal girls ingest between 0.8 to 1.2 g of calcium a day. After twelve years of age, intake declines to between 0.4 to 0.8 g a day in adult woman.[8] Of sixty-four West New York adolescent girls, 55 percent consumed less than two-thirds of the 1973 NRC recommended calcium allowance, i.e. less than 860 mg.[18] The skeletal systems of these girls appear to have developed normally since they attained normal height, but additional longitudinal studies are required to determine if lower than recommended intakes of calcium result in skeletal disorders later in life.

PREGNANCY. The additional calcium needed during pregnancy is primarily for fetal skeletal development. At birth the fetus contains about 28 g calcium.[9] Since small additional quantities of calcium are deposited in maternal supporting tissues and fluids, calcium deposition totals about 30 g in pregnancy. Prior to pregnancy the maternal body contains about 1,120 g calcium. The additional calcium required for pregnancy is, therefore, 2.5 per-

17. M. A. Ohlson and G. Stearns, "Calcium intake of children and adults," *Fed. Proc.* 18:1076, 1959.

18. B. C. Schorr, D. Sanjur and E. C. Erickson, "Teenage food habits," *Journal of the American Dietetic Association,* 61:415 (1972) .

cent of the maternal skeletal content and could probably be provided from that store if necessary.

If maternal dietary calcium was low prior to pregnancy, maternal tissue stores may also be low. Persistence of poor calcium intakes during pregnancy may jeopardize fetal skeletal development as maternal sources will not be mobilized when a critical level is reached. Marginal calcium intakes during pregnancy could also impair lactation. The amount of calcium needed for lactation is greater than that needed for pregnancy and some physiological preparation for lactation is presumably made during pregnancy. To provide calcium for fetal development without depleting maternal tissue an additional intake of 400 mg is recommended during pregnancy.[6]

SUMMARY. If the adolescent continues her own growth during pregnancy, her calcium needs will be great, on the order of 1.6 g per day, but if maternal growth terminates with pregnancy, 1.2 g calcium daily should meet the pregnant adolescent's needs.

4. Iron

ADOLESCENCE. Considerable iron is required during adolescence for the rapid growth in muscle mass, the increase in blood volume and respiratory enzymes, and the maintenance of iron stores (which amounts to about 20% of the total body iron). Additionally, puberty brings on menstruation with attendant blood and iron losses. Balance studies[19] show that 11 to 13 mg of iron daily are needed to cover growth and excretory losses. In 1973 the NRC recommended 18 mg iron a day to allow for variability in iron absorption and to permit sufficient accumulation of iron stores so that iron therapy during pregnancy might not be necessary.[6]

Dietary sources often do not satisfy these iron requirements. In a group of California adolescent girls iron was the most neglected nutrient; their iron intake averaged about 9.5 mg a day.[20]

19. D. Schlaphoff and F. A. Johnson, "Iron requirement of 6 adolescent girls," *Journal of Nutrition*, 39:67 (1949).

20. M. C. Hampton, R. L. Huenemann, L. R. Shapiro and B. W. Mitchell, "Caloric and nutrient intakes of teenagers," *Journal of the American Dietetic Association*, 50:385 (1967).

The iron intake of a group of adolescent girls in New York was only 8.8 mg daily.[18] Low levels of iron intake by adolescent girls are not associated with a high prevalence of anemia in that group. A group of college-aged women consumed similar levels of iron, about 9.2 mg a day, but none of them exhibited iron-deficiency anemia even though some lacked iron stores.[21]

In normal persons during periods of growth, pregnancy, and low iron intake the absorption of iron is more efficient. This adaptation in iron absorption may prevent the onset of iron-deficiency anemia in young women ingesting less than 10 mg iron daily. However, the iron stores necessary for pregnancy will not be maintained on this level of intake.

PREGNANCY. The iron requirement specific to pregnancy is that iron lost by the mother at delivery, i.e. the iron in the fetus, the placenta, and the blood lost. About 370 mg of iron are deposited in the products of conception, and an additional 250 mg of iron are lost at delivery if about 600 ml blood are lost with a hematocrit value of 37.[22] These sources of iron loss total 660 mg. Most of the fetal, placental, and blood iron is deposited during the second half of pregnancy. Therefore, 4.7 mg of iron must be stored daily over the last 140 days in order to meet these needs. Since menstruation ceases during pregnancy, the specific increment for pregnancy is not additive to the nonpregnant requirement. The menstruating adolescent's average iron loss is 0.4 mg a day,[22] so the daily iron increment for the latter half of pregnancy is reduced to 4.3 mg a day.

The iron stores of healthy American women average about 0.3 g,[23] so they are not adequate to supply all the additional iron needed for fetal development. Food or elemental iron must supplement the iron stores. Normally, only about 10 percent of dietary iron is absorbed. The efficiency of iron absorption increases progressively during pregnancy, however, reaching a peak of

21. E. R. Monsen, I. N. Kuhn, and C. A. Finch, "Iron status of menstruating women," *Journal of American Medical Association,* 199:897 (1967).

22. R. E. Shank, "A chink in our armor," *Nutrition Today,* 5 (No. 2) :5 (1970).

23. D. E. Scott and J. A. Pritchard, "Iron deficiency in healthy young college women," *Journal of American Medical Association,* 199:897 (1967).

about 25 percent in the last trimester.[24] Consequently, 4.3 mg of iron would probably be absorbed from diets containing 18 to 22 mg of iron. Diets currently consumed by American women contain on the average 6 mg of iron per 1,000 calories.[8] Pregnant women consume 13 to 14 mg of iron a day. Supplementation of these diets with 30 to 60 mg of elemental iron, such as ferrous sulfate, ferrous fumarate, or ferrous gluconate, would readily satisfy iron needs in normal, healthy pregnant women.

SUMMARY. As it is likely that iron stores are low in adolescent women due to poor dietary iron intakes for several years, 30 to 60 mg of supplemental iron should be given to pregnant adolescents.

5. Other Minerals

Other essential minerals include phosphorus, magnesium, copper, fluorine, sulfur, zinc, selenium, cobalt, manganese, molybdenum, nickel, tin, chromium, iodine, vanadium, and silicon. These minerals have many functions relating directly or indirectly to growth. They contribute to the rigidity of bones and teeth and are important parts of lipid and protein fractions in the body. In addition, they preserve cellular integrity by osmotic pressures and are a component of many enzymes which catalyze metabolic reactions. Thus, all are considered essential for normal growth and development during adolescence or pregnancy.

If the calcium and protein needs are met, *phosphorus* requirements will be covered as foods rich in calcium and protein are the best sources of phosphorus.

Magnesium is an important component of bone and soft tissue, and it is a constituent of many enzymes. A magnesium intake of 300 mg daily will maintain positive balance in college-aged women.[25] An additional 150 mg are recommended in pregnancy.[6]

Copper has a role in blood formation and is a component of many enzymes. An ordinary mixed diet provides 2 to 5 mg of

24. C. A. Finch, "Iron-deficiency anemia," *American Journal of Clinical Nutrition*, 22:512 (1969).

25. F. I. Scoular, J. D. Pace and A. N. Davis, "The calcium, phosphorus and magnesium balances of young college women consuming self-selected diets," *Journal of Nutrition*, 62:489, 1957.

copper a day. Balance is maintained in adults on 2 mg a day[26] and in preadolescent girls on 1.3 mg a day.[27] To date, the NRC has not recommended a daily copper intake.

Extensive evidence suggests that during tooth development a controlled intake of *fluoride* protects against dental caries. In areas where the fluoride in natural water is low, fluoridation at the rate of 1 part per million is highly desirable. No additional recommendation for fluoride intake has been made.

Sulfur is an integral part of coenzyme A, mucoproteins, sulfo-lipid, and many enzymes. Inorganic sulfur cannot meet the sulfur requirement for these compounds. Amino acid sulfur is needed, so the sulfur requirement is closely related to the protein requirement.

Zinc is essential for growth in most mammals and is a cofactor for numerous enzymes. Uncomplicated zinc deficiency in man is not well documented, but patients with anemia, hepatospleno-megaly, short stature and hypogonadism have responded to zinc therapy.[6] Zinc dietary intakes of about 15 mg daily will maintain balance in adults. In pregnancy maternal serum total zinc is reduced by about one-half.[28] This could be due to hemodilution, but a maternal-fetal concentration gradient must be maintained as zinc appears to move across the placenta by passive transfer. An additional 5 mg zinc daily in pregnancy seems to be appropriate, and the NRC Committee made such a recommendation.[6]

6. Vitamin A

Vitamin A is required for formation of retina visual pigments and maintenance of normal epithelial structures. Evidence[29] suggests that vitamin A is essential for the synthesis of mucopoly-

26. R. M. Leverton and E. S. Binkley, "The copper metabolism and requirement of young women," *Journal of Nutrition*, 27:43, 1944.

27. R. W. Engel, N. P. Price and R. F. Miller, "Copper, manganese, cobalt, and molybdenum balance in preadolescent girls," *Journal of Nutrition*, 92:197 (1967).

28. R. I. Henkin, "Newer aspects of copper and zinc metabolism," in W. Mertz and W. E. Cornatzer, eds., *Newer Trace Elements in Nutrition* (New York, Marcel Dekker, Inc., 1971).

29. G. Wolf and P. T. Varandani, "Studies on the function of vitamin A in muco-polysaccharide biosynthesis," *Biochemica et Biophysica Acta*," 43:501, 1960.

saccharides. It may also be involved in the production of adreno-cortical steroids.[30] Vitamin A also appears to have a function in bone growth, but its exact role is not known. During adolescence the NRC recommends 4,000 IU of vitamin A a day to satisfy growth and tissue needs.[6]

Fruits and vegetables, the major dietary sources of vitamin A, are not popular food items of adolescents, and their vitamin A intake is frequently less than 4,000 IU. A group of New York adolescent girls consumed, on the average, 3,500 IU of vitamin A per day and 50 percent of a group of teenage girls in California consumed less than 3,400 IU.[18] Yet, clinical signs of vitamin A deficiency, i.e. xerophthalmia and keratinization of epithelium, are rare, but low serum vitamin A levels have been detected[31] in teenage girls and suggest long-standing low vitamin A intakes or a long history of defective fat absorption.

During pregnancy the NRC[6] recommends an additional 1,000 IU of vitamin A daily to support the requirements of a rapidly growing fetus. As vitamin A maintains cellular integrity, an increased need is expected in a rapidly growing system, but documentation of this need is not available.

7. Vitamin C (Ascorbic Acid)

Vitamin C is required during adolescence for the synthesis of collagen, steroids, norephinephrine, and to maintain certain protein metabolic pathways. The recommended allowance for persons beyond twelve years of age is estimated to be about 2.5 mg per kg body weight to the three-fourths power, representing metabolic body size.[6] This gives a figure of about 45 mg daily for the 44-kg eleven- to fourteen-year-old girl.

Vitamin C intakes frequently drop below the desired level if the adolescent does not include a citrus fruit in her diet. Vitamin C in the diet has been associated in a negative fashion with

---

30. R. L. Jackson, F. M. Hanna and M. A. Flynn, "Nutritional requirements of infants and children," *Pediatric Clinics of North America*, 8:879 (1962).

31. R. E. Hodges and W. A. Krehl, "Nutritional status of teenagers in Iowa," *American Journal of Clinical Nutrition*, 17:200 (1965).

skipping breakfast in a group of Iowa teenagers.[†] This suggests that breakfast furnishes the primary sources of vitamin C. The average ascorbic acid intake of these Iowa teenagers was 82 mg a day, but the standard deviation was large indicating that intake was highly variable.[31] Only a few of these teenagers had low plasma ascorbic acid levels. As plasma ascorbic acid levels may reflect only the most recent dietary intake, leukocyte ascorbic acid assays are a better index of tissue stores, but this test is tedious and not widely used.

An additional 15 mg of ascorbic acid is suggested for pregnancy.[6] In a state of rapid growth and increased metabolism, augmented ascorbic acid requirements for synthetic functions are logical, but the specific increment has not been determined.

8. Folacin (Folic Acid)

Folacin functions as a coenzyme in the transfer of single carbon units in a number of intracellular processes, particularly in the synthesis of thymine, a nucleotide component of DNA. Under conditions of folate deficiency there is interference with DNA reduplication and mitotic activity.[32] The result is retardation of nuclear growth while cytoplasmic growth, for a period of time, seems unaffected. The rapidly dividing cells, such as the red blood cells, are affected the most and macrocytic anemia may result from folic acid deficiency.

Pregnancy is a period of rapid cellular growth, and pregnant women appear prone to develop folic acid deficiency. Even though folic acid occurs in a wide variety of foods of animal and plant origin, folate deficiency is usually due to an inadequate dietary intake. The dietary histories of a group of pregnant women with megaloblastic anemia revealed a low intake of animal protein and almost complete absence of green vegetables. Staple foodstuffs consisted of wheat and corn flour products, beans cooked for a long time, boiled potatoes, soft drinks, and occasional animal protein in the form of chicken, pork, and packaged luncheon meats.[32] Natural food folate in many of

32. D. A. Kitay, "Folic acid deficiency in pregnancy. On the recognition, pathogenesis, consequences, and therapy of the deficiency state in human reproduction," *American Journal of Obstetrics and Gynecology*, 104:1067 (1969) .

these foods was destroyed by the preparation processes, i.e. excessive exposure to heat and hydrolysis during long periods of cooking. The apparent ingestion defect was worsened by anorexia and vomiting associated with pregnancy.

The healthy nonpregnant woman may require only 0.05 to 0.10 mg folacin a day, but the NRC recommends 0.4 mg daily since cooking losses and absorptive capacity are variable. During pregnancy the folate requirement is increased. The NRC recommends an addition of 0.4 mg of dietary folate daily.[6] The frequent finding of maternal folate deficiency has resulted in a trend towards routine folate supplementation during pregnancy. As pure forms of folacin are utilized more effectively than natural forms, a supplement of 200 to 400 μg folacin will protect most pregnant women from folate deficiency.[10]

9. Vitamin B₁₂

Vitamin B_{12} is needed for normal nucleic and folic acid metabolism, and, therefore, is essential for the functioning of all cells. Like folic acid, vitamin B_{12} is concerned with the maturation of red blood cells; megaloblastic anemia also is a clinical sign of vitamin B_{12} deficiency.

Vitamin B_{12} is found in all animal tissues, especially liver and kidney, and in dairy foods, but little is found in plant food. A diet containing 1 cup of milk, 4 ounces of meat and 1 egg has 2 to 4 μg of vitamin B_{12}. Beef liver or kidney increases the intake 15 to 20 μg daily.

In adolescence cellular growth occurs in practically all tissues including marrow, nervous system, and gastrointestinal tract. Vitamin B_{12} is essential for development and normal functioning of these systems. A dietary vitamin B_{12} intake of 5 μg per day will support this growth and replace normal losses.[6]

Vitamin B_{12} needs may be greater during pregnancy due to excessive fetal demands so one additional μg per day is recommended.[6] Serious vitamin B_{12} deficiency during pregnancy is rare even though a gradual reduction in serum vitamin B_{12} is frequently observed. This reduction may occur because of hemodilution. Serum levels usually rise promptly after delivery. The pregnant adolescent who is a strict vegetarian will get only a trace of this vitamin in her diet and may develop megaloblastic anemia due to vitamin B_{12} deficiency. Vitamin B_{12} supplementation may be indicated for the vegetarian pregnant adolescent.

10. Vitamin B_6 (Pyridoxine)

Vitamin B_6 functions as a coenzyme in the metabolism of amino acids, protein, and glycogen. In vitamin B_6 deficiency abnormalities of fat metabolism have been demonstrated, but no definite site of vitamin B_6 function in fatty acid metabolism is confirmed.

Vitamin B_6 denotes three closely related chemical compounds, pyridoxine, pyridoxal, and pyridoxamine. These compounds are widely distributed in a variety of foods; in animal foods largely as pyridoxal and pyridoxamine and in plant foods as pyridoxine. The adult daily intake of vitamin B_6 is from 1 to 2 mg a day.[33] Dietary records from a small group of adolescents[34] showed that they consumed about 1.4 mg a day.[1]

There is some evidence[6] that the requirement for vitamin B_6 is related to the intake of protein. A high protein diet (168 g) required 2.76 mg vitamin B_6 a day to maintain normal tryptophan metabolism, whereas 40 to 50 g of dietary protein required only 0.9 mg of vitamin B_6 a day. Evidence is lacking on the specific vitamin B_6 requirement for adolescents. A daily intake of 1.4 to 2.0 is recommended in accordance with increases in recommended protein intake.[6]

In pregnancy biochemical abnormalities have been detected in toxemic women presumably on "normal" diets which were corrected by vitamin B_6.[35] The specific dietary increment required to satisfy these needs during pregnancy has not been determined. The placenta normally concentrates vitamin B_6 in fetal blood

33. J. F. Mueller and J. M. Iacono, Effect of desoxpyridoxine-induced vitamin B_6 deficiency on polyunsaturated fatty acid metabolism in human beings, *American Journal of Clinical Nutrition,* 12:358 (1963).

34. J. C. King, S. H. Cohenour, D. H. Calloway and S. Oace. Unpublished data.

35. J. A. Klieger, J. R. Evrard and R. Pierce, "Abnormal pyridoxine metabolism in toxemia of pregnancy," *American Journal of Obstetrics and Gynecology,* 94:316 (1966).

compared to maternal blood at delivery.[36] The NRC presumes that an additional 0.5 mg a day will meet fetal needs.[6]

11. Other Vitamins

Other vitamins include thiamin, riboflavin, niacin, vitamin D, vitamin E, vitamin K, pantothenic acid, choline, inositol and biotin. Fortification or restoration with thiamin, riboflavin, niacin, and vitamin D has essentially eliminated deficiency symptoms of these nutrients in this country. The vitamin E requirement is a function of the unsaturated fatty acid content of the diet. Fortunately, the naturally occurring unsaturated fatty acids are associated with vitamin E. The amount of vitamin K required is normally synthesized by intestinal bacteria. Pantothenic acid is present in many foods so a mixed diet usually supplies the amount needed. Choline, inositol, and biotin are all synthesized in the body.

ADOLESCENT DIETARY HABITS

The dietary habits of an adolescent usually reflect patterns learned in early childhood. By two to seven years of age the food habits of children are found to be similar to those of other family members.

The fact that a close relationship often exists between the food habits of college girls and their mothers suggests that these early food habits are preserved into young adulthood. When teenagers are surveyed about their attitudes on food, many view food behavior as a family-centered activity and often name their mother as the "food authority figure."

Adolescent food habits are also positively influenced by the establishment of a routine in living habits. During the winter months when the teenagers are in school better diets are selected largely due to the more regular schedules imposed by school attendance.[37] Also, diet quality is closely related to the number of

---

36. R. Karlin and M. Dumont, "Contribution to the study of the vitamin B$_6$ levels during childbirth in the total blood of the mother and in the total cord blood," *Gynecology and Obstetrics*, 62:281 (1963).

37. M. A. Hinton, E. S. Eppright, H. Chadderon and L. Wolins, "Eating behavior and dietary intake of girls 12 to 14 years old," *Journal of American Dietetic Association*, 43:223 (1963).

servings and variety of foods eaten, and the complexity of the diet increases with the extent of diversification in other areas of life.[18] Factors that are associated with the diversity of adolescent diets include an increase in the father's and mother's educational level, the extent of the teenager's social participation, i.e. the number of extracurricular activities, and his or her employment.

An excessive number of extracurricular activities can have a detrimental effect on the adolescent's food habits, however, and when teenagers are asked why they do not eat better, many say they don't have time.[37] What they are really saying is, "I don't think it's important." Time is found for those things that are considered really important. Meals are often omitted by teenagers merely because their time schedule doesn't coincide with the families' meals, and they don't feel that eating with the family is important enough to warrant a change in their schedule.

Emotional adjustment affects all behavior including eating behavior. Generally, teenage girls who score best in emotional stability, conformity, adjustment to reality, and family relationships miss fewer meals, are acquainted with a wider variety of foods, and have better diets than other girls.[37] Girls who mature late or early often have emotional problems accompanying this deviation, such as feelings of inadequacy and isolation, and they frequently have poorer eating habits than those girls maturing normally.

ADOLESCENT MEAL PATTERN

Many adolescents have little or no food from bedtime to lunchtime the following day. It has been reported that as many as one-fifth of all adolescent girls do not eat breakfast,[38] and an additional 50 percent may have poor breakfasts.[39] One study[40] showed that as students progressed from seventh to twelfth grade, those missing meals increased from 10 to 25 percent and twice as many missed breakfast in twelfth grade as in seventh

38. E. B. Spindler and G. Acker, "Teenagers tell us about their nutrition," *Journal of American Dietetic Association*, 43:228 (1963).

39. E. Spindler, Eating habits in teenagers. *Food and Nutrition News*, 39 (No. 8):1 (1968).

40. C. H. Edwards, G. Hogan, S. Spahr and Guilford County Nutrition Committee, "Nutrition survey of 6,200 teenage youth," *Journal of American Dietetic Association*, 45:543 (1964).

grade. Huenemann[41] asked teenagers to name their favorite meal. Dinner was favored by over 60 percent, lunch by about 30 percent and breakfast by 8 percent. Reasons for their choices are of interest: dinner for food, lunch for freedom and company, and breakfast for its effect in preventing fatigue or hunger.

Breakfast may be the most important meal of the day. The body has been without food for eight to twelve hours and needs fuel. Research[39] has shown that when teenagers omitted breakfast, at 11:00 a.m. they took longer to make a decision on a test, neuromuscular tremor was greater, and their work output on a stationary bicycle was reduced. When students eat breakfast their thinking may be sharper, their neuromuscular reflexes may be steadier, and their ability to work and play may be better in the late morning.

Snacks are popular with teenagers and represent important social functions. Hampton[†] reports that teenagers often eat five times a day; and as much as one-fourth of their total caloric intake may come from snacks and that those who snack frequently are also likely to eat meals of good quality and to have overall good diets. This suggests that teenagers' snacking habits reflect wise choices and should not necessarily be condemned.

MOTIVATING ADOLESCENTS TO SELECT GOOD DIETS

Contrary to expectation, good food habits are unrelated to the number of nutrition information channels available to the adolescent girl[18] or to her knowledge of nutrition as gauged by knowledge of the four basic food groups.[20] Desired food habits represent a set of behavior patterns and are developed from a variety of motivational forces. Adults can only provide good food and attempt to present nutrition information in a way which will motivate adolescents to select wisely from the large variety of food available to them (see appendix). In the end, adolescents must initiate the appropriate action themselves.

Nutritionists working with adolescents should be aware that the sophisticated ones often give answers to questions which they think are correct or which they think are wanted. The nutrition-

---

41. R. L. Huenemann, "A study of teenagers: body size and shape, dietary practices and physical activity," *Food and Nutrition News,* 37 (No. 7) :1 (1966) .

ist and/or dietitian is recognized as a member of the medical team and, consequently, is often viewed with suspicion as an authority figure. Rapport is essential for the acquisition of honest information. To develop this rapport the nutritionist must convince the adolescent that she is not a disciplinarian, but a counselor and educator. If the nutritionist is a woman, she can often relate better to the pregnant adolescent by helping the girl develop her social skills and improve her hygiene and grooming. Teenagers are weight-, complexion-, and personality-conscious.

Other members of the medical team, i.e. the doctor and nurse, must support the nutritionist in her role as a counselor and educator. If adolescents are threatened with a visit from the dietitian when food habits or weight gain patterns are found to be unacceptable, the dietitian will only appear as a disciplinarian.

There is no magic formula for motivating teenagers to select a good diet. One nutritionist's approach may be entirely different from another's. In our study of pregnant teenagers a few novel approaches were tried. To motivate pregnant adolescents to take their supplemental iron, we showed them the differences between their hemoglobin and serum iron laboratory reports and those of a girl who took iron supplements. Serum iron values are very responsive to supplemental iron, and the girls were very pleased to see the positive response four weeks later after they began taking their supplements. We also gave the girls jeweler's ring-size measurers in order to measure the fluid retention in their hands. Small increases in ring-size were normal, we explained, but large, erratic changes might be diminished with a good diet. Most importantly, a "healthy pregnancy diet" was discussed with each girl, and each was shown how she could evaluate the quality of her diet with the use of a point system (see Appendix).

Dr. S. L. Hammar,[42] a physician with the University of Washington Adolescent Clinic, suggests that a nutritionist functioning in the following ways on an interdisciplinary team will make significant contributions to the total care of an adolescent patient:

---

42. S. L. Hammar, "The role of the nutritionist in an adolescent clinic," *Children*, 13:217, 1966.

1. Her consultations and nutritional recommendations are inventive and resourceful, and she is able to sell her ideas to other professionals, particularly physicians.
2. She makes observations on aspects of the adolescent's behavior other than those directly related to nutrition.
3. She is not bound by convention and will try new approaches or methods in dealing with adolescents.
4. She periodically evaluates her accomplishments and continually seeks ways to expand her scope of activities and to broaden her understanding of adolescent behavior and needs.

APPENDIX

Healthy Pregnancy Diet

High-scoring diets mean a healthier mother and baby. You are feeding your baby from your own body while it is in your womb. So it is important that your body be supplied with *everything* it needs to make good flesh and blood for your baby and to keep you well and strong. All through pregnancy every bit of the baby's food comes from you. It is up to YOU to see that he gets everything he needs by eating a high-scoring diet.

Score Your Diet

Score your diet by comparing the points it earned with the perfect "40-point" basic pregnancy diet.

Food Groups	Amount Required	Rating	Total Possible
I. Milk or choices from the milk food list	4 servings	4 points per serving	16
II. Meat or choices from the meat foot list	3 servings	2.7 points per serving	8
III. Vegetables and fruit; dark green or yellow	1 serving	3 points	3
other vegetable, cooked or raw	2 servings	2 points per serving	4
potato group foods	1 serving	1 point	1
citrus fruit	1 serving	3 points	3
other fruit, fresh or canned	1 serving	1 point	1
IV. Bread and cereal	4 servings	1 point per serving	4
			40

How do you rate?

40	Excellent
36-39	Good
32-35	Borderline
Below 32	Danger! You need to improve.

Why, What, and How Much of Each Food Group

GROUP I. Milk is probably the most necessary food in the basic diet given above. Four cups of milk will give you over three-fourths of the CALCIUM you need to build good quality teeth and bones in your baby. Milk also is high in protein as well as in minerals and vitamins.

If you do not like milk or if it does not agree with you, you may want to select something else from the list below that will provide as much calcium as one cup of milk. Different kinds of milk also can be selected to give your diet variety. Select *four servings* from the list of milk foods every day.

Milk Foods	Amount for One Serving
Skim, low-fat, chocolate, or buttermilk	1 cup
Milkshake, malted milk, or eggnog	1 cup
Evaporated milk	½ cup
Cheese—American, Swiss, Cheddar, or Monterey Jack	1 slice or 1 x 1 x 1″ cube
Cottage cheese	1½ cup
Cheese spread	2 ounces (4 tbsp.)
Ice cream	3 cups
Ice milk	1½ cup
Cream soup made with milk	2 cups
Pudding made with milk	1 cup
Yogurt	1 cup (8 ounces)
Special diet food—Metrecal, Nutrement, Carnation Instant Breakfast	¾ cup

GROUP II. Meat or other foods such as fish, eggs, cheese, nuts, and beans are excellent sources of high-quality PROTEIN. These foods are readily used to form your baby's tissues, bones, and blood. Meat and eggs are valuable sources of iron. If you eat an adequate amount of iron during pregnancy, your baby will have good iron stores in his liver to use during the first months of life. (See the list of iron-rich food choices on page.)

Be sure to select *three servings* every day from the list of meat foods below; for example, two eggs, four slices of bacon, one hamburger pattie, and two chicken legs would total three servings. (One serving equals 3 ounces.)

Meat Foods	Amount to Use	Servings Provided
Chicken	1 breast, 2 legs, or 2 thighs	1
Chops—pork, lamb, or veal	3 x 3 x 1″ chop	1
Roast beef, pork, lamb, veal, or turkey	3 x 3 x ½″ slice	1
Steak—any kinds	3 x 3 x 1″ size	1
Cubes (as for beef stew)	Five 1″ cubes	1
Hamburger	3 x 3 ½″ pattie	1
Hot dog	1 each	⅓
Luncheon meat	2 slices	⅓
Sausage links	2 links	⅓
Vienna sausage	3 links	⅓
Canadian bacon	2½″ diameter or ¼″ slice	⅓
Bacon	4 slices	⅓
Fish fillet	3 x 2 x ½″ piece	1
Shrimp, scallops	5 or 6 large pieces	1
Canned fish—tuna or salmon	½ cup	1
Eggs	1 each	⅓
Cheese—Swiss, American, Cheddar, or Monterey Jack	1 slice or 1 x 1 x 1″ cube	⅓
Cottage cheese	¾ cup	1
Refried beans	½ cup	⅓
Black-eyed or split peas	½ cup	⅓
Navy beans	½ cup	⅓
Nuts—cashew, walnuts, peanuts, or mixed	25 to 30	⅓
peanut butter	2 tbsp.	⅓
Chili con carne with beans	½ cup	⅓
Casseroles—chicken chow mein, chop suey, macaroni and cheese	1 cup	⅓

GROUP III. In general, the more fruits and vegetables eaten, the better. These foods not only help give you the necessary vitamins and minerals, but they also make the diet bulky and laxative and help prevent constipation. The dark green and yellow vegetables are necessary to provide vitamin A since little is present in other foods. Vitamin A is used to make healthy skin and eyes. Orange juice and other citrus fruits are needed to supply vitamin C. Vitamin C is a very important vitamin used in the formation of healthy gums, blood, and bones.

> During pregnancy, the vitamins and minerals are so important to both you and your baby that you should remember every day to take the vitamin pills ordered by your doctor. They will help provide the necessary amount of each vitamin that you need every day.

One serving of vegetables and fruit is equal to ½ cup cooked, canned, or frozen, or one medium fresh fruit or vegetable. You may also use ½ cup fruit or vegetable juice. You have a wide variety in each food group. Select the following servings in each group of fruits and vegetables daily.

Dark green or yellow vegetables—one serving per day. Broccoli, spinach, kale, carrots, winter squash, chard, pumpkin, sweet potatoes, yams, tomatoes, and collard, mustard and turnip greens.

Other vegetables cooked or raw—two servings per day. Celery, lettuce, cucumbers, onions, radishes, cabbage, green pepper, peas, corn, beans, beets, asparagus, cauliflower, brussel sprouts, summer squash, zucchini, and artichokes.

Potato or alternate—one serving per day. White potatoes, lima beans, navy or pinto beans, rice, noodles, spaghetti, or macaroni.

Citrus fruit—one serving per day. Oranges, grapefruit, cantaloupe, strawberries, or lemons.

Other fruits or juice—one serving per day. Apples, applesauce, apricots, bananas, cherries, blackberries, blueberries, grapes, pineapple, raspberries, honeydew, nectarine, tangeloes, tangerines, peaches, pears, plums, or watermelon.

GROUP IV. Breads and cereals provide the energy needed to develop a healthy baby. They also supply needed vitamins. Whole wheat breads and cereals are particularly useful in preventing constipation.

A serving can be one slice of bread or one-half cup cooked cereal or three-fourths cup dry cereal. Several kinds of bread can be chosen: white, whole wheat, rye, French, sourdough, raisin, bran, corn, oatmeal, or potato breads. Muffins, biscuits, rolls, waffles, pancakes, crackers, or popcorn also can be used.

What About the Extras?

You can *supplement* the basic pregnancy diet with butter, margarine, salad dressing, or desserts and sweets, but *do not replace* any required foods. Desserts and fats generally contribute energy. Your need for energy will vary with your size and activity. Regulate your intake of extras so that your weight gain is spaced at about four pounds for the first three months, ten pounds for the middle three months, and twelve pounds for the last three months. Studies show that the average pregnant woman should expect to gain about twenty-five pounds. If you are a teenager who is still growing, you may expect to gain about thirty pounds during your pregnancy.

A Favorite Dish

Your favorite dish may easily be part of the basic pregnancy diet. Here are some examples:

Food Items	Amount	Food Groups Supplied
Spaghetti and meat sauce	1 cup	½ meat; 1 bread; ½ vegetable
Tamales	2 each	⅓ meat; 1 bread; ½ vegetable
Tacos	1 each	⅓ meat; 1 bread; ½ vegetable
Enchilladas	1 each	½ meat; 1 bread; ½ vegetable
Spanish rice	1 cup	1 bread; ½ vegetable
Beef hash	1 cup	1 meat; 1 bread
Peanut butter and jelly sandwich	1 each	⅓ meat; 2 bread
Chicken or beef pot pie	1 each	½ meat; 1 bread
French fries	10 each	1 potato
Pizza	3 pieces	½ meat; 2 bread; ½ vegetable
Hamburger with bun, lettuce, and tomato	1 each	1 meat; 2 bread; 1 vegetable
Tomato soup (made with milk)	1½ C	1 milk; 1 vegetable
Vegetable soup	1 cup	1 vegetable
Corn flakes with sliced bananas and milk	1 bowl	1 bread; 1 milk; 1 fruit
Beef and vegetable stew	2 cup	⅔ meat; 1 or 2 vegetable

Iron-rich Foods

Iron is important in your diet. Be sure to select at least one of the iron-rich foods once a day.

Organ meats—liver, kidney, heart, liver sausage and liverwurst

Lean meat—beef, pork, veal, lamb

Dark green leafy vegetables—chard, greens, and spinach

Eggs

Oysters and clams

Dried beans—navy and pinto

Dried apricots

Raisins

Enriched or whole grain cereal—shredded wheat, raisin bran, bran flakes, grapenut flakes, ralston, and wheatena

You cannot eat enough iron-rich foods to supply the iron needed for the average pregnant woman. It is important that you take the iron pills ordered by your doctor every day. Try to take the pills with the meal and they will not bother you.

CHAPTER V

PSYCHOLOGICAL AND EMOTIONAL PROBLEMS OF PREGNANCY IN ADOLESCENCE

Judith Weatherford Shouse

P REGNANT ADOLESCENTS and their problems have been of increasing interest and concern to professionals for some time. There is a rise in the birth rate among adolescent girls, regardless of socioeconomic or marital status, racial or ethnic group, geographic location or current family situation. Adolescent girls are more frequently keeping their babies and attempting to deal with the responsibilities and pressures of the new and often premature roles incumbent on them—mother, wife, woman, student, careerist.

Abortion is being chosen more frequently and adoption less frequently as alternatives to having and keeping a baby. The mother-child dyad is becoming more common and acceptable in all strata of society; the single mother in all age groups is no longer the object of public censure or social stigma. There seems little question by now that this increasingly frequent choice to keep one's baby represents a genuine cultural change which is adding to the more general alteration in the family unit as the basis of our social system. The focus here will be on the adolescent who chooses to continue her pregnancy, bear her child, and rear it herself.

ADOLESCENCE

It is important to understand something of the complex problems of the developmental stage of adolescence, a universal transitional experience bridging childhood and adulthood. The basic task of adolescence is to replace the dependent childhood attachment to one's parents with a mature adult relationship to them

161

and to others. It involves establishment of intimate relationships with others, including a sexual adaptation. The knowledge and power which adolescents must assume to become adult must be internalized as part of their self-concept. Their choices and controls must be self-directed. Incorporation of standards of personal and social morality which are acceptable in adult society are also necessary. This autonomy, self-dependence, and emancipation from parents requires the adolescent to look elsewhere for financial support, thus educational and vocational choices become another task. The tremendous pressure of these conflicts and the hard work that must be done by the adolescent to resolve these conflicts renders a characteristic response which Erikson calls "role diffusion," a temporary phase of role indecision and confusion.[1]

The changes in relationships, specifically separation from the parents, and the burst of physiological growth responsible for these changes present the task of a further advance in defining body image and identity formation. This produces, in Eriksonian terms, a crisis in the way one sees oneself in relation to the outer world.[2] It prompts the adolescent to ask herself questions about her female identity: "Who am I?"; about her relation to others: "How do others see me?"; about her hopes for herself for the future: "How do I want to be?" Identity formation does not begin or end with the fluid stage of adolescence and is never finally achieved, but it is expected to bring about consolidation of an evolving personal identity. Also it must be remembered that successful resolution of adolescent tasks depends largely on successful completion of the tasks of childhood. When these tasks have not been fulfilled, they are carried by the child into adolescence. The tasks of adolescence are accompanied by emotional lability, ambivalence, heightened sensitivity, and a fluid, vulnerable ego state. The adolescent's internal pressures plus the pressures from peers, parents, and society simultaneously impinge on her, insisting on some form of resolution.

---

1. Erik Erikson, *Childhood and Society* (New York, W. W. Norton and Company, Inc., 1950) .

2. Erik Erikson, "Identity and the life cycle," *Psychological Monograph*, 1 (1) (1959) .

Girls who become pregnant in their teens experience simultaneously two major developmental crises: they have not yet fulfilled their female adolescent maturational functions, and imposed on this is the crisis of pregnancy. Some girls also marry prior to or after the pregnancy occurs, adding a third crisis, as the early phase of marriage is also a critical period in feminine life.[3] They are often still students attempting to reach educational goals and are often in the process of making vocational choices and establishing life goals.

PREGNANCY

The touch points of feminine psychological development and experience have been called the development of breasts, menarche, defloration, sexual experience, abortion, pregnancy, mothering, and menopause. Each is a critical phase which creates developmental opportunities—for further growth and fulfillment as a woman or for conflict and disturbance—affecting her total life at present and in the future. Nearly all are characterized by profound physiological and hormonal changes, and fundamental psychological changes, and each phase creates characteristic adjustment tasks related to an individual's entire life history.[4, 5]

Because of the inner emotional life distinctive of the pregnant state, it is universally experienced by women as a psychological crisis. It is also an event of great personal impact in the anthropological sense, as it marks a woman's relationship to society. It is a transitional experience bridging the childless life and the irreversible state of parenthood and in some sense assures one's immortality.

In the early part of a typical pregnancy, a woman usually becomes more regressed and turned inward, incorporating the idea that the fetus is in her body. She is commonly concerned with the past, particularly her relationship with her own mother. The task

3. H. Rausch, W. Goodrich and J. Campbell, "Adaptation to the first years of marriage," *Psychiatry*, 26:368-380 (1963).

4. Natalie Shainess, "Psychological Problems Associated with Motherhood," in Silvano Arieti, ed., *American Handbook of Psychiatry*, Vol. 3 (New York, Basic Books, Inc., 1966).

5. Natalie Shainess, "Let's bury old fictions!," *Psychiatric Opinion*, 9:6-11 (1972).

here is to form a relevant, personal mothering identity, separate and unique from that of her own mother. As the pregnancy progresses, the woman feels the fetus move, forcing her to differentiate between the baby being in her and dependent on her, but not part of her. As it ends, the reality of both the pregnancy and the baby are inescapable. The woman must prepare for separation from the fetus who will soon arrive as an individual. This phase is usually accompanied by feelings of joy and fulfillment as well as fear of the unknown. There are feelings of anxiety about labor and delivery and fantasies about the baby.

Throughout a normal pregnancy, a woman may experience emotional lability, sudden and extreme mood swings, real and irrational fears, bodily discomforts and shifts in body image. She is dependent on environmental supports and finds her unconscious processes highly accessible through fantasy and dreams. Her ego is fluid and vulnerable, as in adolescence. Yet pregnancy at any age level seems to provide its own protection against the occurrence of serious psychiatric problems. Most of the emotional problems of pregnancy seem to emerge from normal reactions to it. By the end of a typical pregnancy, it is expected that a woman who is about to become a mother has begun to consolidate a mothering identity based on her feelings about and relationship with her own mother.[6] Thus the adaptive and integrative task of pregnancy and motherhood—biologically, psychologically, and realistically—is enormous. When this occurs in adolescence and when it is coincident with marriage, the stress and task is even greater.

Both adolescence and pregnancy are temporary transitional experiences, bridges from one life phase to another. Both are characterized by fluid ego states and create opportunities for growth and development—of an unhealthy, disintegrative nature or of a healthy, integrative nature.

THE PREGNANT ADOLESCENT

The psychological factors contributing to adolescent pregnancy and the emotional problems resulting from it are as numerous

---

6. Arthur Colman and Libby Colman, *Pregnancy: The Psychological Experience* (Herder & Herder, New York, 1971).

and varied as the girls themselves. Although there often exist common factors among populations of pregnant adolescents, there is no one causative factor and no one solution for the problem. Each pregnancy is multidetermined and each girl and her family must find the individualized, differential resolution that fits her needs at the time.

Even though they may share some general psychological features, pregnant adolescents and their families, including their babies, boyfriends, and husbands, cannot be stereotyped. There is as much variety in this population as there are geographical regions, cultural differences, and personality styles in our society. Thus it is necessary to understand and deal with the pregnant adolescent in terms of these differences and in terms of her own experiences, and not from preconceived notions and gross generalizations.

The following comments made by four teenage girls about their own and their families' reactions to their pregnancies is excerpted from a panel discussion in which they participated.[7]

SHOUSE:

What did you first do when you suspected you were pregnant? Who did you tell first and how did they react?

JANE:

I told my best girlfriend and then I told my boyfriend, the father of the baby. I told my parents when I was about five months along. I chickened out. I wrote my mother. My parents lived away from here and so I wrote my mother a letter and she didn't write me back for a long time. She was mad. So that was the way it went.

DORIS:

I didn't actually break the news to my mother, the doctor did. I was sick all during the summer of last year with a bladder infection. In August—that is when I got pregnant—they thought it was a setback, an illness. When I went to the doctor he said, "Well, your bladder is all right, it is healed. Your period hasn't

---

7. Judith Shouse, Panel, Adolescents' Point of View, *Social and Health Needs in Childhood and Adolescence* (University of California, Berkeley, 1972), p. 77-95.

come down. Maybe it is because you are pregnant," and he gave me two shots. I said, "No, I'm not." When he said I was pregnant my mother was standing in the room so I denied it. When we got home she asked me, "Doris, are you pregnant?" I held my head down and I told her, "I think so." Then she took me to her doctor and he said that I was. She took it very hard, but she was understanding. She didn't fuss or argue. I heard her crying in her room. That really made me feel bad. But what really helped me the most is that she didn't argue and deny me.

MARY:

I didn't tell my parents right off because I figured if I told mother without being able to tell her what I was going to do about it for myself, it would be a big traumatic thing. So I figured I would wait until my boyfriend and I knew what our plans would be. We told the doctor that I wanted to find out if I was pregnant for sure and that we didn't want anything to come in the mail, that we wanted to tell them ourselves. When I was only about four weeks pregnant the bill for the lab test came and my mother got it before I did. That had to be about the worst way she could find out. She thought it was horribly sneaky and there was still nothing I could tell her that I was going to do. There wasn't really anything I could do because it was so unexpected. When mother came in with the bill, she just handed it to me. She fell apart as much as I did. I was really mad. All I could say was, "I will work it out." But I still didn't know how I was going to do it. I know it was horrible. If I had to do it again I think I would tell her at first. Initially she was a lot more levelheaded than I thought she would be. At first she sat down and said, "Oh, my God." But then she said, "Well, we will just have to work it out." I felt relieved that she knew because it was so good. But I guess the more she thought about it the more horrible it was and the more she couldn't work it out. Being my parents were divorced she just felt that the burden was too much for her and that she couldn't help because there were five of us in the family. I guess the more she thought about it the worse it got, until finally, she told me she wasn't going to do anything. And she hasn't helped me do anything since.

CINDY:

I was a lot different from everybody in that my boyfriend and my mother told me I was pregnant. Sounds kind of funny, but I didn't want to think about it. I had worked the whole summer to buy new clothes for school. I had spent a lot of money on clothes and the next thing I knew I was pregnant and I couldn't wear them very long. So my mother was the first one to ask, "Well, are you pregnant?" I said, "No, I don't think so. My period is not supposed to come for a few more days." The few more days passed and it didn't come. Then my boyfriend said the same thing. So I was kind of up in the air. I started to school that September and Ken and I finally decided to get married in October. I was all mixed up in getting married and trying to face the fact that I was going to have a baby. Then it was harder on me in that my mother didn't want the people on her job to know, and they still don't know. I didn't tell any of my relatives that I was pregnant. They just knew that I was getting married. But I was all confused in trying to accept the fact that I was pregnant, that I had to get married, that I had to change schools, and my whole life would be altered by this. So it was harder for me, I feel, than for anybody in my whole family, although my mother did take it kind of hard.

DORIS:

My father was understanding. He took it better than my mother because she wanted so much for me to become a debutante for our church. That December our church was giving a debutante ball for all the young girls and since I became pregnant I couldn't very well be a debutante. So that hit my mother, too. It is the first thing that came to her mind, then graduation, then finishing school, all that came to my mother's head. But my father thought of me as an individual, how Doris would be, what about the baby, what would the baby need, what he had to do for the house in order to prepare for the baby. I think my father took it very well because he thought about my needs and the baby's needs and didn't think about what people might say. So my father really took it the best.

MARY:

My father was a lot more logical and down to earth, too. When you think about it, your mother looks at it completely different than your father does because your mother is a woman and when you are pregnant you are a woman. All she can see is that she has got daughters and sons, and the whole thing from the time you were a little baby girl is that you are going to get married and get pregnant someday. And I think it is more of a personal thing. She has been pregnant before and knows what it is like. But your father can stand back and look at it and reason it out, where your mother just feels, "Oh, my God, you don't know what it is like to be pregnant and what it is like to be married."

When I told my father he didn't know Bob. He had only met him once because my father wasn't living with us. At first he asked, "Who is this Bob?" But he had us over for dinner. That was the first time he really talked to Bob and he really liked him. We talked about the whole thing, and when we left, we felt he was really going to help us and he has. He has really helped a lot, but I think my mother feels more like I did it against her, where my father just sees it as "Well, you are pregnant and we have to do something about it." But I think all the fathers kind of looked at it objectively. I think that, especially with me, it is because for the last two years my mom has been raising us. She sees all our problems as her failure. She has five children and she just can't supervise all of us all the time, but she just thinks if she had been home maybe she could have helped more. She has to work.

JANE:

My mother takes the attitude that I did all this to hurt her because she said she wanted me to be just like her. She wants me to do the same things she did and have the same kind of life. She wants me to be a replica of her because I am her oldest daughter. So when she found out I was pregnant she took the attitude that I did those things to hurt her. As I told you before, I wrote my mother to tell her I was pregnant and she didn't answer my letter for quite a while. I never hear from my father anyway. He is sort of silent, even lets my mother do all the corresponding and everything. Then for Mother's Day I sent a card and it must have broke mom down because she wrote me right after that. She wanted to know when the baby was due and now she is sort of acting like a grandmother. She came to my graduation and gave me money to buy things for the baby, but she takes the attitude that I am creating problems because she feels she has to lie to the rest of the family about my situation, but my father is understanding and he doesn't take the attitude that I am creating or being a big problem. So he makes me feel a lot better about it.

CINDY:

It was kind of hard for me because my mother and real father are separated and my mother has remarried. My stepfather has never really taken a fatherly interest in my brother or myself. So it was kind of hard for me to go to him to tell him I was pregnant. My boyfriend, Ken, and I went to him when we were going to get married and Ken told him everything. My stepfather was kind of level-headed about it. He said, "This is no reason you have to get married," and all that kind of thing which was nice because I wasn't really ready for marriage myself. Two weeks ago I went to the town where my real father lives to see him. He didn't know about the baby at all and he was totally against my marriage from the start because he felt that it wouldn't work because I was too young—you know, just the same way fathers feel when they give up their only daughter. So it was rather hard for him to accept, but he had to accept it.

The only problem I had was with my stepfather. He keeps throwing up in my face that he feels that six months from now I will be pregnant again. After I graduated and was looking for a job he would say, "Well, the reason these people won't hire you is for one thing you are young and for another thing you have a baby. You are only seventeen years old and they feel that if you are offered a job paying twenty cents more you will go take it, and the other factor is that probably they feel six months from now you will get pregnant again." So I keep hearing this and it is not very encouraging; it makes me feel even more determined to want to push myself to get ahead and prove to people that just because you made a mistake it is not supposed to hold you back.

DORIS:

My brothers and sisters were surprised that I became pregnant but they accepted me. I have a brother attending college and he offered to quit and go to work to help me save up to pay the hospital bill. When he said that I started crying because I didn't think that my brother would stop his education in order to help me. My older brother bought all my baby things and my sister babysits for me. Before the baby was coming they were picking out names and we really had a good time, just the five of us, but my aunties, the older ones, rejected me and, at first, I got mad at this and I said, "I don't care. I don't need them." Then I realized that I need all my people. A family needs to be together. So I made a special trip to where all of them were. They all just looked at me, did real bad things and spit on me, and didn't want to have me around, but I stayed and I told them all I was sorry and that I know I had hurt all of them by becoming pregnant. They all believed me and now we're all back together and they all like me. I have graduated from high school and now I am going on to college, but I have one aunt who constantly says I will become pregnant after six months. I get real mad at her. So I look at her and then turn my head and say, "We will see."

In order for me to live with my family I had a weapon as Cindy did with her father—my self-assurance. My family said, "We don't like you." That made me feel inferior. I expected to be accepted which I was eventually. Also I was determined I had the strength to go on and not to stop when I was walking down the street and people would look at me all funny because I was young and my belly was sticking out. Once when I was going to school a bus driver said, "Well, you are pregnant so you can start paying the adult fare." Everybody on the bus looked at me. I looked back at them and I smiled. The driver punched my student card and I said, "Thank you very much." I saw the bus driver the other day and I said, "Hello," and he said, "Hello." He seemed surprised as though he thought I was going to be mad at him, but I don't hold a grudge against anyone for saying something nasty.[8]

PSYCHOLOGICAL AND EMOTIONAL PROBLEMS

When pregnancy occurs during adolescence, the typical ambivalent strivings for emancipation and self-dependence are both reflected and disrupted. The unpredictable adolescent's attempt to achieve a balance between impulsiveness and control has failed. She is in the process of separating from her parents yet her pregnancy makes her regressed and dependent. She may now be even more ambivalent about leaving whatever material support and emotional security the family has to offer, and this conflict often evokes great anxiety and anger. Most parents also react with anger, disappointment, and hurt on confrontation with the pregnancy. Most held different expectations for their daughters than to become pregnant in adolescence.

It must be reiterated that contrary to popular myth, minority girls and their families do not find it any easier emotionally to accept the initial shock of pregnancy than do caucasian families. It is the choices made in response to the pregnancy, however, that may reflect differences in racial, ethnic, or socioeconomic group, or levels of individual self-esteem and autonomy.

Adolescent development includes a sexual adaptation—developing concepts of intimacy and how one will use oneself sexually. There is obviously much evidence today to suggest an increasing reduction of conflict among adolescents in general about having sex. There is continuous pressure from the media and from peers of the same and the opposite sex to experiment with sex as well as drugs.

Certainly there are girls who use sex consciously to become

---

8. *Ibid.*

pregnant, to hold onto the boy, to force parental permission for marriage, to escape from an intolerable living situation.

> I didn't have any trouble telling my parents I was pregnant. Jerry's and my problem was trying to get married. We wanted to get married. So the only way for me to get married was by telling them I was pregnant, but I wasn't. I told them that for about two months, so they decided to let us get married. Then after we got married, I got pregnant a month later. When I got pregnant, everybody was happy, everybody wanted me to have the baby. So I didn't have any problems.[9]

But in the minds of most girls who become pregnant there is no conscious correlation of intercourse and pregnancy, no conscious choice to become pregnant or become a parent. The girls themselves often prefer to view the outcome as having "gotten caught" or "I just came up pregnant." Even though they may dress and behave in ways which are likely to attract young men, they are surprised and upset when the outcome is pregnancy. One statement often heard from young women who become pregnant is, "I didn't think it would happen to me." The following conversation was with an eighteen-year-old married girl with one child.

> After I had my first baby it took me two months to come down, you know, my weight and all. I was real happy because I got to buy new clothes and look nice again, but after the two months I had one month to look good and I got pregnant again. Now I am afraid I will probably get pregnant still another time so after this baby I will probably use something.
>
> Shouse: Didn't you want to use anything last time?
>
> Answer: I didn't think anything was going to happen.[10]

There is much evidence to suggest that the expectations and means of sexual satisfaction are becoming more similar for both sexes and that mutual satisfaction has become more highly valued. It is also well-known that satisfaction and compatibility require time and maturity to develop. Many girls seen clinically confide they do not enjoy sex play or sexual intercourse; many are

---

9. *Ibid.*, p. 79.
10. *Ibid.*, p. 82.

not orgasmic. Their lack of enjoyment of sex can perhaps be attributed partly to their emotional immaturity, partly to the attitudes toward sex and men conveyed by their mothers, or to their own life experiences as women. A mother's own life history as a female—especially her experiences and attitudes regarding sex and pregnancy—greatly affect a daughter's development.

JANE:

My mother said, "Well, when your father went overseas I was able to wait until he got back to have sex." She treats me like I am a sex fiend or something. Like I just went out looking for sex, like I didn't fall in love with my boyfriend and we had sex then. She said, "Why couldn't you wait? Your father was overseas a whole year and I waited at home," and things like that. Like I said, she wants me to be just like her and she can't see that anybody else can be different from her, that things can happen differently. She wouldn't look at it like I found love and had sex before I got married. She looks at it like I went out looking for sex with some boy.[11]

Many girls use sex for such nonsexual aims as to gain love and acceptance; to express fear and anger about her past, present, or future; to prove her own adequacy as a female; or to flaunt her disregard for parental and social standards—pregnancy can be incidental to these aims. Adolescent pregnancy has seemed most often, in my experience, the result of trying to obtain gratification of these nonsexual needs, needs carried forth from earlier phases of development for security, closeness, acceptance, attention, and affirmation as a wanted, valued person.

With adolescence comes the realization that the original loved objects are forever lost as far as satisfying infantile needs. A girl who arrives at adolescence with these needs unmet or inadequately met feels afraid and alone, helpless about her future. She may somehow feel the state of pregnancy and a baby will be sources of continuing parental love, care, and gratification of dependency needs.

---

11. *Ibid.,* p. 83.

When I was pregnant last year, everyone babied me. My husband really babied me and he said he was going to do all kinds of things for me. Then the baby came. Up to today, he has changed the baby's diapers about two times, and he doesn't help me at all anymore. When I first came home he didn't want me to move around or anything, and about two days later, he just didn't do anything. He doesn't do anything at all.

Nobody cares at all about this pregnancy. He doesn't even know I am pregnant, I don't think. He doesn't care at all. He goes to a drag strip all the time and takes me along and I have to sit in the car when he is going down the quarter mile. So, you know, he doesn't care at all. I have a little boy, so he wants me to have a girl and he says that he wants it to be sexy and stuff, so he doesn't care about it. He doesn't know about the pains or anything. He just thinks "Go to the hospital and have it," and that is it. So he is no help at all.[12]

The fantasy is then carried over to the baby, that it will love and give to her and help her feel better. Thus, there are many instances of bitterness and depression a few months after the baby's birth, when the attention obtained from the environment during pregnancy stops or is withdrawn, and the young mother is left with the realization of all that is entailed in rearing a baby—a dependent, complex human being. She often has a feeling of loneliness with, and total responsibility for, her new baby. This can be a period of sadness and mourning; she is not returned to who she was before, nor is she a new person; she is irrevocably changed. She often feels she has lost her chance to be a teenager, free and having fun, and now has the responsibilities of a woman.

Although adolescent girls and their partners have reacted in a biologically normal way to innate needs for procreative activity and for intimate physical contact, they have failed to defer gratification and to exercise self-restraint, failed to plan ahead and take responsibility for their actions; reality testing is poor. Some girls are self-deprecating and do not care what happens to them. They have few plans or positive directions for their lives. It is often heard, "Well, I wasn't doing anything important anyway, so what difference if I got pregnant." Then when the pregnancy

---

12. *Ibid.*, p. 94.

is confirmed, a common corollary is a self-punitive feeling that she must have and raise the baby, that there is no choice for her but to accept the consequences: "Well, if you don't want to have a baby, you shouldn't have sex in the first place." The needs and expectations involved in sex, pregnancy, and motherhood in these instances are often based on a temporary or chronically poor or disturbed self-image, lack of self-esteem, feelings of emptiness, helplessness and worthlessness, and feelings of hopelessness about themselves and the future.

A positive self-image and self-esteem are direct results of the parents' expectations and hopes, especially the mother's, as conveyed to the child at all developmental levels. Self-esteem in adolescence depends greatly on how a person was treated during infancy and throughout childhood.

People with high self-esteem have been consistently treated by their parents with respect, consideration, and acceptance and have developed self-trust, independence, and self-reliance. They have been reared with the security and guidance provided by clearly defined expectations and values and enforced limits on their behavior. They have experienced a focused, well-structured environment that demanded competence and taught the problem-solving process. They were given a basis for a sense of personal worth, respect, and dignity which could be internalized as part of a positive self-image. They feel they have had fair, nonpunitive treatment which they could see was truly in their best interests. People with high self-esteem have had acceptable models with which to identify. Their parents are described as "benevolent despots" who have had a deep abiding interest in their children.

Obviously, people with low self-esteem have had quite a different experience. They have been treated by their parents with extreme permissiveness coupled with harsh, vindictive, corporal punishment. They consider their parents to be unfair. They feel the absence of dependable, clearly defined standards and limits on their behavior expresses parental indifference to them.[13, 14]

13. Stanley Coopersmith, *Antecedents of Self-Esteem* (San Francisco, W. H. Freeman, 1967).

14. Stanley Coopersmith, *Scientific American*, 218:96-106, 1968.

Often a teenage girl finds it difficult to identify with and communicate with her mother, especially if they have had previous difficulties with their relationship. She is in the process of disparaging her, modifying her view of her mother, and replacing it with an identity of her own. Yet it is the experience of a healthy adolescent to feel her father is reliable and her mother is understanding; emotionally, she feels closer to her mother.

Pregnancy is an opportunity for an adolescent to assess her relationship with and feelings toward her mother, as she begins to define her own concept of mothering. She should be helped to assess her own childhood experiences around her mother's pregnancies and around experiences with siblings and new infants. She should be helped to resolve difficulties that persist or reemerge from earlier developmental levels. She should be helped to find for herself appropriate, adequate role models, so she can become more stable, resilient, and self-reliant as a mother and as a woman and emerge from the experience of pregnancy in adolescence with greater self-esteem and hope for her future.

She should also be helped to assess her feelings about her father and her relationships with men. Many pregnant adolescents were reared primarily by their mothers in homes where fathers were absent or inconsistently present and undependable. Often stepfathers or other men were part of their upbringing.

Adolescence is characterized by a sense of urgency combined with a feeling that each moment is interminable. One must, during this time, continue learning to cope with and sublimate sexual and aggressive impulses, to postpone gratification of or find substitute gratification for these impulses. An adolescent girl must, in addition, cope with the currently controversial ideas about female roles and feminine identity prevalent in our culture, and adolescents must learn to cope with the fundamental change in cultural mores in which direct sexual stimulation and expression through the media are very much part of everyday life, often in the presence of parental confusion about values and priorities.

Parents of adolescents, too, are often caught in an ambivalent struggle. It is difficult for them to accept the fact that they are gradually becoming less vitally necessary in their children's lives and to cope with the adolescent's devaluation of parents. This essential repudiation of parental standards and actions, though painful for those involved, seems to be the best way the adolescent can modify her internalized, infantile notion that her parents are both omniscient and omnipotent.

Parents and other adults need to appraise and help the adolescent appraise her social, intellectual, athletic, and other abilities as realistically as possible. Parents and other adults must remember that it is the adolescent who is pregnant and it is she who must make the choices and decisions regarding her pregnancy and her child. Choices made during pregnancy or adolescence can have more decisive and extensive effects on one's total life than choices made at less critical phases in feminine life. Often these are the first important decisions she has made in her life. She needs patient understanding so she can make reasoned decisions, ones which reflect her needs and are in the baby's best interests. Parents of adolescents can learn to respect the integrity of their grown children and be of assistance where realistically possible through their ongoing vested interest in them.

JANE:

I think it would help if they (adults) treated us like adults. They treat us like a child having a child, but none of us feel like children. Maybe when we first get pregnant, we are immature. There are a lot of girls who are real immature and you see them change. By the time they have their baby they have grown up so much, but some of them were already mature and grown up. We know it is hard for our parents suddenly to change from the little girl attitude to, "You are a woman." But some of them are like my mother who does that now when she talks to me. She talks to me on an adult level and she doesn't try to hide things from me like I am still a child.[15]

Adults can help adolescents alter the harmful mode of making premature or poor choices or no choice at all, which results in passive drifting or becoming a victim of the choices and acts of

15. Shouse, *op. cit.*, p. 95.

others. The fewer choices one feels able to make the greater finality they have. Persons with self-images of passive victims cannot mature to become healthy, positive, assertive people.

To succeed at mothering, just as in any other life undertaking, a woman needs to be motivated and have adequate self-esteem. She needs to be valued and supported by others who sincerely want her to enjoy this phase of feminine development and who really believe she can achieve it. During pregnancy, needs for mothering and solicitude from the environment, especially important to the girl who has felt inadequately cared for, are appropriate and can be met in a variety of ways. Most mothers of pregnant teenagers want the best for their daughters and, after the initial reaction of shock to the news of the pregnancy has lessened, their aid in helping their daughters plan for the immediate future can be solicited. In some families where the girl decides to continue the pregnancy and raise her baby, it serves to lessen some of the hostile-dependent ties, and a more positive, more adult relationship can be established between mother and daughter. There seems to be a correlation between a girl's health and well-being during pregnancy and the amount of acceptance and emotional support she receives from her mother.

SHOUSE:

Since you have been pregnant how has your relationship changed between you and your mom?

MARY:

I don't have any relationship with my mom at all, and now more than ever I need her. I mean every day I need her and I can't even phone up and say, "Hi." And it is just horrible. I haven't seen her for about two months and my sister is the medium. I phone up and say, "How is mom? Can I see her?" They say, "No." On Easter Sunday, I was staying with my father's mother who I don't know or anything, but she is my grandmother, but not like my mother's mother is to me. Easter Day has always been a big family thing like Christmas is; and I really wanted to go home and spend it with my family, so I kind of popped in and walked in the kitchen and I said, "Hi, mom, Happy Easter." She just looked at me and didn't say anything; she just turned around. So I stayed about ten minutes and left. It is like I have done it all by myself from the first day I knew I was pregnant until now. It is so hard on Bob and me and everybody's family, not just my mom, and my mom could be making it so much easier on everybody. It is like the first time you feel the baby kick; you want to say, "Mom, it is kicking!" But you can't. I know now that my mom knows I am happy about it, and I know she knows Bob and I can make it work, but it has been so long since we have talked that I just can't go home and say, "Okay, can we talk now?" And every day it is getting worse. I know when I do have the baby she is going to want to share it; just like I know she wants to share it now, but it is so hard to break down the walls. It is such a big strong wall. I have seen her recently when my sister graduated from high school and asked me to come over so I could fix her hair and her dress and stuff. So I came over and my mom just got home from work when I was there and she came up and was really friendly. She came over and said, "Hi, how are you?" And I wanted to fall down and laugh or something but after she said, "Hi, how are you?" and I said, "Fine, how are you?" there just wasn't anything left to say. It was a really horrible feeling and I know she felt it just like I did, but I don't know how to break it and she doesn't either.

SHOUSE:

It sounds like you want to break it.

MARY:

It does, it has to be broken, but no matter how it gets broken she will always feel that she ran out; and even ten years from now when the kid is ten years old she will still know that when I was pregnant she wasn't there. Of course, it hurts me but I understand why. I just hope if one of my children gets pregnant that I will do exactly what I wanted my mother to do, but I know how hard it was for her because the way she was; she couldn't have taken it any other way, but I still can't forgive her the way she wants to be forgiven because she cannot forgive herself. It is just getting worse, and neither of us can fix it.

CINDY:

Our relationship got a lot better. When girls get pregnant they need their mothers. They realize that the relationship gets stronger between mother and daughter, and it was easier between the two of us. We would converse like women, whereas before I was never able to tell my mother how I felt about anything. I think that another reason that I got pregnant is that I could never go to her and talk. I have never been a person who can express my true feelings to someone. I have just learned to do that this past year at school. Before when my mother and I had to talk it would always be a one-sided thing. She would do all the talking and I would do the listening. She would never really know how I felt. So in going through the adolescent period there were a lot of changes in my life that nobody could really understand. I was ready to give up during that time, just to stop living, and that is kind of hard for a person who is fifteen years old—to want to give up her own life. I just felt that I wasn't being understood and that had my father been around or had my stepfather taken an interest it would have been different.

DORIS:

When I first told my mother I was pregnant, I wanted her to act just the way she did because then I knew that she cared about me but then, being pregnant, I couldn't stay in the house with my mother and father because I had let them down. Every time they looked at me or said something I felt that it was all against me, which it really wasn't. It was just a change I was going through. My mother would call every day and ask how I was doing or if she could call the doctor, but I couldn't face them. It was me. My oldest sisters and brothers went through school without having babies and here I came up pregnant. No cousins, nobody, it was just me. I felt out of place. Even though my mother was understanding, listened to my problems, and wanted to know every ache and pain I had,

I just couldn't face up to it myself. First I wanted the baby, then I didn't want to go through the changes of being pregnant, getting big, letting everybody see me, having friends say, "Oh, you are pregnant, when is the baby due?" I didn't want that and I wouldn't go to the store and buy a maternity dress. That I couldn't do. My brother bought my maternity dress for Christmas and when he brought it in I looked at it and didn't want it, but my mother said, "Isn't that sweet?" I didn't want anything to do with pregnancy. That is all there was to it, and here my brothers, sisters, and aunts were bringing me things showing I was pregnant—maternity girdle, maternity slip and all, for Christmas, and I didn't want any of this. All my sisters were getting nice little skirts and I couldn't have them. So it was me, I was the one that caused the bad relationship with my mother and father. When I was nine months along and sick, I wanted to go home to mama and daddy, and that is when I ran home. My mother and father were with me and my father was telling me some remedies, little old wives' tales that my mother didn't know. So it was really nice with my mother and father. When I went in labor, my father stalled the car, he was so nervous, and my mother was nervous too. After the baby came, I was in the hospital and my father was up there every day. He had dinner with me, he talked to me and told me what I must do to take care of the baby. It was really nice, I had no problem at all. My parents stuck by me.[16]

In some families a girl may give her child to her mother as a peace offering or in order to obtain her freedom from her home and mother. In others, a girl's mother may claim proprietary rights to the baby and the adolescent mother is in a subordinate position in caring for her baby and in making decisions regarding the baby. Some girls want to experience motherhood in their own right after a lengthy period of caring for younger siblings. Others' pregnancies follow a self-fulfilling prophecy, a prediction of her family that she was "fast" and would "sooner or later" become pregnant. Often in this situation a girl's mother

16. *Ibid.*, p. 84-86.

has closely monitored her menstrual periods since the onset of menarche. Still others are in response to pressure from peers of the same or opposite sex. As part of the counseling offered by clinicians during pregnancy, a girl should be helped to assess the meaning of the baby to her and how it will fit into her family situation and view of her future.

Other girls seek the state of pregnancy, the appearance and feeling of fullness, and enjoy that in itself. It is common to hear a girl say after giving birth, "I miss my big tummy." A task of adolescence is to define body image; a task of pregnancy is to accommodate to the natural shifts in body image. Encouraging the pregnant adolescent to value and care for her own body, including her genitals, can contribute lastingly toward a healthier self-image. Encouraging her to evaluate how she feels about her body and how she wants to use it, including her sexuality, can help her significantly to identify and gain mastery over the processes of adolescence and pregnancy and emerge into adulthood with dignity.

Families, schools, and institutions must offer education about social, sexual, and family relationships throughout all levels, and it must include helping growing children develop healthy self-images based on feelings of genuine self-esteem. Without this no amount of exposure to sex education or interdiction of male-female relationships will aid in resolving the problem of adolescent child-bearing.

We must continue working to elucidate more specifically the causes of adolescent pregnancy and must continue to formulate imaginative, therapeutic ways to help young people prevent it. We must help girls prepare themselves for menarche and the successive phases of feminine sexuality. We must help girls in their stressful search for sexual values and feminine identity, to examine the traditional allotted gender roles, the traditional yearning for male approval and judgment, and give up what is no longer relevent and productive to their development as women. We must help them assert themselves, resolve their conflicts around feminine self-concepts, and achieve security and autonomy. We must help them appreciate and enjoy their intellectual strength and their own unique human and feminine qualities.

When a pregnancy occurs, an adolescent girl and her boyfriend and their families need specific services for both the practical and emotional problems that occur. An adolescent girl is often shocked and confused on confirmation of the pregnancy and often has difficulty making a decision regarding continuing it or obtaining an abortion. Often she is in a quandary about telling those close to her—how to tell and who to tell first. She often suffers intense internal conflict over what has happened, guilt about the past, fear of the future.

A girl and her boyfriend often feel under pressure to decide whether or not to marry at the time. Some pregnancies result from casual relationships. In others the couple breaks up coincident with or during the pregnancy, or the baby's father deserts. However, in my experience there is very little promiscuity in the adolescents in this population. Most of the relationships between adolescent parents are fairly stable and ongoing, whether married or not. The couple remains in close contact throughout the pregnancy, share an interest in their infant, and plan their immediate future together. When the baby's father is interested, involved, and is offered services along with the baby's mother, it has been found that she can usually cope more effectively with the problems of parenthood. This makes it even more important that any program for the pregnant adolescent be developed from the concept of offering comprehensive care and teamwork throughout the pregnancy, postpartum period, and through the first few years of the baby's life. The young family needs to be offered contact with adults and peers in pediatric clinics, infant day care programs, schools, and other places where they can become confident in parental skills and which can foster healthy parent-child relationships.

DORIS:

> If you're going to help us while we're pregnant we need a lot of help after we already have had our babies. A lot of girls after they had babies dropped out of school and I wondered why, but after I had my baby I could see why. You just can't do it, trying to take care of a baby and trying to do your homework. It is hard because the baby cries a lot. You have to stop

and see about it, and you lose track. One of your girl friends may come over, and you tell them to go home so you can get back to your homework. It's hard, because you have to have study habits and with a baby and all the noise at home, it is kind of hard to do your homework. If there was somebody at school to listen to your problems maybe things would be better.[17]

If a couple decides to marry, counseling should be made available to help them appreciate that marriage cannot solve their problems, as evidenced by the extremely high divorce rate accompanying teenage marriages. They may need help, too, with the problems in marriage of in-laws, religion, finances, sex, intimacy, and other issues with which marriage counseling can be helpful.

Often the school-age girl is excluded from school and needs to make other educational and vocational plans. She may experience increasing financial pressures and have material needs that must be met. She may need legal help, housing, and help in planning for her recreation and leisure.

It is typical for a girl to feel acutely the physical sensations and discomforts of pregnancy and to have especial difficulty waiting in the last few weeks. She reacts intensely to the changes her body and body-image undergo during the nine months. Many girls reject maternity clothes, saying, "They look like they are for old women" or "They just hang on you like sacks." She needs information and support around the experiences of pregnancy, delivery, and infant care to develop self-confidence and specific maternal skills. Information regarding contraception needs to be freely available, and contraception itself must be readily obtainable.

During pregnancy, a woman is especially susceptible to environmental influences and is more dependent on personal relationships. The quality of human supports, what she gives to and receives from others, is crucial to her maturation into motherhood. A pregnant adolescent may be fearful of social isolation yet ambivalent about wider social contact. She needs help assessing

17. *Ibid.,* p. 91.

her environmental resources and finding social supports among relatives and friends, boyfriend or husband, hospital and community services. She needs to find acceptable role models and ego-ideals. When the environment gives support and reassurance, a new mother is most often able to relax and interact pleasurably with her infant, feel less lonely, and gain perspective on her situation.

Often a person in the midst of a crisis, overwhelmed by the stresses, cannot see the process of it or its meaning. Adolescents who are still to some degree dependent on adults, no matter how turbulent their struggle for independence or how omnipotent they may believe they are, are amenable to help from adults in finding models for identification and verification for their own growing sense of identity and life style. They usually can form trusting relationships from which they can derive help in resolving conflicts, both current and chronic, and which can help them in their struggle to achieve a satisfactory balance of adventure and stability in their lives.

When an adolescent girl feels that not enough which is meaningful and which promotes security is occurring at home within her family, when she feels the school curriculum is irrelevant to her interests, when she is dissatisfied with peer relations, and when she does not feel her life is going in a definite, positive direction, it is then that she often does not care if she becomes pregnant.

Adults can help the pregnant girl develop self-confidence and some realistic goals for her own and her baby's immediate future. We can help her emerge from these multiple crises with more positive self-concepts, compatible with future health and autonomy for each member of the family. Those in clinical work with young people and their families see, everyday, heroic efforts to resolve internal and interpersonal conflicts and reality problems and to emerge into adulthood with esteem. That so many young people do achieve mastery of the tasks of pregnancy and adolescence and move on into personally satisfying adult lives is a tribute to their physical stamina, natural thrust toward maturity, and emotional flexibility and resilience.

Adults can help the pregnant adolescent use her pregnancy as an occasion in which to make decisions and choices about herself, her baby, and their lives and then plan and follow through to achieve what she wants. We can help her internalize and learn to act on feelings of power, hope, and confidence in the future. We can help her realize that a most unique human undertaking is the direction of one's own destiny.

CHAPTER VI

THE COMMUNITY HEALTH NURSE AND THE ADOLESCENT FAMILY

Georgiana M. Selstad

THE COMMUNITY HEALTH nurse's role in working with adolescent families will vary considerably according to her agency,
the area of the country where she is working, and her own interests and capabilities. According to Freeman[1] the community
health nurse is generally taught to (1) provide and promote comprehensive nursing service to families; (2) use nursing as a chan-
nel for strengthening family life and for promoting personal or
family development and self-realization; (3) participate in disease control activities; (4) work with appropriate personnel in
special settings, such as schools and places of employment, to
plan and implement the nursing phases of their health programs;
(5) plan and evaluate nursing services for the population group
under her care; (6) contribute to decision and policy setting in
the community; and (7) contribute to the extension of knowledge in nursing and health care by engaging in surveys, studies,
or research. There is ample opportunity for the community
health nurse to use all of her training and experience in the areas
listed above when working with adolescent families.

The community health nurse's function may also change according to the availability of various professional persons to
work with these families. Some programs are fortunate in having
a complete interdisciplinary team consisting of teacher, nurse, social worker, and physician,[2] while other programs operate with
only one or two professional groups. In the latter case, there will

---

1. R. Freeman, *Community Health Nursing Practice* (Philadelphia, W. B. Saunders Company, 1970) .

2. E. W. Smith, A. Duncan, J. W. Shouse and R. C. Brown, "Adolescent maternity
services: a team approach," *Children*, 18:209 (1971) .

be overlapping of functions, especially in the area of health teaching and counseling. The role that is described here is that which any community health nurse is generally able to assume in a school, clinic, or community program for adolescent families.

COMMUNITY HEALTH NURSE'S SERVICES TO SCHOOL PREGNANCY PROGRAMS

1. Community Health Nurse's Role in Starting Programs

The community health nurse can assume a very important role in proposing or initiating school pregnancy programs. This may be in the form of gathering statistics on the extent of the problem, especially statistics related to health problems of this group, or she may assume the role of coordinating the efforts of various persons or agencies to support new or proposed programs.

Documenting Need

This can be done in numerous ways but in Ventura County, California (population 450,000) where I work, a questionnaire (see Table VI-I) was sent to all school nurses through their principals, to probation officers, community health nurses, the County Hospital prenatal clinic, delinquency prevention, adoption and welfare units. Specific names of girls were not requested but, by using initials and birthdates, duplication was prevented. Information on ages, residence, grade in school, type of current schooling, where prenatal care was being received, marital status, and ethnic background was tabulated. This type of information proves invaluable in documenting the need for programs to administrative personnel who seemingly are most impressed by statistics. At the same time, information can be solicited regarding each school's written policy towards pregnant girls.

In larger communities, there are usually Departments of Vital Statistics which may supply the required information on adolescent pregnancies.

Coordinating Efforts to Organize a Community

Community health nurses are traditionally active as coordinators between health disciplines, other health services, and the

TABLE VI-I

SURVEY OF SCHOOL AGE PREGNANCIES

Name of school district .... Name and position of person completing survey ....
Name of school ....

A	B	C		D	E	F			G			H		I		J	
		Ethnic Group		Com-munity or City	Grade Level	Present Schooling			Pregnancy Status			Marital Status		1st Preg.		Hlth. Care	
Girl's Initials	Birth Date	Anglo	Mex. Neg. Oth.			Home	None	Unk.	Preg.	Deliv.		Wed	Unwed	Yes	No	HD*	Priv.
1.																	
2.																	
3.																	
4.																	
5.																	
6.																	
7.																	
8.																	
9.																	
10.																	
11.																	
12.																	

* HD = Health department

community. They are generally knowledgeable about people in the community who are influential and who might support a school pregnancy program. Organization and support from the community may take various forms—group meetings of interested professional and lay people and official agencies, speeches, letters of support, and panels of adolescent family members to speak to different groups.

In large communities it is necessary to first elicit the support of all the official agencies, such as departments of health, welfare, and education, and any public or private agency that deals with any aspect of care or services to adolescent families. After support has been obtained from these groups, it is possible to request support from other community groups and people.

Group meetings can be effective, if well planned, especially in the early organizing phase. Representation should be encouraged from the schools (administrators, principals, counselors, school nurses), welfare, adoption agencies (public and private), the health department, all involved official agencies, and any local physicians and church representatives who might be supportive. Such a group meeting should bring forth a decision that the group supports the general idea of a school-age pregnancy program and should appoint a subcommittee charged with documenting the need. Later, other subcommittees may be needed to look into funding sources, physical location, and the type of program needed. In Ventura County, the health department served as the organizing point for the development of the surveys, the compiling of all statistics, and the physical location of the meetings; however, this function might be assumed by the schools or another agency. It is an enormous task and unless it is headed by someone who has the time and energy to devote in the beginning, it is not likely to succeed.

Speeches to community groups can be used effectively to mobilize support. Such organizations as local Rotary and Optimist groups, women's clubs, American Association of University Women's groups, church groups, ministerial associations, and school boards are frequently interested in hearing about youth problems. Generally, men's organizations are more likely to respond to information such as the cost of raising a child on welfare when the mother hasn't been able to finish her education, while women's organizations are more responsive to the problems of raising a child alone and the medical and emotional problems faced by the girls.

Letters of support for beginning programs can often be obtained from the groups and organizations after speaking to them and should be addressed to whichever agency is going to be responsible for starting the program, usually the school district. However, letters from individuals—taxpayers and voters—who are parents of a pregnant girl, her minister, or physician can be very effective. Parents of pregnant girls are often willing to go see school administrators to offer verbal support to a school program. Administrators generally respond to indications of public pressure and interest in a program.

Panels of pregnant or newly delivered adolescents can be used, although this must be handled carefully. The panel might contain one married girl, one unmarried, one who was planning to keep her baby, and one who has chosen adoption. Only first names of the girls should be used. The girls can usually be chosen from outside the community where they would be speaking; however, most girls do not object to seeing people they know. These girls are remarkably frank and open and the expression of their needs, strengths, and weaknesses is often much more effective coming from them than from a professional person. The panels might also contain grandparents or adolescent fathers. Because the problem of pregnancy is less visible for the expectant father or grandparents than it is for the girl, it is easier to overlook the problems of both these groups. The boy who must often drop out of school in order to support a child, whether married or not, is also a serious problem. In all school programs, there must be built-in ways of assisting both young parents to look at realistic alternatives and future plans for themselves and possibly a child.

Thus, meetings, speeches, letters and panels can all be effective in mobilizing public opinion to support the concept of school pregnancy programs.

2. Community Health Nurse's Duties in Established Programs

Once approval has been received to start a program, the community health nurse again has a definite role. If the program is a school-based one, the direction and running of the program will fall under the school's jurisdiction. This is the case in Ventura, but it was quickly discovered that most teachers feel unprepared to teach the rather specialized areas of pregnancy, labor and delivery, childbirth exercises, breast and bottle feeding, and child care.

Preparation of Health Curriculum Guide

In order to assist the teachers, a health curriculum guide may be jointly prepared by the teachers, by school and community health nurses, and by health educators and physicians—either interested local doctors or perhaps a representative from the health department. Special input should be obtained from the students themselves so that the guide represents areas of special concern to them and not just what professionals feel they should be interested in. The outline for one such guide is shown below:

Reproductive system
    Anatomy and menstrual cycles
    Venereal disease
Pregnancy
    Alternatives
    Physical and emotional changes
Labor and delivery
Postpartum period
    Physical and emotional changes
    Family planning
Infant and child care
    Physical care
    Emotional development of children
    Nutrition

For each of the topics, packets may be prepared that contain lists of films and visual aids that are available; samples of the pamphlets carried by the health department; suggested speakers and community resource people, such as Lamaze instructors; samples of quizzes that can be given on health information; and suggested classroom activities, such as visits to local hospitals or nursery schools and topics for special reports written by the girls.

Direct Teaching Services

When the programs were very new in Ventura, most of the teachers wanted the community health nurse to attend the class whenever there were any health-related activities (such as showing films on labor and delivery) and, generally the health department was able to provide this through the community health nurse in the district where the program was located. However, as the teachers listened to the nurses repeatedly discuss these topics, most of the teachers soon felt competent in handling most of the subjects. Many of the teachers still feel more comfortable if the nurse is present for discussions on labor, delivery, and anesthesia.

In some places this kind of direct teaching may be provided by the school nurse, if there is one, or by Red Cross instructors or visiting nurses, if they are available and have time and expertise to do such teaching.

Provision of Consultation Services and Coordination

Consultation services by the community health nurse can be provided in addition to, or instead of, direct teaching services. In many cases, it is the community health nurse who is most knowledgeable about sources of care for the pregnant adolescent including pregnancy diagnosis, prenatal care, therapeutic abortion services, and venereal disease treatment. When the community health nurses cannot provide direct teaching service, they may still provide teaching aids, pamphlets, films, or resource persons for the programs. Community health nurses may also be used as co-leaders in group discussions with the girls related to both physical and emotional health. Other co-leaders might be the teacher, social worker, or mental health consultant. Groups can also be used to work with the expectant father or with the couples together. Much more attention needs to be paid to strengthening the family unit, whether this unit consists of a mother and her child or includes the presence of a man and whether this unit is legally recognized or not. The negative attitude that society generally has toward early childbearing and marriage may in itself be the most destructive force towards these relationships.

Evaluation of the Health Portion of School Programs

The community health nurse is in a position to assist in developing measurements or indexes of health for students and their babies in a pregnancy program. The nutritional status of both mother and baby, rates of prematurity, morbidity and mortality, length of labor, amount of medication, and weight gains are all information that can be gathered by the community health nurse or are available to her through hospital records and birth certificates. This information may be useful in measuring the impact of the educational program on the health of mothers and babies, depending on how the programs are organized.

3. Community Health Nurse's Duties in Adolescent Pregnancy Clinics

Community health nurses are frequently one of the first groups to recognize the need for specialized health and prenatal services for the pregnant adolescent. Community health nurses can be useful in documenting the need for such clinics; in the coordination, running, and teaching in these clinics; and in the follow-up or continuity of care from the clinic, to the hospital, and into the patient's home and community.

Documenting the Need for Special Clinics

Community health nurses, more than any other professional group, are in a position to see the need for specialized medical care for adolescent expectant mothers and their babies. This need can be effectively documented, in relatively small areas such as Ventura County, by monitoring the birth certificates. Each state prescribes the amount of information required on a birth certificate, but in California it is possible to document the number of those who delivered who are seventeen or younger; the month in which they registered for prenatal care; where delivery occurred; complications of pregnancy, labor, or delivery;

marital status, age, and occupation of father of the baby; the baby's weight; and any fetal complications. This information is useful in documenting the need for specialized prenatal clinics and in evaluating the effectiveness of a specialized clinic, by comparing the pregnancy outcome of girls in special clinics to those of the same age who receive care from other sources.

This kind of analysis is time-consuming if done by hand, but a system can be instituted with the registrar's office by which the information is automatically recorded when the birth is registered. In areas where birth certificates are not available or it is not practical to record information at registration, the records of hospitals that serve large numbers of girls in this age group might be available or might already be analyzed. The gathering of this kind of data should be built into the preplanning of any program.

Coordination of and Teaching in Adolescent Prenatal Clinics

Community health nurses often conduct and teach in specialized adolescent prenatal clinics. These clinics may be conducted in connection with school programs or in a separate medical facility within a general or private hospital. If they are operated as separate clinics, they can serve as a feed-in mechanism to school programs as well as vice versa. Wherever they are operated, a community health nurse may be the clinic instructor for group teaching. The subjects for group sessions might include labor and delivery, prenatal care, nutrition, breast and bottle feeding, formula preparation, bathing the baby, selecting a layette, tour of hospital, venereal disease, family planning, and child development (discipline, spoiling, early stimulation); these can be covered in loosely structured classes that encourage participation from the girls. These sessions should encourage attendance by the patients' boyfriends, husbands, mothers, and sisters. Valuable dialogue between all of these groups is often carried on in the waiting rooms after the class is finished. It is important to keep the personnel working in these clinics as stable as possible. Frequently the physician must be rotated, but the rest of the personnel should be kept constant to provide continuity of care.

Follow-up from Clinic to Community

Home visiting, included in the traditional role of the community nurse, is invaluable for the adolescent mother. No matter how informal and open the clinic or school, there are often things that girls wish to discuss privately. The most frequent topics of this sort include sexual relationships during pregnancy, complex family situations such as incest, or lack of adequate food or money. By visiting in the home and establishing a good relationship, the community health nurse is often able to encourage a girl to make her first contacts with official agencies, such as welfare or adoption.

The home visiting community health nurse is also in an ideal position to do case finding. Many referrals come from neighbors or relatives and it is amazing how often the sister or mother of a pregnant adolescent is also pregnant. In the home, health teaching can be geared to the level of understanding of the patient and can meet her particular needs. Home teaching should be supplementary to that received in schools or special clinics; it is important that communication be maintained with each of these places so that special needs can be identified.

Probably the community health nurse's most important home visiting role is in the home after the baby is delivered. The immediate postpartum period, one of the most crucial times, is the time when most other resources are skimpy, since the girl hasn't returned to school and there is often no clinic or hospital follow-up until six weeks postpartum. If the girl has relinquished her child, she will undoubtedly need someone to talk with. If she has a family, they often want her to forget about it as soon as possible and not discuss her experiences. There is, however, a desire for all newly delivered mothers to recount their hospital experiences and to talk about their feelings.

If the girl has brought her baby home, this is a period of tremendous adjustment and physical and emotional exhaustion, whether she is married or single. Rubin[3] describes in detail the physiological changes after delivery such as the need for sleep, food, and information and the mother's psychological need to

---

3. R. Rubin, "Puerperal change," *Nursing Outlook*, 9:753 (1961).

review the labor and delivery and to have some dependency as well as to cope with the autonomy of her own body. Bozian[4] describes the role of the community health nurse as developing a helpful relationship with the family, physical inspection of the baby, and an assessment of the mother's knowledge of the infant's physical, social, and emotional requirements. The nurse must be aware of all these things in order to be most effective in meeting the new mother's needs for support, information, and instruction.

The community health nurse can also play a vital role in the transfer of information about the postpartum or prenatal period to other appropriate places like the clinic, physician, or school. However, extreme attention must be paid to confidentiality, with legal releases of information signed when information is exchanged.

Community Services for Adolescent Families

The community health nurse has a variety of roles to play in working with and for adolescents in her own community. She may perform such functions as serving on advisory boards for school based programs or on boards of private adoption agencies or homes for unwed mothers; she may teach community based programs about pregnancy or parental skills under such sponsors as the YWCA, Red Cross, health department, or adult education; and, most importantly, she may become active in the area of pregnancy testing, referral, and primary prevention.

Serving on Advisory Boards and Committees

Because of her unique contribution to both community-based activities and patient-care services, the community health nurse can contribute much to the advisory boards that most school-age pregnancy programs have established. She can make certain that proper attention is paid to the physical and emotional needs of the students and their babies and can serve as a liaison between the school and the health department or agency where she works.

Adoption agencies, especially private ones, and/or homes for

---

4. M. Bozian, "Nursing care of the infant in the community," *Nursing Clinics of North America,* 6:93 (1971).

unwed mothers also frequently have advisory boards; here, again, the community health nurse is helpful as a liaison person and as the person to focus attention on the need for continuity of care and services following delivery. She may also be instrumental in identifying the need for health teaching, including contraception, in these agencies and institutions.

Teaching in Community Based Programs

The community health nurse may teach in community programs that are sponsored by such groups as the Red Cross, YWCA, adult education, health department, or in privately sponsored groups such as La Leche or Lamaze classes. Adolescents are often idealistic and desire to do everything "naturally," so these classes are often very attractive to them. In a larger community there may be enough girls in the adolescent age group to form a separate class. Community health nurses may choose to do this teaching on their own time or as a combined service with the YWCA or other organized group.

4. Working in the Area of Prevention

Pregnancy Testing

In many areas, local health departments provide free pregnancy testing, counseling, and referral services. Many state laws, as in California, provide that tests or examinations related to pregnancy or venereal disease may be done without parental consent. In Ventura County, free pregnancy tests, counseling, and referral are obtainable in the main health department, in the three outlying district offices, and in the free clinics, which are staffed partly by volunteer community health nurses.

Extreme care must be taken in performing the pregnancy tests since the results carry enormous implications. In most instances, it is wise to do both the rapid (two minute) screening test and follow this by the two-hour tube test making certain that the patients understand the first test is *only* a screening test. Explicit instructions must be given to the girls so that the test is carried out according to the manufacturer's directions. The results should never be given to anyone except the girl. The quick tests may be done by clinic or community health nurses after proper training, but the more elaborate tests are usually performed in a laboratory.

Counseling and Referral

No person should be told the result of a pregnancy test without someone being immediately available to counsel with her regarding the findings. The community health or clinic nurse must be aware of all the legal alternatives that are available to each girl and her boyfriend, and she must be a person who can discuss these alternatives in a nonjudgmental manner. Generally, the alternatives include (1) marriage (the nurse should be aware of the state laws regulating age of consent); (2) staying single, but keeping the baby; (3) adoption (the nurse should know both the private and public agencies in her area); and (4) abortion (depending on the legal availability in each state).

Community health nurses, because of their ability to do home visiting, are also in a good position to work with boyfriends, husbands, and parents of pregnant adolescent girls. Many girls need assistance in telling their parents that they are pregnant; this support may be provided by the community health nurse. Both the girl, her boyfriend, and any grandparents involved must be assisted in looking realistically at all the alternatives as well as the future both of the young parents and a possible child. Girls and their boyfriends are always encouraged to confide in their parents, when possible, although legally in California they do not need to in order to seek care (either prenatal or abortive). In a few instances, the girl is supported in her decision not to tell her parents, if there is a history of or realistic fear of severe physical punishment to the girl.

Both the girl's parents as well as the young persons involved face many difficult problems and emotions when a pregnancy is discovered. Parents frequently feel guilty ("What did I do wrong?") as well as anger or hostility ("How could you do this to me?"), and they must be helped to recognize and deal with these emotions. Young people may also have mixed emotions of guilt as well as of pride saying, "You mean I'm really going to

have a baby?" Unfortunately, all too often the pregnancy and/
or baby becomes a pawn or tool in the hands of either the grandparents or the parents. Young girls may say, "I know I'm not
ready to have a baby and I really don't want one, but this will be
the only thing I have that my mother can't take away from me."
Grandparents may use the baby to punish the girl saying, "You've
sinned so now you pay for it by staying home all the time and
taking care of this baby." If both groups are able to accept counseling assistance, the pregnancy may be the first time that a girl
and her parents have really been able to communicate and it can
be a growth experience for all involved. If no help is sought or
received, it can be a destructive period for everyone, including
the new child. The community health nurse who is skilled in
listening and in interpersonal relationships can be a source of
strength to all parties and can serve as a referral person when the
problems are deep-rooted and serious. Because she is physically
in the home, she is more likely to see and hear these emotional
conflicts and is in the best position to make appropriate referrals
when necessary.

Community health nurses generally have up-to-date information concerning all of the alternatives and are able to counsel
about the possibility of obtaining welfare assistance and the
costs and availability of both therapeutic abortions and prenatal
care.

Availability of Family Planning Services

If a pregnancy test is negative or if a girl seeks contraceptive
services, the community health nurse should know if and where
this may be obtained. In many areas there are planned parenthood associations that can supply care or possibly private physicians, although many private physicians are reluctant to provide
contraceptives without parental consent. In many communities
the health department provides contraceptive services at little or
no cost. Again, state laws, local restrictions, or agency policy can
severely limit the availability of contraceptives for adolescents.
However, even if no actual devices can be obtained, the community health nurse can talk with each girl and her boyfriend about
anatomy, physiology, the availability of nonprescription methods

and about the decision to be sexually active. In our experience, few girls are able to use the rhythm method successfully because of irregular periods and the fantastic fertility that most young, healthy females possess. The IUD has been the most accepted and effective device used in the Ventura County Health Department so far, mainly because the girl has to decide only once that she is going to need contraception—at the time of insertion. Few adolescents are able to make the decision daily that, not only are they going to have sex, but that they will use birth control; this is the kind of motivation that effective use of an oral contraceptive demands.

The community health nurse can also be useful in talking with each girl and her boyfriend about responsible sexuality and what this means. In group discussions with girls who are in school pregnancy programs, the community health nurse can discuss effective contraception, and more importantly, the emotional aspects. No matter how good the contraceptive or how available it is, if the girl does not accept her sexual activity, family planning will not be used effectively or even begun.

Encouraging Family Life Classes

Many areas of the country are still fighting antiquated laws or public opinion that prohibit classroom discussion and teaching of subjects related to sexuality, responsible parenthood, and readiness for marriage. People must be licensed to drive cars, own pets, and even ride bicycles, but anyone who is biologically producing ova is allowed to give birth to and rear children with no formal instruction or, indeed, assistance in doing this. Instead, enormous amounts of money and energy are spent in attempting to institute legislation, as in California, that would punish them by removing these children from them after they have been born. How much better to expend that energy and money to prevent these pregnancies from occurring.

The community health nurse is in an ideal location to provide testimony, formal and informal, on behalf of the need for family life classes and to assist in providing in-service training for those who should be teaching the classes.

It must be repeated that the roles and services that have been described as being appropriate for a community health nurse may frequently be assumed by any one of the team working with adolescent families; however, the duties that have been discussed can be handled effectively by most community health nurses.

As a community health nurse who has worked with this group of young people, I feel strongly that more attention must be paid to primary prevention in such organizations as the National Alliance Concerned with School-Age Parents, Consortium on Early Childbearing and Childrearing, and the Inter-Agency Task Force. No matter how much welfare, health, or educational support is given, ten-, eleven-, and twelve-year-olds are not, and probably can never be, prepared to become responsible parents. Until persons in the health, education, and social service fields are prepared to accept that fact and accept the existence of adolescent sexual activity, no headway will be made against the problems of children bearing and raising children.

Meanwhile, active steps must be taken to assist the adolescent parents and their children who are here now and who are likely to be here in the next few years. Whether in the community, the hospital, or the school, and whether in beginning or established programs, the community health nurse can be an effective force in working with and for adolescent families.

CHAPTER VII

A SOCIAL PSYCHIATRY VIEW OF FEMALE ADOLESCENT CONTRACEPTION

Patti Tighe

ADOLESCENT SEXUAL ACTIVITY AND CONTEMPORARY ATTITUDINAL CHANGE

M OST STUDIES of female sexual activity prior to 1972 assessed behavior or attitudes but not both. They described specific, often minor subgroups of the population by widely varying methods. Liben[1] noted that white middle-class women are studied by psychoanalytically-oriented methods that find intrapsychic explanations for sexual activity and pregnancy. Lower-class nonwhites, on the other hand, are studied by sociological and epidemiological approaches and are seen to be motivated by social factors.

The following examples illustrate the variability of the findings regarding the frequency of sexual intercourse. Kinsey[2] reported on the sexual lives of 6,000 adult white educated Northeastern women. He reported that 50 percent had had premarital sexual intercourse. There was a similar incidence for lower class women of corresponding age. Burgess and Lawlin,[3] reporting on the sexual activity of 650 married high school and college educated women of the 1930's and 1940's, claimed a 47 percent rate of premarital sex. Helax[4] claims a 20 percent report of intercourse experience in white middle-class college students by the fourth

1. F. Liben, "Minority group clinic patients pregnant out of wedlock," *American Journal of Public Health*, 59:1868 (1969) .

2. A. C. Kinsey, W. B. Pomeroy, C. E. Martin and P. H. Gebrand, *Sexual Behavior in the Adult Female* (Philadelphia, W. B. Saunders Company, 1953) .

3. E. W. Burgess and P. Wallen, *Engagement and Marriage* (Philadelphia, J. B. Lippincott Company, 1953) .

4. S. Hallek, "Sex and mental health on the campus," *Journal of the American Medical Association*, 200:684 (1967) .

year. Gebhardt[5] on the other hand, reports 60 percent of grammar school-educated lower-class Negro girls reporting sexual intercourse by age fifteen and over 80 percent by age eighteen.

Sorenson[6] more recently published a detailed behavioral and attitudinal study of adolescent sexuality with greater comprehensiveness. The data was drawn from 411 statistically quantifiable questionnaires and 200 personal interviews of American adolescents. This sample was drawn from 103 representative areas of the United States as determined by Response Analysis Corporation, and the respondent samples corresponded with the adult and adolescent national distribution by sex, age, geographic region, locality size, race and with representative household incomes. Of all adolescents in the study 52 percent reported having had sexual intercourse (45% of the females and 59% of the males). Of these, 56 percent of the girls and 71 percent of the boys reported sexual intercourse by the age of fifteen, with a 90 percent total positive response by age sixteen.

It is probable that contemporary adolescents are initiating premarital sexual experiences at an earlier age than previous generations. The major attitudinal characteristic of this generation of teenagers seems to be a refusal to be forced into marriage in order to initiate and maintain a sexual relationship. They are seeking affectional and sexual satisfaction without a marriage bond and in many instances without inordinate guilt.[6] Several recent studies confirm the finding that at least two-thirds of adolescents accept premarital intercourse between two consenting people or in the context of a relationship of mutual concern.[7, 8] Although this permissiveness does not seem to reflect the current thinking of adults, as will be shown, there are clear evidences of attitudinal shifts in society—sexual frankness in the media, mixed col-

5. P. Gebhard, *Pregnancy, Birth and Abortion* (New York, Harper & Row Publishers, 1958).

6. R. C. Sorenson, *Adolescent Sexuality in Contemporary America* (New York, World Publishing Co., 1973).

7. J. E. Morgenthau, and N. J. Sokoloff, "The sexual revolution: myth or fact?" *Pediatric Clinics of North America,* 19:779 (1972).

8. E. A. Suchman, "Accidents and Social Deviance," *Journal of Health and Social Behavior,* 11:4 (1970).

lege dormitories, and public and private health clinics dispensing contraceptives to unmarried adolescents.

This attitude correlates with two behavioral changes. First, because of the earlier age of first sexual intercourse without a corresponding decrease in marriage age, young women are participating in increasing numbers of monogymous stable ongoing relationships, including sex, before settling on a marriage partner (serial monogamy). This is in contrast to the premarital sexual behavior of the women from the 30's to the 50's, which was likely to be limited to their eventual husband. Second, Reiss[9] and others believe that there is a contemporary shift away from the double standard to a greater belief in female-male equality and the greater acceptance by both women and men of female premarital intercourse. Clearly, girls are more frequently entering into relationships without the expectation of marriage and boys are becoming interested in emotional as well as sexual satisfaction. This is supported by the finding of common adolescent interest in relationships of emotional commitment as the optimal context for sexual activity.

Sorenson[6] reported that 55 percent of all nonvirgins and their partners (the youngest persons sampled) use no birth control methods on first sexual intercourse. Numerous other studies support the findings that most adolescents have their initial coital experience without contraception.[10, 11] Most surveys of unmarried women seeking therapeutic abortions report that from 50 to 80 percent of them used no contraceptive device at the time of conception. The range is similar for pregnancies carried to term.[12] Sorenson[6] also reported that 78 percent of those initially using contraception continued the practice and that 51 percent of initial nonusers continued to ignore it. He found contraceptive use

9. I. L. Reiss, "Premarital sexual standards," in C. B. Broderick and J. Bernard eds., *The Individual, Sex and Society* (Baltimore, The Johns Hopkins Press, 1969).

10. I. L. Reiss, "The influence of contraceptive knowledge on premartital sexuality," *Medical Aspects of Human Sexuality*, 4:71 (1970).

11. K. E. Bowman, "Selected aspects of the contraceptive practices of unmarried university students," *Medical Aspects of Human Sexuality*, 5:76 (1970).

12. R. Finklestein, "Program for the sexually active teenager," *Pediatric Clinics of North America*, 19:791 (1972).

relatively constant for girls but decreasing with age for boys. In his sample, teenagers with one consistent partner were more apt to use contraception than those with serial partners. In Miller's[13] sample of California women entering hospitals for therapeutic abortion, of whom 37 percent were nineteen years old or less, 54 percent reported no contraception around the time of conception.

A recent study of seventy-eight adolescents followed up after abortion indicated that less than one-third were using contraceptives.[14] Stated reasons included: "I couldn't be pregnant twice at such a young age" or "I won't ever have sexual relations again."

One follow-up of unwed pregnant adolescents indicated that twenty-six of the original seventy-eight project participants were pregnant again within one year. None had consistently used contraceptives.[15] This is a marked contrast to Sarrel's[16] and Osofsky's[17] groups of adolescents who had comprehensive contraception counseling with high success.

Statistics about the level of illegitimacy among adolescents vary, but the National Center for Health Statistics[18] reports that these levels haven't changed in thirty years—stating that in 1940, 48 percent of the recorded illegitimate births were to teenagers. In 1965 the figure was 44 percent. All of the earlier studies, including those of the 60's, attempting to document illegitimacy, were limited to special groups and nonrandom samples, i.e. white, middle class, college students, lower class black pregnant women

---

13. W. B. Miller, Psychological Antecedents to Conception in Pregnancies Terminated by Therapeutic Abortion (in press).

14. P. Barglow and S. Weinstein, "Therapeutic abortion during adolescence: psychiatric observations," to appear in the *Journal of Youth and Adolescence* (1973-74).

15. P. Barglow, M. Bornstein, D. Exum, M. Wright and H. Visotsky, "Some psychiatric aspects of illegitimate pregnancy in early adolescence," *American Journal of Orthopsychiatry*, 38:672 (1968).

16. P. Sarrel, "The university hospital and the teenage mother," *American Journal of Public Health*, 57:1308 (1967).

17. H. Osofsky, Adolescent out-of-wedlock pregnancy: an overview, *Clinical Obstetrics and Gynecology*, 14:442 (1971).

18. National Center for Health Statistics, *Trends in Illegitimacy—United States, 1940-1965* (February, 1968).

in public hospitals, delinquents. These statistics do not apply to adolescents of all socioeconomic and geographic groups, because of sampling biases, better reporting in minority groups, the tendency for older women to marry once they learn of pregnancy, and the larger number of women in the reproductive years.

According to a U. S. Department of Health, Education and Welfare report,[19] the frequency of out-of-wedlock births increased from 7.4 per 1,000 unmarried women in 1940, to 16.7 per 1,000 in 1965 for fifteen- to nineteen-year-old adolescents. Whatever the real rate and trend changes might be, these figures support the contention that the absence of effective measures of contraception does not stop sexual activity in adolescents. The benefits of providing contraceptive information and services to adolescents obviously are greater than the hazards of not providing them.

A major contributory factor to earlier sexual activity is earlier fertility with many young girls now reporting menarche at ten or eleven years old.[1] For adolescents a normal healthy curiosity about one's self leads to sexual experimentation. As sexual desires begin to develop, a tendency toward experimentation becomes greater.

Societal objection to sexual activity in the unmarried is beginning to disappear. The resultant ambiguity is communicated to the adolescent. Lack of firm standards and guidelines is particularly difficult for the developing superego to manage and probably enhances earlier sexual experimentation.

Changes in behavior have resulted, at least to some extent, from a loosening of family restrictions. Sexual activity frequently takes place with one or the other parent at home, either sanctioning or ignoring what is going on. Blakes' study[20] supports this shift toward permissiveness in behavior codes, particularly

19. U. S. Department of Health, Education and Welfare, National Center for Health Statistics, *Natality Statistics Analysis—United States, 1965-66* (Washington, D. C., Government Printing Office Publisher #1000).

20. J. Blake, "The teenage birth control dilemma and public opinion," *Science*, 180:708 (1973).

in young adults; 42 percent of the women and 65 percent of the men under thirty in her sample answered that it was not wrong for a man and a woman to have sex before marriage. In Sorenson's study[6] half of the adolescents believe that young people participate in sex in the service of peer group conformity, although less than 25 percent admitted to being so influenced themselves.

FACTORS OPPOSING SUCCESSFUL CONTRACEPTION USAGE

Sexual intercourse is the final common pathway for at least three activities having different goals: (1) the sexual drive with its goal of pleasure and tension release; (2) the reproductive drive with its goal of offspring; and (3) the expression of adult love and affection as it manifests itself in close, intimate dyadic heterosexual behavior.

Ideally, successful contraception should not interfere with the sexual pleasure-seeking drive, should use reality principle operations of postponement of immediate satisfaction until the optimal conditions for heterosexual activity are present, and should not involve, unless chosen, permanent impairment of fertility or procreative ability.[21] What elements interfere with such success?

Misinformation About Sex

Sexual attitudes and contraceptive information are always acquired somewhere. For modern adolescents too often they originate from the peer group or the popular communication media. Most studies report a pervasive absence of sex education in the presence of regular early unsupervised dating. Several studies of pregnant adolescents show that 75 to 90 percent of them believe they wouldn't have become pregnant if birth control measures had been available to them. While statistical data is generally unavailable, the literature is full of contradictory unsubstantiated statements about the availability of reproductive and birth control information to various segments of the population.

Most studies of adolescents indicate a widespread lack of ac-

---

21. G. Pollock, "Psychoanalytic considerations of fertility and sexuality in contraception," *The Israel Annals of Psychiatry and Related Disciplines,* 10:203 (1972).

curate information about contraception and a great poverty of understanding about the real nature of sexual activity. Typical is a report by Carter and Ostendorf[22] of questions asked by junior high school students in inner-city schools. These demonstrated a high degree of misinformation about menstruation, sexual intercourse, and oral contraception. The girls asked questions such as, "Does intercourse hurt?," "Does a boy know when the girl is pregnant?," "Does not having enough intercourse lead to mental illness?," "How does the baby get out?" and "Do young boys produce sperm?" One study of lower socioeconomic pregnant adolescents showed that none of the subjects had had any formal sex education. Of these 80 percent received their sex education from the peer group or sex partner and 20 percent claimed home as the source. Less than 10 percent had any knowledge of the physiology of sex and none of the emotional development of sexuality.[23]

Distortions and superstitions are passed from generation to generation. Ideas that diaphragms or IUD's can be "lost inside" and that sexual desire is hurt by the use of oral contraceptives are still popular in many adolescent groups. However, good studies on the level of information and understanding in middle and upper middle-class groups are particularly lacking. Gabrielson[24] reported a high positive correlation of general sex knowledge and birth control knowledge in a nonpregnant group of adolescents seeking contraception in contrast to groups seeking abortion and planning to carry a pregnancy to term.

Availability of birth control information and services to American adolescents is incomplete and spotty at best. This is particularly true for the medically indigent and those too unsophisticated to negotiate the usual complicated procedures required. In Sorenson's[6] sample, 30 percent of adolescent girls (46% of the thirteen- to fifteen-year-olds and 18% of the sixteen- to eighteen-year-olds) reported knowing of no available

22. I. Carter and M. Ostendorf, "The awakening of adolescent femininity," *Journal of School Health,* 40:203 (1970).

23. J. Rovinsky, Abortion recidivism. *Obstetrics and Gynecology,* 39:649 (1972).

24. I. W. Gabrielson, S. Goldsmith, L. Potts, V. Mathews and M. Gabrielson, "Adolescent attitudes toward abortion: effects on contraceptive practice," *American Journal of Public Health,* 61:730 (1971).

facility for obtaining contraceptive services; 68 percent of the girls and 80 percent of the boys in his sample deny that their parents ever discussed contraception with them.

Cost of services is also frequently reported as a deterrent. Many studies report fear of and misinformation about the side effects of most forms of contraception. Fear of side effects is sometimes reported to be greater in uneducated and sometimes in better educated groups. Despite the frequency of report of the use of rhythm, most women surveyed using this method are found to be grossly misinformed about ovulation and proper timing. Many users consider the most fertile period to be during menstruation, and consider midcycle days to be the safest.

Adolescents frequently report that conception cannot occur without pleasure. There is a belief that fertility is absent because of their young age and that failure to conceive in the past also indicates subfecundity. Although these explanations are frequently used in the service of denial and rationalization, it is probable that most young adolescents are unclear about these facts.

Adolescents have been exposed since early childhood to the exploitation and mechanization of sex presented by the mass media. The pejorative and degrading presentation of sexuality which unfortunately constitutes a major aspect of most adolescents' sex education is restricted, superficial, and distorted. It adds to the adolescents' confusion, increases the sense of guilt and shame about sexuality, and discourages the obtaining and use of accurate contraception information.

External (Extrapsychic) Reasons for Avoiding Contraception

PARENTAL ATTITUDES. External prohibition against premarital sex is still prevalent for contemporary adolescents in the form of continued disapproval by their parents. Blake[20] evaluated the attitudes of younger, middle-aged, and older American women and men concerning sexual permissiveness and birth control information and services. Less than one-third of white adult American men and women answered No to the following question: Is it wrong for a man and woman to have sexual relations before marriage?

Adolescents frequently report unwillingness on the part of their parents to discuss the subject of sex or sex education and feel that their parents do not communicate openly what they believe their children should know. It is clear from several studies that parents whose children already do know and are curious about sex still believe their children to be too young to know. Hence, they are reluctant to take the initiative in discussions. Adolescents in turn are reluctant to volunteer what they believe will be unacceptable ideas and questions to their parents. Only 31 percent of the girls and 18 percent of the boys in Sorenson's[6] study report that their parents told them anything about birth control.

Large segments of society tend yet to support the attitude that all sex is bad. However, it is "less bad" if it is spontaneous. This implies that to anticipate a pregnancy risk is to admit forethought for sexual activity. The results of such parental inhibitions and prohibitions are avoidance of contraception for fear of parental discovery. This explains why most adolescents living at home report the use of rhythm and withdrawal methods. In Sorenson's[6] sample 57 percent of the girls claim one reason for not using oral contraceptives is the fear of parental discovery.

All studies of all groups indicate an overwhelming lack of openness on the part of the parents with their children about sexual activity and values. Many parents still claim that contraceptive education will lead to amorality. Even well-intentioned parents are frequently uncomfortable in discussing matters of sex and contraception, feeling embarrassed and inept. Because of the natural deep emotional involvement of parents with their own children, rationality and objectivity are even more difficult to achieve. Parents frequently demonstrate greater tolerance of the sexual aspects of adolescent relationships in others, but attempt to forbid them in their own children. Additionally, sexual problems, repressions, and fears of the parents can be a further deterrent to free communication with children.

Parents are still the main purveyors of attitude to their own children and sexual immaturity and inhibition in parents are communicated to the child from his earliest days. The same parents who demonstrate minimal involvement in control of adolescent sexual behavior frequently refuse to provide or sanction contraceptive information service.

The influence of the parent is also crucial in indirect ways. "A capacity to plan ahead and a conviction that one has the power to control one's life have been related to effective family planning. Responsible, competent marital couples plan their families effectively."[25] Such parental capacities may become part of the adolescent's self-image.

On the other hand, parents may provide negative models as well as the absence of supervisory support for the self-control required for contraception use. Grossack[26] has described parents of the poverty culture as inconsistent, authoritarian persons who quickly resort to harsh corporal punishment and who "relax closely monitored supervision much earlier than their middle-class counterparts." Lewis[27] has commented that the lower-class parents "disapprove of adolescent sex" but "feel that their child's fate was out of their hands." They "seemed to feel helpless in regard to controlling their child, considering their cultural influences and their precarious economic stability."

RELIGIOUS, CULTURAL, AND SOCIETAL INFLUENCES. A variety of cultural, social, and religious factors and values influence sexual activity and contraceptive use. For example, the Catholic church prohibits premarital sex and all forms of birth control except rhythm. The sanction against premarital sex is apparently easier to ignore if it can be experienced as spontaneous, unplanned, or the result of strong passion. The use of birth control, on the other hand, implies premeditation. Yet Sorenson[6] reported that only 16 percent of children of Catholic families reported that they would not use birth control for religious reasons.

Blake[20] found that there was no significant difference between Catholics and non-Catholics approving of nationwide programs of birth control education in public high schools and also birth con-

25. P. Barglow, "Psychiatric aspects of contraceptive utilization," *American Journal of Obstetrics and Gynecology.* p. 94 (1972).

26. M. Grossack, ed., *Mental Health and Segregation* (New York, Springer Publications, 1963).

27. H. Lewis, Child rearing practices among low-income families. Casework Papers. p. 82. 1961. op. cit. 15.

trol services being made available to teenagers. The difference between Catholics' and non-Catholics' Yes response to the question about sexual relations before marriage was less than 5 percent.

Other cultural and ethnic attitudes toward fertility constitute barriers to the acceptability of contraception in some populations. The standards, ideals, and values of minority groups may act to facilitate or inhibit the wish for children. For example, the cult of machismo (virility) is usually a psychological bar to reduction in family size. If a group wishes to gain political power through numerical increase, large families might be associated with high prestige. This was true in Germany during World War II. The barren woman is considered accursed in the Bible and is a person to be shunned in the Islamic religion.[25]

A contemporary black leader recently told a federal commission that birth control "is a form of genocide . . . the destruction of the black people."[28] The stigma of unwed motherhood may constitute a pseudomoral barrier to contraceptive usage.[29] Blair[30] found that 25 percent of blacks considered family planning methods harmful to health. Contraception services are often unpopular in rural, isolated communities with low educational levels and high unemployment. Members of these groups often evidence an attitude of fatalism and mistrust of professional services.

PHYSICIAN ATTITUDES. The ethical position and attitude of the physician toward adolescent contraception is crucial. Emphasis in the relevant medical literature of the early 60's was on the physician's moral and ethical dilemma in providing contraception to minors. In the 70's it is clear that the problem for the medical community has evolved to dealing with the growing number of out-of-wedlock teenage pregnancies.

In April, 1971, the American Academy of Pediatrics[31] recommended that "the teenage girl whose sexual behavior exposes her

28. *The Chicago Sun-Times,* June 23, 1971, p. 42.

29. *The Chicago Sun-Times,* February 9, 1971, p. 24.

30. A. O. Blair, in D. J. Bogue, *Sociological Contributions to Family Planning Research,* Community and Family Study Center, 1967, p. 1.

31. American Academy of Pediatrics—Committee on Youth, "Teenage pregnancy and the problem of abortion," *Pediatrics,* 49:303 (1972).

to possible conception should have access to medical consultation and the most effective contraceptive advice and methods consistent with her physical needs; the physicians so consulted should be free to prescribe or withhold the contraceptive advice in accordance with their best medical judgment and in the best interest of the patient." Their counsel on child health further states that "contraceptive advice and prescription for the sexually active teenage girl should be accompanied by investigation and alteration of contributing issues wherever possible. Continuous long-term support directed toward facilitating personality development is an integral part of the care situation. Abortion must never be allowed to replace adequate preventive care or contraceptive measures."

In May of 1971 the American College of Obstetricians and Gynecologists[12] issued a statement substantially in agreement with the above which goes further to suggest that the legal barriers, which restrict the provision of these services to unemancipated minors who refuse to involve their parents, should be removed—this within the context of counseling the patient to involve her parents.

Despite these official position statements, the individual physician still brings his various attitudes, moral judgments, and psychological biases to the treatment situation. Nationwide statistics on physician attitudes and their effect on contraceptive dispensing are not available. Pauly and Goldstein[32] report the results of a questionnaire surveying 937 Oregon physicians about the acceptability in their minds of premarital intercourse. A third reported acceptability often or always, one-third sometimes, and one-third seldom or never.

Physicians frequently are still unable to admit their own discomfort with sexual behavior in minors. Those who do approach this as a moral issue sometimes indicate that their refusal of contraceptive services will inhibit the sexual activity of the patient. It is obvious, however, that this sexual activity will not be affected at all despite lack of exposure to contraception. The physician

---

32. I. Pauly and S. Goldstein, "Physicians' attitudes toward premarital and extramarital intercourse," *Medical Aspects of Human Sexuality,* 5:32 (1971).

by such a stand places himself in the position of fostering patient irresponsibility toward herself and her community. The physician who attempts to impose his own standards of morality or religion on the adolescent patient also runs the risk of destroying the doctor-patient relationship and seriously undermining that person's willingness to participate in responsible, medically-advised contraception in the future.

Most practicing physicians today are educationally deficient in all aspects of human sexuality including the various methods of contraceptive practice. The average physician is not familiar with available community facilities, hospital and local health department adolescent clinics, and Planned Parenthood clinics. A sense of inadequacy in sexual counseling is frequently the basis of a physician's reluctance to involve himself with his patient's contraceptive needs. This can be complicated by the physician's own sexual anxieties which can be ultimately deleterious to the adolescent patient.

Also, the possibility of litigation is still a real one in the minds of some physicians. In most states adolescents over eighteen or under eighteen and married are legally able to give their own consent for contraception. There are now laws in almost all states allowing various forms of medical treatment *without parental consent,* and several states have passed laws permitting minors to give their own informed consent without parental involvement. Local health departments can provide the current legal status of medical provision of contraceptives to minors without parental consent. Pilpel and Weschler[33] contend that it would be extremely unlikely that a suit could be successfully prosecuted against a physician who provided for his patient in this way. Our review of the literature has found no report of such a suit.

All physicians today must be prepared to be confronted with sexually active teenagers who are not going to be counseled out of their sexual activity authoritatively, morally, ethically, or religiously. The physician offering contraceptive advice is certainly, at least to some extent, sanctioning the sexual activity of his pa-

33. H. F. Pilpel and N. F. Weschler, "Birth control, teenagers and the law: a new look, 1971," *Family Planning Perspectives,* Vol. 3 (July, 1971) .

tient. If he finds this attitude in himself unconscionable, he must be prepared to refer the adolescent patient to a colleague who can objectively assess her motives, ambivalence and mental, social, and medical condition and who can counsel her and provide contraceptive methods appropriately. (Sorenson[6] found 24% of adolescents who reported no contraceptive use stated that their physician's attitudes contributed to contraceptive nonuse.)

Psychological (Intrapsychic) Reasons for
Avoidance of Contraception

Most studies report the adolescent desires that sexual intercourse be a spontaneous, unpremeditated event. Spontaneity and naturalness, the cardinal virtues of the current generation, are said to contradict the artificiality of chemical or mechanical intervention. More frequently, however, this serves as a rationalization for an, as yet, poorly developed capacity for impulse control, typical of this developmental period. Adolescents are not always ready to assume the responsibility for behavior which they espouse so vocally.

The capacity to plan ahead or to project one's self into the future is also a developmental goal of this period for the younger adolescent. It seems to be easier for older adolescents, who have acquired a greater sense of being in control of their own lives, to guard against the risk of pregnancy in their sexual activity. Numerous studies report large numbers of adolescents unwilling to admit to themselves that they are having intercourse regularly or that there is even a remote possibility of becoming pregnant. Adolescent girls, who have intercourse irregularly accompanied by contraception, usually believe that the wish not to have a baby would somehow prevent conception despite the lack of contraceptive use. Also frequently reported is the idea "I've had intercourse before so many times without contraception and never got pregnant; it won't happen to me." This as yet poorly developed reality testing capacity is not atypical for early adolescents.

In one sample of adolescents who were sexually active,[34] 45

34. L. Nilsson, and L. Solvell, "A randomized, double-blind, cross-over study of four different preparations," *Acta Obstetrica et Gynecologica Scandinavica, Supplement* 8, 47:31 (1967).

percent reported carelessness and forgetfulness as reasons for intercourse without contraception, and 38 percent reported that it was simply too much trouble. This demonstrates the typical early adolescent ambivalence toward accepting one's sexuality, which is at first characterized by denial of the existence of sexuality. Adolescents are curious about themselves and beginning to experience unfamiliar and powerful new feelings which must be gradually accepted, integrated, and explored. They frequently don't experience the sexual relationship or their partner as real but rather as if they were engaging in a fantasy. "It is almost as if I wasn't really having intercourse." Many adolescents are maturationally ill-equipped to handle the situations in which they find themselves and the new sensations and wishes for intimacy which they experience.

Contrary to adult populations in which the need to prove reproductive capacity is frequently seen as the cause for contraceptive failure, adolescents more commonly demonstrate disbelief about their own reproductive capacity. To use contraception is to plan ahead. This implies an acceptance of these as yet not totally acceptable wishes and capacities. For this reason, adolescents frequently prefer to tell themselves that they were not really actively participating in sexual activities but were simply surprised by the passion of the moment.

This normal internal conflict about emerging sexuality is increased by the external prohibitions against acceptance of sexual impulses and the initiation of sexual behavior. As reported above, Blake[20] demonstrated that less than one-third of white, adult, American men and women approve of sexual relations before marriage. The adolescent's ambivalence is heightened by the mixed message from parents reluctant to admit obvious sexual activity of their own children.

This societal disapproval of sexual activity in adolescents, particularly girls, produces a marked sense of guilt and negative anticipation. In Sorenson's[6] group, about one-third reported worry, guilt, embarrassment, and disappointment. Girls are taught that sexual activity is acceptable for them only within the context of an emotional relationship. Society places a premium on virginity in girls as opposed to boys in whom virginity well into adolescence is practically a liability. Most girls demonstrated their guilt over sexual activity by offering rationalizations that their first sexual intercourse was viewed in the context of relatively strong affective ties and even the possibility of marriage.

Girls are taught that their bodies are sacred, "gifts to be given," and so the first sexual experience is described in terms of a loss and, in fact, constitutes a threatened loss of the previously experienced nonsexual self-system. Experiencing sexual drives and desires is thus traumatic to the adolescents' previous sense of self. The external prohibitions placed on this natural experience greatly increase the sense of guilt and feelings of stress necessary to accept her sexuality.

The culturally reinforced expectation of deriving a major component of her new identity from a close relationship with a loved man is deleterious to a girl's independently seeking contraception. This kind of independence—to plan for making love— is still a threat to the male (although attitudes are changing) and still produces the accusation of promiscuity in the girl from which the boy, in similar circumstances, is saved. To be assertive in this way is frequently reported as feeling like a violation to the role of the girl.

One of the most important developmental tasks of adolescents is emancipation from parental control and establishment of an independence and separate sense of identity. To establish themselves as adults, adolescents must renounce the still present but less acceptable dependency wishes towards their parents. This takes two forms. Adolescents must not only challenge what they've been taught to accept from their parents but also evaluate the effect that this has. They have to compare their own developing ideas and opinions to established institutions which have externally determined their ideas in earlier years. As this process unfolds, they begin to feel genuinely qualified to make decisions of a moral and ethical nature for themselves. This necessarily leads to conflict as their lives are still essentially regulated from outside.

Within this context, it is normal for adolescents to believe that their values are different from and superior to those of the adult generation. This is frequently experienced by the latter as the flaunting of authority. At the same time, however, residual dependency strivings result in vacillations in the attempts at parental rejection. Acceptance of birth control advice in this context can be difficult and conflicted even for the adolescent who believes it would be good for him. If a parent is unable to tolerate this insistence on independence before the child is actually prepared to assume all the concomitant responsibilities and responds with exaggerated restrictions in an effort not to lose the child, a reaction of oppositional behavior can be even more intensified.

The struggle for independence is further complicated for the female adolescent in the society by the cultural valuing of passivity and dependence for women. To transgress this role, especially in relationship to the male, and take the initiative in birth control planning for herself may produce a threat to the girl's self-esteem and externally sanctioned self-image.

Parental ambivalence about pregnancy can influence contraceptive practice even if the parent overtly disapproves of premarital sex and out-of-wedlock pregnancies for her daughter. Simultaneously, a parent may encourage these by deliberately withholding sex or birth control information, refusing money for the cost of such services, or by suspiciously checking closely on the monthly menstrual period. In some segments of the population, adolescent pregnancy is frequently the acting out by the child of a parental wish. Premature sexual activity can also be reinforced by overt messages from the parents that remaining single or not having established heterosexual relationship by late adolescence is abnormal.

The influence of peer group pressure on adolescents must not be underestimated. Most young people will correlate their behavior to the mores of the group. Pressure on girls to be attractive, to please, to acquire and keep a boy subjects the adolescent girl to the psychological conflicts of her male partner. Boys during this age period are struggling with the internal issues of developing a sense of masculine identity compounded by cultural pressure to demonstrate virility. For some cultural subgroups this can best be done by repeatedly impregnating a woman. Boys, too, can have an unconscious fear of sterility. Contraceptives used by the girl, especially methods that the boy can't see or control, can constitute an unconscious threat to his masculinity and potency. A small number of girls in the studies reported no use of contraceptives because of pressure from their boyfriends.

Rejection or failure of contraception can be in the service of the transference reaction to mother or father or even physician. Producing a child can unconsciously represent to a girl a bond, with a gift to or a punishment for a parent. The oedipal conflicts of childhood are resurrected in the adolescent period. This reawakened attraction to father substitutes can be made more difficult by the addition of erotic sensations. The resultant avoidance of the father can result in overt or covert seductive behavior on his part in an understandable but exaggerated attempt to delay giving up "his little girl." In an attempt to resolve this situation, the daughter commonly makes an exaggerated search for nonincestuous sexual partners to replace the father as the loved object, to provide a wished-for baby from the father, and to relieve the oedipal guilt.

Occasionally, out-of-wedlock pregnancy appears to be a repetition of a parental pattern, either in the service of maternal identification or as a defiant demonstration of hostility to one parent. Acting out of conflicts with parents around the issue of birth control can be extended to manipulative use of transgressions in this area to punish parents who are withholding privileges or who are not understanding. Unfortunately, deliberate but unwanted pregnancy is sometimes used as a way of removing oneself from an intolerable home or family situation.

A girl who has adjusted well to the image of herself as a sexually active being may still be conflicted about pregnancy and childbearing with resultant "forgetfulness" about contraception or denial of the possibility of pregnancy. The conscious wish for pregnancy in this population as reported in most studies is negligible. Anecdotal material, however, sometimes reveals the unconscious wish or need for pregnancy. This wish or need can sabotage an effort at contraception. The motivation to inhibit reproduction must be consistently stronger than the wish for a child, for even short term contraceptive success.

PREVENTION

Attempts to achieve prevention of conception in adolescents must consider the realities of normal developmental adolescent states and tasks and also the realities of society. Changes in anatomy and body image and the new emotions characteristic of the maturing adolescent are often experienced traumatically. These changes, conflictual attitudes towards sex, and spurts in emotional growth are crucial and largely ignored factors in conception prevention. Most adolescent girls are not adequately equipped with physiological, psychological, and sociological facts to grasp the meaning of their own sexuality and its repercussions for themselves and others.

The physician must be integrally involved in the training of teachers in the biology, physiology, psychology, and sociology of sexual activity. These teachers need a great sensitivity to the anxieties aroused by the didactic material presented. Since adolescents are not ordinarily seen by physicians, medical involvement in school programs is particularly important.

The objective presentation of the advantages and disadvantages of all contraceptives with demonstrations and a description of all major moral and ethical alternatives of sexual behavior should be offered. Beyond this, the burden of moral persuasion and the engendering of a specific value system is the task of the parent. There is clear-cut evidence demonstrating the adolescent's abysmal lack of knowledge of the basics of sex and contraception and the inability of parents alone to provide this information.

Refusal to provide adolescents with adequate programs offering sexual and contraceptive information will not stop sexual activity in this group. It is clear from many studies that knowledge of pregnancy risk does not interfere with continued nonuse of contraception. Pregnancy risks are still repeatedly ignored and home remedies are relied on (i.e. soda pop douches, Saran-wrap® condoms).

Blake[20] found that policy making about contraceptives is subject to two trends, normative values and pragmatism. The normative value view holds that provision and legal sanction of birth control information and services is unconscionable and immoral because of the implied sanction of premarital sex. This view is embodied in President Nixon's response to the report of the Commission of Population Growth and the American Future. In it he refused to support unrestricted distribution of family planning services to minors, because it would do nothing to preserve and strengthen close family relationships.

The Commission itself represents the pragmatic view that adolescent sex is a current and continuing reality. Therefore, birth control information and services should be made available in appropriate facilities. National surveys conducted by the Gallup organization show that in August 1972, 71 percent of all adult white men and women approved of nationwide programs of birth control education in public schools. At the same time, 54 percent of men and women approved of making birth control services available to teenagers. The conclusion is that despite disapproval of premarital relations, there is a growing public permissiveness and pragmatism about protecting the adolescent population from unwanted pregnancies.

Adolescents only gradually develop a capacity for mutuality, intimacy, and maturity in a relationship. The use of sexual activity to nurture a sense of devotion and commitment in a relationship must replace superficiality and casualness. The inclusion of sexual activity in developing these maturational capacities can be productive only within the context of freedom from unwanted childbearing. Adolescents are not prepared emotionally for the requirements of good childrearing but often are unaware of this. Lacking the capacity to project themselves into the future, they also fail to realize the extent of the emotional, occupational, and developmental handicap which premature parenthood produces.

Adolescents need help with concretizing the future. They must be educated to their own need for financial and emotional stability before becoming parents. They need to recognize the loss of freedom and mobility that such early childbearing inflicts on them. They should be factually exposed to the statistics of the high U. S. divorce rate, the disadvantage of emotional and financial dependence, and the lack of education predominant in young, unwed mothers. The adolescent girl must be taught to desire the development of her own fullest potential.

Some youngsters can benefit from sexual experimentation, others from waiting or limited sexual activity. The physician or teacher and the individual adolescent should reflect together on what would constitute responsible sexuality for that person and support for a realistic attitude must be provided appropriately. In one study among lower-class adolescents, girls were given the opportunity to discuss these matters openly with peers and understanding adults. Usually they were able to recognize the lack of emotional maturity and the presence of serious emotional conflicts in their peers who were unwed mothers.

In order to minimize the denial of sexuality which occurs at its first appearance, adolescents must be carefully prepared ahead of time for impending strong impulses and desires. The premature rush into sexual intercourse which bypasses the gradual unfolding of sexuality can be avoided. Orgasm is not necessary for or desired by all adolescents at an early age but rather affection and intimacy.

To provide contraceptive information and services need not be construed as sanctioning casual and superficial relationships. With appropriate adult guidance that encourages emotional maturity, the adolescent can develop a capacity for intimacy and responsibility to the self, to the partner, and to the larger society. The provision of birth control information and services must be a natural outgrowth of a progressive educational experience that fosters adaptation to the emotional impact of dramatic physical changes and the concomitant strange emotions.

Today's early sex activity confronts the adolescent with intimacy for which she is not maturationally prepared. Earlier exposure to sexual activity and the possibility of multiple partners increases the probability that the adolescent girl will experience herself as being treated not as a person but as a sex object. She may become conditioned to a degraded sense of sex rather than sex as an integral part of a meaningful relationship.

There are some indications that openness about sex with parents may be greater in adolescents whose first intercourse experience occurs later than average. This kind of frankness is difficult for most parents because of their own unresolved conflicts about sexuality and the general societal attitude of shame and secrecy. Listening to their offspring promulgate ideas which are contrary to their own may prove difficult for most parents who commonly wish for children to develop in their likenesses.

Another difficulty results if parental attitudes are the result of deeply felt moral principles with which the children disagree. The uneasiness experienced by a parent at repudiation of his or her values can foster concealment of adolescent attitudes and increase the related guilt. About one-third of the adolescents interviewed by Sorenson[6] believed that their sexual activities were probably harmful to their relationship with their parents. The fact that concealment is felt to be necessary obviously impedes closeness.

Suitable emotional settings must be provided in which adolescents can integrate their own developing feelings and opinions with the contradictory values of their parents and those of society at large. Today's adolescents will not respond to moral judgments. Provision of comprehensive educational facilities then must confront the needs, drives, and impulses of the sexually active or potentially sexually active adolescent, must accept the drives, and make realistic assessment of possible consequences, especially that of pregnancy.

Contraceptive information and services must reach all sexually active adolescents. Programs must be designed with full knowledge of the contemporary sexual mores and activities of the specific group involved. Approaches must be appropriate to the real life situations of each population. Continuous methods of reevaluating assumptions about activities and effectiveness of programs must be developed. Reports are now beginning to appear in the literature describing methods of identifying and isolating the characteristics of groups toward whom these services can be suitably directed with detailed descriptions of optimum hospital and clinic settings for various types of groups.[12, 35] Studies con-

35. C. B. Arnold and B. E. Cogswell, "A condom distribution program for adolescents. The findings of a feasibility study," *American Journal of Public Health,* 61:739 (1971).

cerning deterrents to the acceptance and optimum use of contraceptives by specific groups are now emerging.

Most of the various clinic and school approaches described in the literature consider a sex-segregated group setting, including peers and nonjudgmental adults and indigenous workers, to be an integral part of the success of their programs. Hearing others' ideas and exposing one's own in an accepting nonjudgmental setting often produces a decrease of sexual activity and/or a conscious need for contraception in the members.[24] Other studies show apparent trends towards reduction in repeated pregnancies as a result of contraceptive education and counseling.

The results of these programs also suggest the need for comprehensive medical, social, and educational care and staff constancy along with sex education. In some groups, encouraging appropriate aspirations and offering practical assistance in achieving goals and in continuing education are crucial and significantly enhance self-esteem in deprived persons. Various methods of providing exposure to adequate role models for both boys and girls have also been attempted.[16, 36]

Sexual activity in an adolescent may be provoked by problems of emotional growth and interpersonal relating. A request for contraception can be a covert search for help with these difficulties and should be managed as such. When evaluation reveals provision of contraception to be indicated, what should be considered? The successful use of any family planning method presupposes adequate age-appropriate ego functioning. During adolescence, transitory decompensations or regressions occur with predictable regularity from unusual psychic stress, blows to the self-esteem, or major conflicts with parents or the peer group.

The capacity for impulse gratification delay, good reality testing, the ability to project oneself into the future, and a stability in object relations are directly related to contraceptive success. Acting-out tendencies, overwhelming object hunger, magical thinking, and precarious self-esteem produce contraception failure.

How well does the adolescent patient regulate drives, needs,

---

36. H. Babikian and A. Goldman, "A study in teenage pregnancy," *American Journal of Psychiatry*, 128:755 (1971).

impulses? How does she react to the likelihood of transient loss of the procreative function? What specific contraceptive method best engages her reality principle operations and avoids the influence of neurotic conflicts and symptoms? Answers to these questions determine the outcome of contraceptive efforts.

CHOICE OF CONTRACEPTIVE AGENT

The methods of contraception reported in Sorenson's sample closely parallel those of more limited studies.[6] Of adolescents reporting contraceptive use 33 percent claim they always use oral contraceptives (65% never use them); 17 percent report withdrawal of the boy's penis, 4 percent use either condom, contraceptive foam, rhythm, or an IUD and 27 percent trusted to luck or didn't think about it. Virtually no respondents used a diaphragm. Miller in his study of a group containing one-third adolescents reported the use of rhythm (14%), foam (9%), withdrawal (5%), oral contraception (5%), diaphragm (5%), IUD (3%), condom (3%).[13]

Each of the above methods have advantages and disadvantages that must be openly and often repeatedly discussed with adolescent patients. The impulsive, promiscuous, or sexually very active teenager requires contraceptive means such as the IUD or the contraceptive pill. Often the well-adjusted, mature adolescent is able to use intercourse-related devices which reinforce a sense of self-control and the meaningfulness of sexual union.

ORAL CONTRACEPTIVES

The medical and psychic hazards involved in the use of oral contraceptives specifically in adolescence are not predictable. The long range and diffuse somatic effects of the hormones are in part unknown and certainly not reliably documented in adolescents. The FDA has warned about the use of the pill in adolescents who have not yet completed bone growth.[36] Speculation that subsequent fertility especially in the subfecund can be negatively affected is yet undocumented. The serious disadvantage of oral contraceptive use in adolescents is the frequency of abnormal uterine bleeding, difficult to distinguish from dysfunctional bleeding associated with anovulatory cycles. Throughout the earlier years after menarche, this latter diagnosis cannot be automatically assumed. Oral contraceptives definitely should be withheld from adolescents who haven't yet established clearly normal menstrual patterns. Psychological consequences of this method are uncertain with both positive and negative findings often reported.

The early taking of the pill requires a full recognition of the probability of frequent sexual intercourse. If an adolescent has fluctuations in her positive feelings for her partner or toward her own sexual activity, the use of the pill may be likewise irregular.

Oral contraception has been found to be effective in reducing unwanted pregnancy in some settings. Follow-up studies of pregnant teenagers receiving contraceptive education and pill prescription postpartum generally show a decrease in the rate of repeated pregnancies. Sarrel[37] reports that within five years, 100 postpartum adolescent patients had a 95 percent repeated pregnancy rate with many having several such pregnancies. Contraceptive services reduced such an incidence to near zero.[16, 38] Osofsky[17] reports only fifty-nine of 325 adolescents becoming pregnant a second time with one month to four year follow-ups, within the setting of a comprehensive oral contraceptive and counseling program.

The Intrauterine Device

The use of the IUD in adolescents has been attempted and studied only recently. There is an almost universal aversion in the adolescent group to pelvic examination and implantation of the device. Widespread use of it would require much vigorous education. The IUD has been particularly recommended in adolescents with low contraception motivation, inability to follow instructions and previous oral contraceptive failures. One study[39]

---

37. P. Sarrel, "Young unwed primipara. A study of 100 cases with five-year follow-up," *American Journal of Obstetrics and Gynecology*, 95:722 (1966).

38. P. Sarrel, "Teenage Pregnancy," *Pediatric Clinics of North America*, 16:347 (1969).

39. L. Johnson, R. Burket, and J. Rauh, "The successful use of an intrauterine device," *Clinical Pediatrics*, 10:315 (1971).

of adolescents age eleven to twenty reports generally painless insertion with some patients experiencing cramping, uterine pain for up to twenty-four hours. In this age group, the expulsion rate of plastic devices is very high but with the use of a metallic spring device they report only three out of sixty expulsions in five- to eighteen-month follow-ups. Pregnancy is possible with the device in place and spontaneous expulsion frequently unnoticed. The often-reported short-term bleeding and pain can be a particular problem in the adolescent group. This technique seems to be indicated only for specific adolescents with difficulties in self-control.

Intercourse-related Methods: Diaphragm, Foams, Condom

The diaphragm is not an effective means of contraception in girls with conflicts about genital touching and masturbation. The advantages are lack of immediate and long range side effects. The disadvantages in adolescents relate to the need for a high degree of motivation, some skill in use, and the need for a prescription from a physician, which may reveal sexual activity to the restrictive parent.

Spermicidal foams have the advantage of being available over-the-counter without a prescription. The requirement of application an hour before intercourse and with each recurrent act is a distinct drawback in all but the less sexually active teenager. Effectiveness of foam used in conjunction with a condom is great. The condom has the disadvantage of requiring the girl to rely on her partner for contraception. This method is difficult to use for boys who have impotence and sterility conflicts, but it is available without a prescription and is inexpensive. A recent feasibility study was done by Arnold and Cogswell in which free condoms were distributed throughout commercial outlets such as barbershops and pool halls in an inner-city area in North Carolina.[35] Reported results were an increase in use from 19 percent to 68 percent and an increase in those who reported its use during the last episode of intercourse from 20 percent to 91 percent.

Abortion

Abortion is always a last-ditch method, not a primary contraceptive device. Reliable recent studies conclusively demonstrate abortion to be a relatively harmless procedure from the psychiatric point of view.[40-44] These findings are in marked contrast to those documenting the sequelae of unwanted motherhood.

Levene[45] states that unwanted motherhood probably affects an adolescent more profoundly than any other event in her life. These girls tend to drop out of school and to remain uneducated, with minimal realization of their personal potential, arrested emotional and social development, and severe financial dependence. Hook[46] in an eight- to ten-year follow-up of 294 women denied an abortion found 24 percent had continued significant negative emotional sequelae. Most of them had demonstrated pathological reactions including frequent punitive hate reactions against the child and major social difficulties connected with care or placement of the child; 31 percent were judged to be providing an unfavorable environment for their child.

Forssman[47] compared 134 refused abortion children with a group of self-selected wanted children. The refused abortion children had less education and showed more family instability, antisocial and criminal behavior, need for psychiatric care, and requests for public assistance. Caplan[48] describes disturbances in the relationships of mothers to children who are the product of refused abortions.

The American Academy of Pediatrics Committee on Youth

---

40. N. Simon, A. Senturia and D. Rothnon, "Psychiatric illness following therapeutic abortion," *American Journal of Psychiatry*, 124:59 (1967).

41. S. Patt, R. Rappaport, and P. Barglow, "Follow-up of therapeutic abortion." *AMA Archives of General Psychiatry*, 20:408 (1969).

42. J. M. Kummer, "Post-abortion psychiatric illness—a myth?" *American Journal of Psychiatry*, 124:59 (1967).

43. G. Walter, "Emotional Consequences of Elective Abortion," *Obstetrics and Gynecology*, 36:482 (1970).

44. M. Eklund, "Induced abortion on psychiatric grounds—a follow-up study of 479 women." *Acta Psychiatrica et Neurologica Scandinavica Supplement*, 30:99 (1955).

45. H. Levene and F. Rigney, "Law, preventive psychiatry and therapeutic abortion." *Journal of Nervous and Mental Disease*, 151:51 (1970).

46. K. Hook, "Refused abortion," *Acta Psychiatrica Scandinavica Supplement*, 168:1 (1963).

47. H. Forssman, and I. Thuwe, "One hundred thirty children born after application for therapeutic abortion refused," *Acta Psychiatrica Scandinavica*, 42:71 (1966).

48. G. Caplan, "The disturbance of the mother-child relationship by unsuccessful attempts at abortion," *Mental Hygiene*, 38:67 (1954).

states that it prefers not to sanction nor forbid the use of abortion in a teenager to terminate pregnancy, but admonishes a physician considering this course to provide appropriate counseling and support.[31] In fact, adolescents have acquired abortions legally and illegally, medically and nonmedically and will continue to do so. What is known about psychopathologic predisposition and possible psychological reactions should be utilized to provide optimum management and follow-up and minimize potential trauma. Additional studies of psychiatric problems and consequences of adolescent abortion will be published soon and will provide the facts for further assessment of this procedure.[14]

CHAPTER VIII

LAWS RELATING TO FAMILY PLANNING SERVICES FOR GIRLS UNDER EIGHTEEN

Harriet F. Pilpel*

G IRLS UNDER EIGHTEEN can consent to birth control services in two-fifths of the states.

By mid-1972, thirty-nine of the fifty states had affirmed the right of unmarried girls who were not legally emancipated and who had reached the age of eighteen to consent to their own contraceptive care; and in nineteen states they could clearly do so at considerably younger ages or with no age restriction at all, according to a recent national survey (see Table VIII-I).

The survey was supported by the National Center for Family Planning Services, Health Services and Mental Health Administration, Department of Health, Education and Welfare. It examined federal and state laws and state health and welfare department policies affecting contraception, family planning, voluntary sterilization, and contraceptive and general health services to minors. The study was conducted by Planned Parenthood's Center for Family Planning Program Development.

The survey found a strong trend in recent years for states to pass legislation giving minors access to effective birth control ser-

* Reprinted from the November, 1972 issue of *Family Planning Digest,* a publication of the National Center for Family Planning Services, Health Services and Mental Health Administration, U. S. Department of Health, Education and Welfare. Based on a study prepared pursuant to Contract No. HSM 110-71-271 between the Center for Family Planning Program Development, the Technical Assistance Division of Planned Parenthood-World Population, and the National Center for Family Planning Services and Mental Health Administration, U. S. Department of Health, Education and Welfare. The Project Director for the study was Attorney Harriet F. Pilpel. Numerous important developments have taken place in this field since 1972. For example, the Utah decision with respect to the constitutional right of minors to contraceptive sources discussed in the article was revised by the Utah Supreme Court in 1973.

TABLE VIII-I
AGE OF CONSENT

(Ages under 21 at which state legislation, court action, Attorneys General's opinions, and Health and Welfare Department policies affirm the right of certain categories of minors to consent for their own medical treatment for medical care in general, for contraceptive services and for examination and treatment for pregnancy and venereal disease; and age of majority if under 21.)

State	Age (Majority is 21)	May Consent for Medical Care in General — No Limitation	May Consent for Medical Care in General — Married or Emancipated	May Consent for Medical Care in General — In Emergency	May Consent for: Contraception	May Consent for: Pregnancy Connected Care	May Consent for: VD Care	Policy for Contraception — Health Department	Policy for Contraception — Welfare Department
Ala.	19, MF	14	E[9], M	X		X	X	X	
Alaska	18				11, 12	15[17]	X	19	19
Ariz.	18, F		E, M	X[10]			X	18	18
Ark.	18 & M[2]			X			X	18, F[23]	18, F
Calif.			15, E[6], M	X	15[13]	X	12	X	X
Colo.	18	18	15, E[6], M		X[3]		X	X	X
Conn.	18	18	E, M				X[18]	18[26]	25
Del.	M		E, M			12	12	18[23]	X
Fla.		18[3]	E, M	X	X[20]		X		
Ga.			M[3]	X	XF[3, 14]	X[14]	X	X	X
Hawaii	20					14	14	20	20
Idaho	18F						14	18, F[23]	X
Ill.	18[1]	18	M[7]	X	X[15]	X	12	X	X
Ind.			E, M	X			X	25	
Iowa	M		E, M	X			16	25	X[22]
Kans.	18 & M[1]	X[4], 16[5]	E, M[8]	X	12	X	X	18[22]	
Ky.	18		E, M[8]	X	X[3, 14]	X[14]	X	18	18
La.	M	X[21]	M	X	12		X		
Maine	18		E	X			X	18[23, 24]	18
Md.		18	M[8]	X	X[3]	X	X	X	23

State									
Mich.	18	X[4]	E, M	X	12		X[19]	—[25]	18
Minn.			E[6], M[8]	X			X	X	X
Miss.		X[4]	E, M	X	X[16]	X[14]	X	—[25]	X
Mo.			E, M[8]			X[14]	X	—[24]	18
Mont.	19		E, M[7]		12	X	X	19[23]	19
Nebr.	20, M	M	M				X	—[25]	X
Nev.	18F	X[4]	E, M	X[10]			X	18F[23]	X
N. H.		18	E, M[7]			X	14	X	18
N. J.	18						X	—[25]	X
N. Mex.	18		E, M	X[10]	12	X[17]	X		X
N. Y.	18	18	E, M[8]	X			X	—[25]	X
N. C.	18	18	E, M	X			X	—[25]	X
N. D.	18		E, M				14	18	18
Ohio		X[4]					X	—[25] X	
Okla.	18F	15	E, M	X	12		X	18F	18F[23,24]
Oreg.	18[1], M	18	M		15[14]	X	12	X	
Pa.	18		E[9], M	16, M			X	—[25]	X
R. I.			E	X			X		
S. C.		16	E, M				X	X	
S. D.	18		E, M		X[3]		X	18	18
Tenn.	18			X			X	X	18
Tex.	M		M	X			X		X
Utah	18F, M		E, M			X	X	18F	18F
Vt.	18	18	E, M				12	—[25]	X
Va.	18	18[3]	E		X[3,14]	X[14]	X	X	X
Wash.	18	18	E	X	12		14	X	X
W. Va.	18			X			X	X	X
Wis.	18		E, M				12	—[25]	
Wyo.	19[2]			12	12	X	X[19]	—[25]	X
D. C.				X	X			X	X
Number of states	35	20	40	27	12	20	49	32	36

Note: The fact that no affirmative legislation, court decision, or attorney general's opinion or policy has been found in a particular state does not mean that it is not permissible in that state to provide contraceptive services to some categories of minors on their own consent. For example, it is likely that every state would recognize the right of emancipated and married minors to consent to receive services and of the physician to render services without parental consent in an emergency; and health and welfare departments do, in almost all cases, offer services to minors on their own consent if they are emancipated and/or married.

M = married, F = female, E = emancipated, X = any age.

(Continued page 234)

1. For purposes of signing contracts.
2. As of May 25, 1973.
3. Excluding voluntary sterilization.
4. If mature enough to understand the nature and consequences of the treatment. See discussion in text of the mature minor doctrine. This is a new doctrine and the fact that there is no case or statute in a state affirming it does not mean that it would not be accepted in that state.
5. If parent not immediately available.
6. Emancipated defined as living apart from parents and managing own financial affairs.
7. And/or pregnant.
8. Or parent.
9. Emancipated defined as a high school graduate, a parent, or pregnant.
10. If no parent available, others may consent in loco parentis.
11. Information only.
12. Comprehensive family planning law permits (or does not exclude) services to minors without parental consent.
13. If a present or potential welfare recipient.
14. Excluding abortion.
15. If referred by clergyman, physician or Planned Parenthood or if failure to provide such services would create a serious health hazard.
16. If referred by clergyman, physician, family planning clinic, school or institution of higher learning, or any state or local government agency.
17. Examination only.
18. In public health agencies, public or private hospitals or clinics.
19. In publicly maintained facilities.
20. If married or pregnant or may suffer, in the opinion of the physician, probable health hazards if such services are not provided. Surgical services excluded.
21. If minor is or believes himself to be afflicted with an illness or disease.
22. But parental consent desirable.
23. If had out-of-wedlock children.
24. If had previous pregnancy.
25. Policy locally determined.
26. Or if head of a family.
27. Except for an operation not essential to health or life.

vices on their own consent and initiative. While states do not expressly prohibit the provision of contraceptives to minors, young people have often had great difficulty in obtaining medical contraceptive services because of the old common law rule requiring the consent of a parent or guardian before a doctor could treat a minor for anything. Doctors felt that to treat minors without such consent might expose them to suits for technical assault or malpractice, making them liable for damages and possibly to criminal charges as well.

There were always exceptions to the old common law rule, such as emergency treatment and treatment of legally emancipated minors.* What is more, no case has been found in which either a doctor or a layman has been successfully prosecuted criminally or held liable for damages for providing contraception to a minor without parental consent. Nevertheless, doctors, hospitals, and health agencies have been reluctant to proceed without specific legal protection.

The survey found that states in recent years have been providing such specific legal protection, both through legislative enactments and court decisions. Increasingly, the survey found that "the federal government and the states have recognized the rights of mature minors to make their own decisions about their lives generally and about their medical care in particular."

The courts and state legislatures were found to "have gotten away from the old common law rule . . . through the exception for emergency medical treatment of minors . . . the doctrine of the emancipated minor and by new exceptions for the mature minor and the abused and neglected minor. In addition, numerous statutes have been enacted giving broad categories of minors the right to consent to medical services in general and to contraceptive services in particular."

---

* Marriage and entering into military service have been held to emancipate minors in almost all states, and minors are generally deemed emancipated if they live apart from their parents, support themselves, and control their own lives. In some states minors are held emancipated if they live apart from their parents even though their parents still support them. Other states have held that minors are emancipated even though they live with their parents if they work and keep some of their own earnings or make most of the major decisions affecting their lives.

So far as emergency treatment of minors is concerned, courts throughout the country have held that a physician need not wait to obtain parental consent where an emergency endangers the life or health of a minor. Twelve states have codified this principle into statutes. Contraceptive services might fall into the emergency category, the study suggested, if "failure to provide . . . service is likely to result in a pregnancy" which may endanger the life or health of the minor or the child who might be born. Support for this argument, the study pointed out, may be found in numerous data documenting the increased risk to the life and health of mother and baby of births to teenagers.

EMANCIPATION

Some states protect doctors who treat minors from liability if they reasonably rely on the minors' representation that they are emancipated even if this turns out not to be true. Since minors may be partially emancipated for particular purposes, including consent to medical services, the study indicates they may, in some circumstances, be partially emancipated to give consent for contraceptive services.

MATURE MINOR RULE

A more recent exception to the common law rule has become known as the "mature minor rule" and provides that a minor can effectively consent to medical treatment for himself if he understands the nature of the treatment and it is for his benefit. This rule has been incorporated into the Mississippi statute and, in effect, has been recognized by the New Hampshire legislature. Kansas, Ohio, New York, Michigan, and Washington courts have also acknowledged this rule in regard to medical treatment of minors.

Almost all states, the survey found, have statutes which provide for medical treatment of neglected or abused children, usually holding that the courts may order medical care for such children where the child's health, safety, or welfare requires it.

At least eleven states (California, Colorado, Florida, Georgia, Illinois, Kentucky, Maryland, Mississippi, Oregon, Tennessee, and Virginia) and the District of Columbia have enacted statutes specifically authorizing doctors to give birth control service without parental consent to all minors or to broad categories of minors. Eleven other states have laws authorizing publicly sponsored family planning programs which may permit services to at least some minors without parental consent. In seven of these states (Iowa, Michigan, Nevada, New York, Ohio, West Virginia, and Wyoming), the health or welfare departments report provision of contraceptive services to minors without parental consent (see Table VIII-I).

Since passage of the twenty-sixth amendment allowing eighteen-year-olds to vote, there has also been a strong nationwide trend to reduce the age of majority to eighteen. The survey pointed out that Arkansas, Idaho, Nevada, Oklahoma, and Utah had long differentiated between men and women, providing by statute that women reached majority at eighteen, men at twenty-one. But more recent statutes have reduced the age of majority to eighteen for both sexes in eighteen states (Arizona, Connecticut, Delaware, Illinois, Kentucky, Maine, Michigan, New Jersey, New Mexico, North Carolina, North Dakota, South Dakota, Tennessee, Vermont, Virginia, Washington, West Virginia, and Wisconsin). Alaska, Montana, and Wyoming have lowered the age of majority to nineteen, and Nebraska to twenty. In Delaware, Illinois, and Oregon, eighteen-year-olds may now enter into binding contracts; while a Washington statute provides that all persons of eighteen are deemed of full age for most purposes, including consent to medical services.

In addition, eleven states (Colorado, Connecticut, Georgia, Illinois, Maryland, New Jersey, New York, North Carolina, Pennsylvania, Virginia, and Washington) have specifically reduced the age of consent to medical services to eighteen. It has been reduced to sixteen in South Carolina, to fifteen in Oregon, and to fourteen in Alabama. In Louisiana, a minor of any age may consent to medical treatment if he believes himself to be ill. In Kansas, a sixteen-year-old may consent to medical care when no parent is available; and in Mississippi, Ohio, Michigan, and New Hampshire any minor may consent who is "mature." Twelve states (Alabama, California, Colorado, Georgia, Illinois, Kentucky, Louisiana, Maryland, Minnesota, Mississippi, North Carolina, and Pennsylvania) have enacted statutes regarding comprehensive medical care of minors.

One of the first areas of state action permitting minors to consent to their own medical care was for diagnosis and treatment of venereal disease. Forty-eight states and the District of Columbia now permit minors to consent for their own VD care. In more than half of these states, enabling legislation has been enacted since 1968 and, according to the survey, similar developments in the law giving all minors the right to consent to contraceptive services seem in process, supported, as in the cases of the VD legislation, by medical endorsement from such groups as the American Medical Association, the American College of Obstetricians and Gynecologists, the American Academy of Pediatrics, and the American Academy of Family Physicians. Most recently, the U. S. Commission on Population Growth and the American Future strongly endorsed state legislation giving teenagers the same right to consent to contraceptive services as is enjoyed by adults.

At least seventeen states now provide specifically that minors may consent to medical and surgical treatment related to pregnancy. While this has been held by a court in at least one state to include therapeutic abortion, it is not clear to what extent "treatment related to pregnancy" will be construed to include contraception, i.e. the prevention of pregnancy. The one judicial statement found on this question was that the prevention of pregnancy is not included.

The survey found no case in which a doctor was held liable for providing contraceptive services to a minor without parental consent, and no case holding him liable for supplying *any* medical service to a minor without parental consent where the minor was older than fifteen and the treatment was for the minor's benefit and performed with the minor's consent. Neither did the survey find any case where a doctor or health facility treating a minor without parental consent was prosecuted for assault or for endangering the welfare of a minor. Two cases where laymen were charged with distributing or displaying contraceptives to minors were held without merit. In sum, the authors of the study found that there seems little likelihood of prosecution of physicians or other authorized persons who provide minors with contraceptive information or services.

The survey found that twenty-eight states have statutory provisions regarding confidentiality of at least some medical services to minors (mostly pertaining to VD treatment). Four provide that the physician who treats a minor must notify the parents and sixteen specify that he *may* notify them. Most states, however, do not have statutes applicable to the confidentiality of contraceptive services to minors and provide no clear guide for the physician as to the extent to which he may or must respect the confidence of the minor for whom he provides contraceptive services.

The survey pointed to decisions by the U. S. Supreme Court and lower courts that children are "persons" within the meaning of the Bill of Rights. Only in one such case, in Utah, however, has there been a specific determination that minors fourteen and older have a constitutional right to request and consent to medical contraceptive services.

The survey found that thirty-seven state health agencies and the District of Columbia had some type of written or unwritten policy on eligibility of minors for family planning services. Seventeen of these states and the District of Columbia authorized services to minors of any age on their own consent (see Table VIII-I). The rest imposed restrictions based on age, marital, previous pregnancy or parenthood status or left determination to local jurisdictions. Similarly, welfare departments in twenty-one states and the District of Columbia indicated that they provided medical services or referrals to all minors without restrictions, while thirty states imposed restrictions of varying kinds.

In Massachusetts and Wisconsin, welfare policy barred services to unmarried persons, apparently on the basis of state statutes. The Massachusetts law has since been declared unconstitutional by the U. S. Supreme Court—a decision which would appear to cast doubt on the constitutionality of the Wisconsin law also. Connecticut and Maryland forbid all services to unmarried, unemancipated persons, on the basis of administrative policies which appear to be inconsistent with the federal regulations, according to the survey.

The survey found that social eligibility requirements mandating that persons be of "a stated age, be married, have children, have been pregnant, or give evidence of venereal disease . . . severely limit access to family planning services to certain types of minors." It found that the trend toward removal of such restrictions by state legislatures, health departments, and welfare agencies shows that state officials increasingly have come to realize that such restrictions do not have the intended result of discouraging behavior regarded as undesirable, but rather expose minors to the manifold risks of unexpected or unwanted pregnancy. (For a related story, see "28 Percent Had Sex; Half Risk Pregnancy," *Family Planning Digest,* Vol. 1, No. 5, 1972, p. 6.)

BIBLIOGRAPHY

National Center for Family Planning Services, HSMHA, DHEW, *Contraception, Family Planning and Voluntary Sterilization: Laws and Policies of the United States, Each State and Jurisdiction* (U. S. Government Printing Office, Washington, D. C., 1972, in press) .
Family Planning Reporter, Vol. 1, No. 1, 1972.

CHAPTER IX

BRINGING ABOUT CHANGE: A NATIONAL OVERVIEW WITH RESPECT TO EARLY CHILDBEARING AND CHILDREARING

Marion Howard

W HENEVER A CONCENTRATED effort to effect social change meets with reasonable success, there is a question as to whether the change (1) would have come about without intervention, (2) would have occurred but would have taken much longer, or (3) came about due to the effort. The examination and synthesization of the complex factors that contribute to specific social change is difficult. Even when such analysis is undertaken, the results rarely satisfy those who are knowledgeable about the change since versions of what occurred and how it occurred often vary widely.

As director of a national research utilization and information sharing project aimed at achieving social (primarily, institutional) change with respect to school-age pregnant girls, I was very close to one of the more interesting and exciting areas of social change that took place in the 1960's. The fact that it did take place and is still proceeding has been a source of gratification and also a certain amount of wonderment. The following is a partial analysis of some of the changes that occurred.

THE PROBLEM

Looking at the problem of school-age pregnancy early in the 1960's from the perspective of today is almost like looking into another century. Pregnant school-age girls throughout our history have had little or no help from society. Their treatment has been not only neglectful but often punitive. The two most meaningful institutions in the life of a young girl—the family and the school system—have often been harsh and unresponsive.

Within the family context, pregnancy out-of-wedlock has been held to be a shameful occurrence spelling ruination for the girl. In some areas of the country, for example, mothers still tell comprehensive service program personnel, "My daughter's been spoilt." In the past, to avoid total condemnation by society, girls were most often hastily married by their families, often with little or no regard as to whether the marriage was suitable or appropriate. Even in the late sixties as high as 60 percent of all girls giving birth under the age of eighteen were married by the time the child was born even though very few were married at the time of conception. Looking at divorce statistics it is not difficult to understand that, although an immediate solution, ultimately this was no solution at all since more than 50 percent of such girls were divorced within five years. Although an unknown number of families undoubtedly helped their daughters obtain abortions, other girls were sent away from and by their families —many of them hidden in maternity homes to give birth with the expectation they would return without their child and act as if nothing had happened.

School systems have been equally horrified by adolescent pregnancy. Until changes came about in the 1960's, banishment was the almost universal policy of school systems. As soon as it was found that the girl was pregnant, she was excluded from school and was not encouraged to return following the birth of the baby. The result was a young adult with incomplete education and little or no job potential. The banishment from school was not based just on an out-of-wedlock pregnancy. Married students becoming pregnant incurred similar penalties. Marriage itself was at times a cause for dismissal. If married students were allowed to remain in school, they were minimally excluded from extracurricular activities.

However, other institutions or systems that touched on the life of the pregnant girl were also negligent or punitive. Health care systems were rarely sympathetic to the plight of the young pregnant girl. Parental consent was required before the girl could be tested to determine if she was indeed pregnant. Prenatal care was not given without parental consent. Fear of parental disapproval or fear of public disclosure leading to punitive actions, such as dismissal from school, led many girls to hide their pregnancy. They were thus prevented from obtaining essential early health care. Even with parental consent, birth control was not usually available to adolescents. Further, for those girls under health care, the hostile attitudes of health staff often made a frightening confusing experience even more so for the young patients. Prenatal, postpartum, delivery care were many times handled in an unfeeling manner. "If they suffer enough, they'll know not to do it again." "Let them pay for their mistakes."

Social service institutions responded primarily to the girls who wanted to place their baby in adoption. As with the maternity homes, once the baby was placed, the mother was usually dropped from service. There was no continuing follow-through to help her reintegrate into society, get back into or stay in the educational mainstream, find employment or job training, or prevent further unwanted pregnancies. Most importantly, the highest proportion of young mothers kept their babies. The majority of these received little or no professional counseling at all. These mothers—the ones most in need of follow-through services—were the least likely to have access to them.

Thus rejected by family, isolated from peers, ostracized by the school system, barely tolerated by the medical establishment, and mostly ignored by the social service system, it is no wonder that young mothers showed up so disproportionately in a negative way in divorce, health, educational, employment, and welfare statistics. Indeed society had been reaping the rewards of its own neglect and hostility.

THE SOCIAL CONTEXT

For the first half of this century the situation with respect to school-age pregnant girls in the United States remained relatively static. Then in the 1960's, a number of significant changes occurred. The Federal Government launched a substantial effort to see that the nation was made aware of the problem of early childbearing and childrearing and the consequences of neglect in this area. States passed legislation and changed policies dealing with the subject and communities initiated special multiservice programs for pregnant adolescents. What caused this change after decades of neglect?

In order to fully appreciate what occurred, it is useful first to examine the context within which these changes took place. Several important movements gained momentum in the early sixties —women's liberation, the sexual revolution, civil rights, student rights, consumer control, concern about population growth coupled with technological advances in birth control, and demand for day care services. Many of these movements were interrelated and influenced one another. They also contributed to the movement with respect to dealing with adolescent childbearing and childrearing and were in turn influenced by it.

What is now called women's liberation was in general a reexamination of the rights and roles of women in society. Inequities in relation to both position and pay for women in the work force were pointed out. In particular, the large numbers of women who suffered under this system and yet were the sole support of their families gave testimony to the greater need to prepare women for careers outside the home and to prepare the business world to accept them fairly. The fact that school-age mothers were systematically denied an education when it was clear that many of them would be expected to support their children either immediately or within a few short years became an issue.

A further issue was raised by the fact that young women who became pregnant were forced to leave school on discovery of their pregnancy while the young men who caused the pregnancy were allowed to remain in school. While society spoke of this as "boys will be boys" and appeared to applaud a male youth sowing a few wild oats so he could be properly considered a man, the girl involved was viewed as disgraced, shamed, and unfit for peer companionship. As part of the consciousness raising efforts made by women's liberationists, this was cited as yet another example of a discrimination based on sex in our society. Thus such policies came in for a reexamination.

Distinctly separate yet interacting with women's liberation was the so-called sexual revolution. In the sixties the "new freedom" allowed people to talk about sex more freely, to consider openly the naturalness of its existence. There was an increased interest in bringing out into the open what was really going on. Surveys indicated the traditional male preference for marrying only a virgin had altered. Attitudes toward sexual experimentation outside marriage became more realistic and more relaxed. Studies of the incidence of sexual activity among younger age groups were made. Among other things, they revealed that the discrimination against the pregnant girl was grossly unfair in that her sexual activity was not an isolated incident but symptomatic of the experimentation in which many young people were engaging. Public awareness of a rising venereal disease rate also contributed to the new ability to think and talk about pregnancy in adolescence and possible solutions.

Beginning in the fifties and continuing into the sixties, the civil rights movement impressed on public consciousness the inequities of our society with respect to various racial groups. The war on poverty and the Great Society programs of the sixties were in part a response to this. They attempted to provide minority groups with the kind of care and services that would bring them into the mainstream of the "good life." One area of concern was that of the poor pregnancy outcomes associated with the lack of basic health education, nutrition, and sound health care services among the poor. Since the younger the pregnant girl the greater the health risk, and since the greatest proportion of those giving birth under age sixteen were members of minority groups, it became apparent that some priority for service had to be assigned to adolescent pregnant girls, particularly those from low income homes.

The apparent discrimination, that allowed the girls from middle and upper class homes to afford abortions or go away to maternity homes where they could receive excellent health care, continuing education, and counseling services while girls from poor homes and/or minority groups lived at home with no services, was exposed. Agencies that gave service only to middle class girls or those poor whites most likely to place their babies, while making no effort to develop adoptive homes for babies of minority group girls, also came under scrutiny.

Another movement of the 1960's that affected and was affected by the area of adolescent pregnancy was that of student rights. Following the historic Supreme Court decision which affirmed the legal rights of minors, a new era opened up. In general, the relationships between young people and the institutions that came into contact with or served them came in for reexamination. Test cases, such as those concerned with whether or not male students had the right to wear long hair or certain style clothes in school, took place around the country. Exclusion of young mothers and pregnant schoolage girls from school thus was bound to be one of the issues to come to the attention of those interested in student rights. Two landmark cases—one in Mississippi which assured that young mothers could return to school (Perry vs. the Grenada Municipal Separate School District) and one in Massachusetts in which a young mother retained the right to remain in school while pregnant (Ordway vs. Hargraves) were the natural outcomes of this movement.

The trend toward consumer control came out of the civil rights movement. This was a basic attempt to secure the rights of those receiving services to participate in the decision-making about what services were given and how they were given. Federal legislation requiring client participation in various kinds of policy-making bodies in some of its programs gave this movement status. One of the results of the general movement was that service delivery was rethought and more of those giving service were sensitized to and/or trained in an understanding of how to deal with the consumer in more constructive ways. Out of this area in part came the awareness that adolescents receiving what had heretofore been thought of as adult services—prenatal care, delivery, postpartum care, birth control services—could not and should not be treated in the same manner as older women. It became clear that, in order for the services to be used successfully, they had to be delivered in age-appropriate ways. Sensitivity to the needs of clients led to specialized adolescent clinics and other health programs for youth.

Growing interest in and concern about the lack of day care services also peaked in the 1960's. The press of women for day care services, particularly women who were heads of households, women on welfare, and those who otherwise had pressures to work, grew during the sixties. Among the examples of those for whom day care seemed essential were school-age pregnant girls. Without such care, in many cases, they could not return to and complete school. Although the effects of group infant day care services on the infants were just being studied at the beginning of the sixties, pressures to set up or find such services for adolescent parents were such that near the end of the sixties more infant day care centers were being operated to meet the needs of school-age parents than of any other single category of consumers.

One of the most important movements to affect the area of school-age pregnancy was that of concern about over-population coupled with technological advances in conception control. The fact that something could be done about undesired or unwanted pregnancies through relatively simple safe birth control methods allowed people to more openly discuss child spacing, limitation of family size and determining the beginning of family life. Federal support of family planning added impetus to this consideration. Thus it was natural that the often inappropriate and most often unplanned pregnancies of adolescents would come under discussion. Beginning with attempts to prevent repeated pregnancies among adolescents who had already born one child, by the latter part of the decade open efforts at primary prevention were being discussed and implemented.

THE NATIONAL THRUST

Because these tides of change which swelled in the early sixties were so interrelated with and had such a direct impact on the area under discussion, it could be argued that the changes in policy and practice that occurred with respect to school-age pregnant girls were the natural outcome of such events. On the other hand, there is no assurance that public awareness of or interest in any given area necessarily leads to changes in policies and practices.* It is unlikely that the number of comprehensive programs for pregnant school-age girls would have developed naturally

---

* For example, due to rising crime rates and the assassination of nationally prominent persons, opinion polls in the late sixties showed the public to favor some kind of gun control but no such law was passed.

from the tides of change. Even if they had, there is doubt that they would necessarily have developed in the early stages of these movements as opposed to occurring long after these movements had passed their peak.

It is clear from history that there is a wide gap between knowledge in existence and knowledge in practice. All too often research studies which have utilizable conclusions sit on the shelf unread and unimplemented. Therefore one of the more interesting facts concerning the history of the development of programs for school-age pregnant girls is that a successful research and demonstration program to provide services for this population was launched by the Federal Government followed by a national effort to implement its findings. Before describing that effort, it will be helpful to review the Federal Government's interest in adolescent pregnancy and how this interest ran parallel to, but was to some degree quite different from, what has been referred to as the ground-swell reasons for change.

The Federal Government probably became involved in the area of early childbearing because (1) data indicated in the early 1960's that despite our being the richest nation on earth, the infant mortality rate of this nation was higher than that of a score of other nations and that the young age of many of those giving birth in this country contributed substantially to that rate; (2) the country was becoming increasingly angry about the large welfare burden it was carrying, particularly as in the public's mind it was erroneously connected with illegitimacy;* (3) the nation's school dropout rate was a source of concern and dissatisfaction to those in the Federal Government, particularly as there were few jobs for young people who dropped out of school. Studies indicated that lack of education led to underemployment, unemployment, and welfare dependency. Data showed that pregnancy was the major known cause of school dropouts among young women.

Thus the Federal Government had three concerns about the

---

* Although a high proportion of school-age mothers were married, data did show that a disproportionate number of those giving birth at school age entered the welfare rolls later.

negative effects of early childbearing and childrearing which fell
into the traditional categories of health, education, and welfare.
In an effort to see whether or not impact could be made to effect
better results in the lives of school-age mothers, a demonstration
and research program which provided comprehensive health, education, and social services to pregnant school-age girls in the District of Columbia was begun. Based in the public schools but involving cooperation from the local health and welfare departments, the program provided continuing education during pregnancy. This was done in the hope that following the birth of the
baby the girls would be more inclined to complete high school,
achieve independence, and have the capacity to become self-
supporting. The program also provided health care during pregnancy in an effort to produce a healthier mother and infant.
Through the provision of social services it was hoped sufficient
impact could be made on the girls' lives and problems so as to
prevent repetition of pregnancy and to foster the development
of a satisfactory life for both mother and child. The degree of
improvement in the outcomes of enrolled girls when contrasted
with those of girls not in the program encouraged the Government sufficiently to finance an effort to share this knowledge with
other communities struggling with similar problems.

With initial funding from the Maternal and Child Health
Grants Program of the Children's Bureau, a consortium effort
was developed among Yale University, the University of Pitts-
burgh, and George Washington University to promote nationwide development and improvement of comprehensive service
programs for school-age pregnant girls. Based in Washington,
D. C., this project was first known as the Cyesis Programs Consortium and later as the Consortium on Early Childbearing and
Childrearing. Its focus was research utilization and information
sharing among those concerned with the problems of adolescent
childbearing.

The project's initial thrust was confined largely to those already involved in or concerned with the problems of early childbearing. The purpose was to see that those operating in the field
were using the most recent research findings in their efforts, were

aware of the comprehensive service program model that had been developed, and had channels through which to share clinical findings as they emerged. Later the thrust was extended to informing those who were not actively involved in the area in an attempt to gain interest and support for the movement, to remove inhibiting restrictions on the pregnant adolescent, and to develop new and meaningful services for young families.

To accomplish these objectives both outreach and reactive mechanisms were used. Reactive mechanisms included developing a project capability for responding to community requests for information and technical assistance. Knowledgeable practitioners in the various fields associated with programs providing services to pregnant adolescents—obstetricians, social workers, educators, pediatricians, community organizers, nurses, and others—were identified and used either singly or in teams as nonresident consultants to states, communities, and various gatherings. These persons were not paid for their time but were reimbursed for travel expenses. The project thus, in part, relied on the good will and dedication of the professionals in the field to promote change. Their generous sharing of talent and expertise was one of the most important elements in the project's early success when its funds were very limited.

Project staff (at first primarily the project director and later specialists in areas such as child development) also provided consultation on request by responding either through the mail, by telephone, or on site. Materials thought to be useful to those practicing in the field were developed and made available without charge. Useful articles published in the health, education, and social welfare fields were reprinted as part of this strategy. In addition, a newsletter, *Sharing*, summarizing information about the provision of services to school-age pregnant girls, was published periodically.

The requests for information and help received by the project were used in part as guidelines for what was needed in the field. When possible the project tried to build its responses into its activities. For example, when a number of communities asked about what books or films were helpful to pregnant adolescents, it conducted a survey of audiovisual materials in use by the comprehensive service programs and then distributed the information through *Sharing*. When unable to incorporate necessary activities in its own work, the project tried to interest others in picking up some of the responsibility.

Outreach mechanisms included developing project capability for creating public and professional awareness with respect to both the high risks of adolescent childbearing and childrearing and the need for developing programs to reduce such risks.

Small workshops aimed at widening the knowledge base of those actively involved with or planning to be involved with services to pregnant girls and young families were held. Larger conferences were opened to a broader base group yet still retained the aim of informing those who had the capacity for influencing change. Efforts were made to stimulate articles in such magazines as *Life, Reader's Digest,* and *Seventeen*. When possible, articles written by project staff were published in magazines and journals aimed at reaching professional audiences such as *Clinical Obstetrics and Gynecology, Journal of School Health, Today's Education, American Education,* the *Family Planner,* and *Children*. The staff also presented papers at various meetings and conferences—for example, the Minnesota State Welfare Association, the American Orthopsychiatric Association and talked with special groups such as the Health and Welfare Councils of St. Paul, Minnesota and Tulsa, Oklahoma. Mass mailings (for example, one mailing went to every school system in the United States serving 10,000 or more pupils) were undertaken. Such mailings informed school systems and other community organizations of the problem and what other communities were doing about it. Inquiries were made as to whether they or their communities had plans to undertake or already had undertaken action in this area.

Although the research utilization and information sharing thrust was funded by the Federal Government to acquaint practitioners with the latest developments in the field and to stimulate their use of them, efforts were also made to encourage a greater commitment on the part of the Government to use its power and prestige to help communities solve problems related to adolescent childbearing and childrearing. It was felt that guidelines for funds and services available through a number of different federal programs could be amended to specify or interpreted to include pregnant school-age girls. (Often girls eligible for services or programs eligible for funding in one part of the country were denied such eligibility in other parts of the country.) It was also felt that certain Federal programs (such as those aimed at reducing infant mortality and morbidity, preventing unwanted pregnancies, reducing school dropouts, or providing rehabilitative services such as vocational training in a counseling-oriented framework) should give some priority for service to the young parent or potential young parent.

A major boost was given to both the research utilization effort and the commitment of the Federal Government when in September 1971, the then Secretary of the Department of Health, Education, and Welfare, Elliot Richardson, approved an enlarged information and technical assistance effort to bring more school-age parents under nationwide comprehensive services. This led to expansion of the Consortium on Early Childbearing and Childrearing (the research utilization and information sharing project) and the establishment of a Federal in-house effort to coordinate and improve the use of the Department of Health, Education, and Welfare's funds with respect to school-age pregnant girls and young families.

ACTION AT THE COMMUNITY LEVEL

Although the effectiveness of the research utilization and information sharing project effort has yet to be thoroughly evaluated, some measures of its usefulness can be made. For example by the fourth year of its existence, requests for assistance were pouring into the project at the rate of ten to twenty a day, many of them the result of referrals by others who had contacted the project. A more concrete measure is found in the fact that, by the end of the first five years of the project's existence, close to 250 communities had set up multiservice programs for pregnant school-age girls—a growth rate of almost one a week. Many of these programs were copied after the first model developed. Others, although varying in program format, indicated they had been influenced by the thinking that came out of the model and its evaluation. A high proportion cited material or substantive matter developed by the research utilization project in their own program literature.

Ripple effects of the project's activity may also be found in the vast numbers of positive changes made in policies and practices of local school systems with respect to allowing pregnant girls either to remain in their regular schools or participate in meaningful educational alternatives. Changes also occurred in policies and practices of local health departments with respect to loosening or dropping requirements for parental consent with respect to pregnancy testing, prenatal care, and birth control services for young people. Liberal education and health laws were also passed in some states. Back-up information, provided by the project to school systems, health departments, and state legislatures as they considered making such changes, is known in many cases to have been helpful.

Despite the obvious impact of the research utilization and information sharing project, it would be highly suspect to assume that a federally funded effort which did not have direct programmatic funding, could solely bring about the kind of far-reaching changes that occurred with respect to attitudes about and programs related to pregnancy in adolescence. The effort could obviously initiate changes in some areas and could help them along in others, but in some instances it could only uncover what changes were taking or had taken place and publicize them.

In other words there is some evidence to support the contention that many of the kinds of change that came about were the natural outcome of social movements. However, we have also seen that a federally funded project, riding on the climate of social readiness created by these movements, undertook to bring about predetermined kinds of change with respect to adolescent childbearing and childrearing. Since the results achieved approximate what was attempted, it can also be argued that the project was a major cause of the change. There is additional evidence, however, that some comprehensive service programs for pregnant school-age girls would have evolved without the federally funded project.* One effect of the project on these programs may have been to speed their development. In some cases it may also have helped to improve either their conceptual framework or their service design and delivery, but it is clear that in some cases the project had little or no effect.

To understand this position takes some awareness of how the comprehensive service programs developed in many communities. There are almost as many varieties of programs, foci of services, and methods of funding as there are programs. Basically, however, all the comprehensive service programs for school-age pregnant girls have three common elements: (1) early and consistent prenatal care and postpartum and pediatric health services are given to improve the health of mothers and infants, (2) continuing education during pregnancy and following the birth of the baby is given on a classroom basis to assure uninterrupted education, and (3) counseling on a group and individual basis is given to help solve problems that either may have led to or been caused by the pregnancy.

These three elements generally come in the form of program components—that is, the services are available to those enrolled in the program and considered part of program services, but they can all be offered in different locations, under different auspices. For example, education classes may be provided by the school system in a regular school building, while health services may be offered by the health department in a maternity clinic near the school and social services by a family and children's services agency in their own offices. Another program may be organized in such a way that education classes taught by teachers provided by the school system are held in a hospital, where counseling by the hospital social service staff along with prenatal care by the hospital physician and nursing staff can be provided. In some cases a YWCA houses the education and social service components of the program, both provided by the school system, while

---

* For example, the District of Columbia research and demonstration comprehensive service program model, which antedated the research utilization project, received many inquiries in its first years and similar programs were started almost immediately.

health care is given at various public and private locations throughout the city.

Some programs use the small center approach. Several locations throughout the city or county are used to offer special education classes that often tie in closely with health and social services. San Francisco, California, has most of its six special services centers for pregnant school-age girls in various hospitals around the city, while Los Angeles, California bought mobile classrooms and moved them onto the grounds of health department clinics to facilitate health care. The greatest number of programs, however, use one center both for education and for the provision of most of the social services. At times health services are given there as well (such as in Minneapolis, Minnesota, and Jackson, Mississippi), although often they are given either in one major clinic (Patterson, New Jersey) or at various locations throughout the city as in Baltimore, Maryland.

Central to all these programs is their ability to coordinate and integrate various community resources in such a way as to see that the basic education, health, and social service needs of school-age pregnant girls are met. A few of the programs have chosen to incorporate independently so that the coordinating body is not responsible to any community agency. More often, however, a key community agency—the school system, the health department and occasionally the welfare department, or other social service agency—takes responsibility for the coordination of the program. To a large degree these programs rely on some kind of agreement among agencies that the program is important and that they will provide staff or funds to see that the girls are served. A high proportion of the funding of such programs is thus donated or "in-kind" services. Cash funding is likely to be used to augment program coordination or to provide services not normally available to school-age pregnant girls in the community.

Such programs have been begun by communities in ways as diverse as the ways in which they are organized. In the early years of the development of such programs, it was often one person in the community who became interested in the problem of pregnancy in adolescence, took responsibility for interesting first his own agency in actively doing something about it, and then, through that agency's involvement, interested others. The motivated person varied from community to community. Because pregnant girls were classified as physically handicapped by the education departments of many states, sometimes the catalytic person was a homebound education teacher concerned about the isolation and lack of counseling of the girl she was tutoring. On the other hand, it was equally likely to be the school system's director of special education, who was overwhelmed by the numbers of pregnant girls to be served through the home-teaching program. Other people in the educational system, such as a board of education member, a school health director, or a director of guidance and counseling also turned up as program originators. Public health nurses, who made home visits and found many young girls at home after the birth of the baby with little or no support for mothering or for their own growth and development; obstetricians, concerned because in many cases the first time the girls saw a doctor was when they appeared in the hospital emergency room to deliver; group workers in YWCAs or agency social workers, who saw bored young mothers who should have been in school and were unable to find jobs due to their age and lack of training, also became program originators.

Who it was did not seem to matter so much as that they were able to involve the others required for starting such a program. Each of these persons was, to some degree, greeted with hostility or rejection from various parts of the community. Attitudes, such as "You're rewarding sin" and "You'll make it so attractive other girls will want to become pregnant," had to be dealt with in each community. Program originators had to stress repeatedly the various risks the young pregnant girl was facing and the fact that the community ultimately paid for this in human wastage as well as dollars and cents. In particular, they had to stress that education is a basic need of everyone—especially today. Education is not a commodity that can be used as a reward. Although their task eventually was made somewhat easier by the materials and information available from the research utilization project (in particular, information about what had been done in other communities), the amount of time, effort, and selling it took in each community to bring about the establishment of each comprehensive service program should not be underestimated.

It is interesting to know that the people who developed these programs many times were not paid. Even when service to the girls fell within their general jurisdiction, it was most often a labor of love squeezed from both professional and personal time that brought the programs into existence. As one program originator said, "In order to persuade my community to go along with our program, it took going on the 'fried chicken and green pea circuit'—that is, talking to every church group, Rotary Club, Lion's Club, or women's group that I could find. I spent lunch, evening, and weekend hours for months just getting community acceptance before I could even begin to set up the program." In one rural program, the future program director visited every doctor, minister, and almost all of the other community leaders she could think of before her pioneering program began.

SOLIDIFYING THE CHANGES

Programs that were once startlingly new and innovative are now being perfected and worked back into the fabric of the community in such a way that they become an accepted part of community service. The research utilization and information sharing project is typical in that from its original university base it has now come under the auspices of the Child Welfare League of America, a national body with a long history of interest in the problems of families, mothers in difficulty, and most of all children from families in need of help. In addition, a national membership group, the National Alliance Concerned with School-age Parents, is also emerging to play a watchdog role over the quality of programs and those local and national events which could help to bring about further changes in this area.

The message is clear—climate readiness, combined with effective national leadership able to learn from and communicate with concerned professional and lay persons on state and local levels, can bring about needed changes. A more complete description of the mix needed to accomplish such changes will have to await more definitive analysis but, based on the experience in the field of early childbearing and childrearing, we now know change can be brought about. That should give heart to all of us who are concerned with improvement in our society—particularly those interested in the prevention of adolescent pregnancy and in services to young families.

BIBLIOGRAPHY

Daniel, James: The case of the pregnant school girl. *Reader's Digest, 97*:581, September, 1970.

Girls under 18 can consent to birth control services in 40 percent of the states. *Family Planning Digest,* Vol. 1, No. 6, November 1972.

High school pregnancy. *Life,* Vol. 70, No. 12, April 2, 1971.

Holmes, Myra and Howard, Marion: How communities finance programs for pregnant school-age girls. Information series #2, Consortium on Early Childbearing and Childrearing, Washington, D. C., 1972.

Howard, Marion: Comprehensive community programs for the pregnant teenager. *Clin Obstet Gynecol,* Vol. 14, No. 2, June, 1971.

Howard, Marion: A discussion of state laws and local policies as they relate to education of pregnant school-age girls. Information Series #3, Consortium on Early Childbearing and Childrearing, Washington, D. C., 1972.

Howard, Marion: Model components of comprehensive programs for pregnant school-age girls. Consortium on Early Childbearing and Childrearing, Washington, D. C., 1972.

Howard, Marion: Pregnant school-age girls. *Journal of School Health,* September, 1971.

Howard, Marion: School continues for pregnant teenagers. *American Education,* Vol. 5, No. 1, January, 1969.

Howard, Marion: Teen-age parents. *Today's Education,* February, 1973.

Howard, Marion: The Webster School, a District of Columbia program for pregnant girls. Children's Bureau Research Reports #2, U. S. Department of Health, Education, and Welfare, 1968.

Howard, Marion and Eddinger, Lucy: Beginning a program for pregnant school-age girls. Information Series #1, Consortium on Early Childbearing and Childrearing, Washington, D. C., 1972.

Osofsky, Howard J., M.D.: *The Pregnant Teenager.* Springfield, Thomas, 1968.

Wurtz, Frances and Fergen, Geraldine: Boards still duck the problem of pregnant schoolgirls. *American School Board Journal,* April, 1970.

CHAPTER X

A COMPREHENSIVE SERVICE PROGRAM FOR SCHOOL-AGE PREGNANT GIRLS

Mrs. Lee Ryan and Mrs. Ruth Sharpe

HISTORICAL BACKGROUND

IN RECENT YEARS much attention has been focused on the problems of pregnant, unmarried teenagers. In 1968 in the United States, there were 339,200 out-of-wedlock births. Of these, about 82,000 were to girls under eighteen. These are the latest definite figures available on births out-of-wedlock, but in 1969, more than 200,000 school girls under eighteen, married and unmarried, had babies.[1] In Chicago, 10,216 girls under the age of eighteen had babies during 1971.

Since the early 1960's this group has shown a steady gain, with the largest numbers coming from the disadvantaged nonwhite communities. A significant statistical fact related to this problem is that in the City of Chicago from September 1961 to August 1962, 680 pregnant girls, the majority of whom were under sixteen, the compulsory school age, were reported excluded from public schools. Less than 30 percent of the girls excluded from school because of pregnancy returned after enforced absence.[2] (The policy of Chicago Board of Education was changed effective May 1972, so that pregnant students now have the option to remain in their regular school or transfer to one of the special schools for pregnant girls.) Besides contributing to the number of school dropouts, these young girls are almost invariably ill-equpped for the responsibility of parenthood. The results that an interruption in schooling could have on the girl, her child, her family, and the community at large are disastrous.

1. Background paper for the AMA Congress of the Quality of Life, 1972.
2. Harold M. Vistotsky, M.D., Mattie K. Wright and Paulette K. Hartrick, *Proposed Plan for a Comprehensive Service Program for Pregnant School Age Girls in Chicago,* Mental Health Division, Chicago Board of Health, January 1965.

Other dimensions of the problem were being recognized. The public health clinic, which provided prenatal care, was experiencing the failure of many of these young expectant mothers to keep regular appointments. At the same time, the nursing staff of the clinics had no link with a community resource to assist them in following up on medical care. The lack of adequate community services to provide educational, medical, and social services was clearly demonstrated.

Concern over the lack of coordinated services for these girls prompted the Mental Health Division of the Chicago Board of Health, in February 1963, to set up the Community Services Project. This pilot demonstration was designed to meet on a small scale the comprehensive needs of a selected number of unwed pregnant adolescent girls. During its three-year period of operation the Project served 108 elementary-school-age girls from areas of the city characterized by poor housing, crowded schools, minimal job opportunities, and family disorganization—a population of people who have been described as "untreatable," "poorly motivated," or "impervious to standards of socially acceptable behavior." However, tentative conclusions at the end of the Project demonstrated that, if offered, a comprehensive program, which includes educational, medical, and mental health services, does make a significant impact toward improving the lives of the young girl, her child, and her family.[3]

The pilot project served as the catalyst for the creation in November 1966, of a new community-based agency, the Crittenton Comprehensive Care Center. As a result of the contract entered into by the Florence Crittenton Association of America (FCAA) and the Chicago Board of Health, the FCAA undertook to administer the new program. Funding of the program was made possible by the Chicago Board of Health under its maternity and infant care project from the United States Children's Bureau for Maternal and Child Health Services. The program was established for the purpose of providing comprehensive services to an

---

3. Mattie K. Wright, "Comprehensive Services for Adolescent Unwed Mothers," *Children*, Vol. 13, No. 5, U. S. Department of Health, Education, and Welfare, Washington, D. C., September-October 1966.

expanded number of both elementary and high school girls who were pregnant out-of-wedlock. Therefore the Chicago Board of Health maternity and infant care project, the Chicago Board of Education, and the Florence Crittenton Association of America entered into a collaborative relationship to meet the purposes of the comprehensive program.

The program was expanded in 1970 when a second center was opened. This second center, funded by the Model Cities Chicago Committee on Urban Opportunities, has a specific geographic target area designated by Model Cities as high risk in terms of potential individual, family, and community disorganization and in terms of the paucity of resources to meet community needs.

Specific program goals were established: (1) to provide uninterrupted educational or vocational opportunities for each individual, (2) to provide quality prenatal and postnatal medical care for both mother and baby, (3) to provide assistance with practical problems surrounding the pregnancy in those psychological, social, and environmental aspects important to the client and her family, (4) to provide, whenever possible, an appropriate plan of service for the father of the baby, and (5) to identify through a systematic evaluation plan the degree to which the goals of the program are met.[4]

THE SETTING

The Crittenton Comprehensive Care Centers (the 4Cs) has a center on the south side and one on the west side of the inner city of Chicago. At the South Side Center, which was the initial center, a staff of professionally trained nurses and social workers provide services to girls enrolled in one of the two special schools for pregnant girls.

These special schools are funded by Title I, Elementary and Secondary Education Act, and administered by the Chicago Board of Education. The schools offer instructional activities and services on a regular full-day school schedule during a twelve-month school year. The capacity of the school is 250 to 300 pupils at a given time and the pupil/teacher ratio is 15 to 1. The

---

4. Crittenton Comprehensive Care Center Manual.

basic objectives of these schools are to (1) provide uninterrupted education for pregnant girls, (2) provide an opportunity for participation in curriculum activities geared to the needs of the pregnant adolescent, such as child care, home management, and personal adjustment, (3) achieve maximum academic or vocational skills, and (4) encourage continuation of schooling after leaving the program.

One of the schools, the Harriet Tubman School, is located on the south side of the city and makes full use of 4Cs for special services and supportive services. Although the service to girls participating in the Tubman School is a basic component of the work of the South Side Center, counseling is offered on a voluntary referral basis to girls not attending the Tubman School.

The West Side Center staff is composed not only of professionally trained nurses and social workers, but also includes paraprofessionals who bring the added dimension of knowledge of the community, its composition and its needs. All known school-age pregnant girls in the target area are contacted through an outreach program by a staff member who assesses their situation and determines the service needs. Much of the service to these clients is carried on in home visits. By reaching out to the girls in their homes, the workers can more readily appreciate the numerous interfamilial and environmental stresses.

Both centers are staffed with a part-time psychiatric consultant and group-work consultant. The program provides a range of services including social casework and group work, nursing services which includes maternal and child health discussion sessions and health planning, psychiatric evaluation, when advisable, and follow-up services.

Two types of group service are offered to girls in the program: in-school and voluntary groups.

1. The in-school groups are built into the girls' school curriculum and every girl in the Tubman School participates in two groups: one group called the therapeutic discussion group (TDG), which is conducted by a social worker, and the other called the maternal child health group (MCH), conducted by a nurse.

   Each of these groups, which have memberships of about

fifteen girls, are mandatory and are carried on throughout the period of the girl's stay in the school program. The girls are grouped according to their due date, generally spanning a three-month period. Since girls return to their home school at the marking period in the academic program following delivery, these groups are of short term duration, generally taking in a girl's prenatal period. Depending on the due date and the date of commencement of the next marking period, some girls, who come to the school early in their pregnancies, can return to the Tubman School following their homebound delivery period to participate in group services postnatally.

2. Voluntary group services are designed to meet special needs of girls who are not in school or who are in a school program where services are not currently available. From time to time special interest groups have been planned, such as groups to meet the unique concerns of girls in their second pregnancy or with weight problems, or to provide postpartum assistance or premarital counseling to young couples, etc. The size and duration of these groups have been more flexible. Voluntary groups meeting in the respective agency center office have provided opportunities for a wider range of program activity. Handicraft and trips to hospitals and other community agencies have been used as tools in working with these girls.

No matter which of the centers is providing the service, there is a basic philosophy which undergirds the delivery of that help. Adolescent girls in the crises of unplanned pregnancy require focused and flexible approaches to meet their wide range of medical, educational, emotional, and social needs. The 4Cs, using an interdisciplinary team approach, is responsible for providing and facilitating a broad array of these services. It is essential that there be open communication for sharing and exchanging individual and collective knowledge at all levels. A workable blend of the skills of the total staff is necessary to be of most benefit to the clients served.

To be effective, a worker must be a sensitive, empathic, and flexible person who is astute in his psychosocial diagnostic skills and who is able to use eclectic treatment methods from his wide therapeutic repertoire. The goal is to help the girls, their families, and young fathers get through the pregnancy satisfactorily and to provide an opportunity to heighten self-esteem, enhance ego functioning, and increase potential for emotional, intellectual, and social growth.

The pregnant school-age girl represents a high risk group from the point of view of her medical, social, and educational needs. When pregnancy is superimposed on the adolescent developmental tasks, the rate and the intensity of psychobiological and social changes are overwhelming to the girl. Since the stresses and demands placed on her are beyond her adaptive range, she experiences a series of crises. Conflicts usually occur when the pregnancy is suspected or is known to the girl, when her parents and sexual partner are informed, when she may need to leave regular school because of the pregnancy, when she goes into labor, when the baby arrives and a shift in family roles is needed to incorporate the baby into the family structure, and when the young mother returns to regular activities and assumes the dual role of being both a parent and an adolescent.

It is essential that a program designed to meet the needs of adolescent pregnant girls consist of well-coordinated comprehensive services that relate to the whole being. Multitudes of needs and problems must be faced by the girl at a time in the adolescent developmental stage when personality reintegration is one of the major tasks.

CLIENT PROFILE

As in most groups served by any social agency, the clients served by the 4Cs are as diverse as the general population in terms of their backgrounds, their self-concepts, their goals, their response to services, etc. This is not to say that there are no similarities.

The average client is in the fourth month of pregnancy at the time of her first contact with the 4Cs. Most 4Cs clients are black and reside in poverty pockets of the city where housing is deteriorated and overcrowded and physical and mental health problems are numerous. The mean age of the girl is sixteen years and the average age of the baby's father is eighteen years. The girls range in age from twelve to nineteen, while the fathers' range from fifteen to thirty-five.

The average size of the family is six members, with the number of family members living at home ranging from two to fourteen. These families often represent two and three generations living in the same dwelling. Most of these families are faced with a multiplicity of problems such as conflict with the law, school failure, juvenile delinquency, and a high degree of instability with respect to living arrangements for adults and children.

Girls from all levels of age and family status seem to have limited social experiences. They have limited opportunities to expand their social activities outside of their neighborhood. Their knowledge about themselves, both their physical and emotional selves, is very limited. There are numerous fears and superstitions which frequently limit the expansion of their thinking and activities. The clients range from the intellectually slow to the very bright, although there are more of the former. Their academic and intellectual performance is not commensurate with their innate ability. They come from underexposed, nonverbal families that are confined to the ghetto, and that experience all the problems inherent in it. These factors contribute to the intellectual and socialization deficits observed in these girls.

Many of these girls have experienced a breakdown in family relationships and many come from homes with histories of illegitimacy. The girls cover over and deny their feelings about these two elements in their lives unless they are in distress or in a situation in which they can risk expressing their longings for intact families and their hopes (as well as that of their mothers) that they could escape out-of-wedlock pregnancy. Many of them come from matriarchal, one-parent homes. It has been noted that where the fathers may be present marital and relationship problems continue. The girls, as a group, have problems regarding their own femininity. Many of them have become sexually involved as a result of their search for meaningful relationships and for their identities as women. Many of them equate love and being admired, accepted, and cared about with sex. Some of them are concerned about their ability to give their boy friends satisfaction and look to sexual relationships as a solution. There is a great deficit in their knowledge about the expectations men have of women and their own expectations of men.

Shame and guilt about their out-of-wedlock and/or unwanted pregnancy is expressed in overt and covert ways. Before a girl or mother has her defenses up, there may be much talk about abortion and/or threats of rejecting the girl from her family; but as pregnancy becomes a reality, planning for the girl and her baby tend to obscure the hostile feelings. However, this program experience shows continued evidence that out-of-wedlock pregnancy is not desired by the girls. They feel that they are "bad girls" and expect all others, especially adults, to feel the same about them. Fantasies of being punished by difficult labor and delivery frequently result in physical complaints and fear of death. Particularly the younger girls, whose defenses are less intact and who are more readily able to express their feelings of shame and embarrassment, express these fears.

The vast majority of the girls, because of their strong need and because they are encouraged by their families, plan to and do keep their babies. Having inadequate child care plans, the focus of family relationship problems frequently shifts after delivery to child care problems. Many mothers refuse to help with the child care out of their own need to punish or control the girl and the girl frequently reacts by acting out; thus a vicious cycle is created. Planning for the girl and her baby is better and more stable where her parents are actively involved.

Most girls have a notion that an education—a high school diploma—is a way out of many of their problems. The notion seems to be, "If I can get a job, make my own money, not be dependent, I am safe." Many of them find out about the special school for pregnant girls on their own. Many pregnant girls seem to feel a new sense of responsibility, although vague and ill-defined, and to hope to be responsible, good mothers to their expected child. They are often heard saying that they want something "different and better" for their babies. Because of an increased sensitivity and awareness of what being a responsible and adequate person and mother involves, many girls express their desire to prevent another teenage pregnancy. However, they have many misconceptions and fears about using birth control devices.

In spite of the multiple conflicts and problems they are facing, many of the girls have potentials for healthier ego development and have many adaptive capacities. It is evident that when a person actively reaches out to help them in their need and when they clearly understand the purpose, they do make use of therapy. A large number of girls, remembering a positive helping experience, do take the initiative by coming back to us for further service with a variety of requests not necessarily related to another pregnancy. Many have voluntarily kept the staff informed on how things are going with them, perhaps only once a year or on a specific occasion. For example, a girl who had learning problems wrote to us at Christmas to say she has been on the honor roll at school; another girl who had been in the program three years ago and had been about to drop out of school, wrote about her employment and her plan to work toward a college degree in the evenings.

SOME THEORETICAL CONSIDERATIONS

The 4Cs program is based on the premise that pregnancy for a school-age girl represents a crisis in the lives of the girl, of her family, and of the father of the baby.

Her age—the period of maturational development she is experiencing—is as much a fact for concern for the girl and the designing of service as is the fact of her pregnancy. Adolescence is a time of experiencing and adjusting to physiological and psychological changes; it is a turning point in the normal maturational process. The resolution of the adolescent crisis must be successful if the girl is to develop into a relatively mature adult. According to classical psychoanalytic theory, the complex process of adolescence has its beginning in earlier childhood; sexuality does not begin at puberty. In order to discuss the development of the girl with whom we are concerned, we must turn to the primary interactions with her mother, who provides the initial nurturing.

The shift of her infantile attachments from the mother to the father is said to be related to the girl's early awareness of the anatomical differences between herself and boys. The absence of a father interferes with the childhood establishment of clear self-object differentiation. Because the girl continues to need nurture from her mother, her hostility toward her mother is unconscious. As she increasingly realizes that she cannot compete with her mother for her father, it is thought that the girl postpones her affection for her father to her choice of a heterosexual partner.

In early adolescence the girl is faced with a resurgence of many earlier childhood conflicts. The psychological processes are accompanied by enormous physical and hormonal changes. The adolescent girl faces at least three important tasks: the integration of the new bodily changes into a new concept of self, the definition of a feminine identity and a place in the world, and breaking childhood attachment to her parents and transferring it to a mate.

Bibring[5] compares the process involved in the adolescent crisis with the period of crisis which a woman experiences in a pregnancy, especially with her first child. Pregnancy involves profound endocrine and general somatic as well as psychological changes. These physical and psychological phenomena are seen as having specific libidinal and adaptive tasks which seem at times diametrically opposed to the central tasks and functions of preceding developmental phases. Pregnancy, like adolescence, seems to reactivate psychological conflicts of earlier developmental periods that require new and different solutions. It represents a turning point in the life of the individual. "Any normal girl, though she might love the man who will be father of [her] child, still must make a major developmental move in becoming a mother. This step takes place between her being a single, circumscribed, self-contained organism—to producing herself and her love ob-

5. Grete L. Bibring, Thomas F. Dwyer, Dorothy S. Huntington and Arthur F. Valenstein, "A study of the psychological processes in pregnancy and of the earliest mother-child relationship," in Ruth S. Eissler *et al.*, *Psychoanalytic Study of the Child*, Vol. XVI (New York, International University Press, 1945-1969) , pp. 9-44.

ject in a child who will from then on remain an object outside of herself."

It is to this compound, complex nature of the school-age pregnancy that 4Cs services bring a range of medical, social, and mental health services to bear. In addition to helping the girl cope with her pregnancy, the treatment approaches take into consideration a need for her to continue the learning tasks of adolescence: formal education; developing the ability to maintain satisfying peer relationships; better understanding of self and others in the social situation surrounding her; understanding the process of physical and psychological maturation; and developing the ability to make reasonable choices, for example a vocational choice, that would begin to fulfill her self-realization.

Benedek[6] writes of parenthood during the life cycle describing how as a child experiences the various maturational turning points in her life her parent has parallel "critical phases." Clearly the child's adolescence represents one of these critical periods in which significant emotional transactions between parents and children occur. Additionally, the pregnancy of a school-age girl is felt acutely by the parents, especially the mother.

Some parents, who during a daughter's childhood felt satisfaction with her control of muscular coordination in preparation for walking and moving away from the crib, feel threatened by signs of primary and secondary sex characteristics. Their own adolescent conflicts aroused, many mothers wish to protect the child from their earlier difficulties and/or mistakes. When the adolescent pulls away to define her world, many parents are stirred to struggles with their own dependency feelings. A teenage daughter's pregnancy and the subsequent birth of the baby require that parents consider new roles and new self-concepts. How parents, or a family, handle these crises depends in large measure on the crises-handling resources available to them.

When 4Cs enters the situation, the crisis event is presented in relation to the family's learning of the girl's pregnancy. Frequently, as staff and family work together, the crisis is more

6. James E. Anthony and Therese Benedek, *Parenthood, Its Psychology and Psychopathology* (Boston, Little, Brown & Company, 1970), pp. 173-174, 185-206.

sharply defined in terms of the parents' and girl's upheaval over attempts to handle her adolescence. The most vulnerable area parents experience is their conflict over the girl's sexuality. When the parents present themselves, the pregnancy is a crisis and calls on the family's crisis-meeting resources (coping mechanisms and adaptive ability) to produce some solution. The strength of these crisis-meeting resources will vary from family to family depending to a large extent on its basic ego strength. Treatment approaches, or interventions, flow from the worker's assessment of the family and the interactions of the family with the girl in view of her pregnancy crisis.

Although the crisis of pregnancy involves the young fathers, he is frequently excluded from planning because the girl and her parents are reluctant to make an issue of his participation if he does not volunteer to play a role. The question of what an adolescent boy should be expected to do is essentially whether he is to act as an adult when he is not one. In men as in women there are two goals of the reproductive drive: the wish to become a parent and the ability to be one. Men, in contrast to women, "have to overcome their regressive tendencies to assert their virility in the heterosexual act and they have to integrate active, extroverted psychic potentials to fulfill the role of father as protector and provider."[6]

The adolescent tasks, according to Erickson,[7] are to establish a heterosexual identity and to make a vocational choice. The two goals of the reproductive drive in men flow logically and organically from the achievement of those adolescent tasks. However, as Benedek states, fatherhood is not only a biologic fulfillment, it is also the means for further evolution of the parents' personality. Thus, fatherhood carries with it the implicit potential for growth and conversely for failure. In this sense, fatherhood is a crisis which, with the proper intervention, could promote the emotional and social growth of the young fathers in the 4Cs program.

In emphasizing fatherhood as a crisis, however, it should be

---

7. Erik M. Erickson, *Childhood and Society* (New York, W. W. Norton & Company, Inc., 1963) .

pointed out that young men struggle with many of the same adolescent conflicts previously described for the young girl. His development, Benedek states, "toward sexual maturity, toward male identity, implies not only heterosexual maturity, but also acceptance of its consequences by becoming a father, i.e. protector-provider, and the ability to fulfill these functions with empathic quality of fatherliness."[6] Parenthood, over and above the biologic act, is learned behavior. The emphasis is on the boy's identification with his own father as a prerequisite for the acceptance of/ and patterns for fatherhood. The vast majority of the adolescent fathers in the 4Cs program come from fatherless homes. When and if father is at home, he plays a rather marginal role. Without adequate role models and with the adolescent struggle for heterosexual identity, it would seem that the biologic role of fatherhood takes precedence over the function of providing.

In terms of designing a program to serve young fathers, the focus is on them as adolescents first. If they can be helped with that struggle, fatherhood, either in relation to the first child or subsequent children, will be a more rewarding experience. Constructive and productive experience would heighten their self-esteem and self-confidence, which in turn would serve as the source of mobilizing motivation for higher levels of adaptation.

It should be emphasized that the girls served in the 4Cs, their families, and young fathers are struggling with crisis situations, new situations for which they have no adequate coping behavior. Lack of resources or unfamiliarity with how to solve the particular problem is not necessarily indicative of a pathological state. At the base of the treatment approach is the assumption that, when client and resources are linked and when information and responses to questions and needed support to use them are given, the crisis can be dealt with and opportunities for growth-producing experience can be provided. In this context the clients are viewed as being at a crucial turning point in their lives which will have a profound effect on their maturation and growth. Their psychic maturity will in turn have a direct bearing on the child's development, since they are the primary caretakers of the child.

COMPLEMENTARY USE OF CASEWORK AND GROUP WORK

The Crittenton Comprehensive Care Centers accept referrals from local public health clinics, schools, other social agencies, relatives, friends, and the girl herself. Initially all the girls are seen individually, with their parent(s) or parent surrogate, to determine urgent needs that might require immediate casework intervention. Immediate and focused casework intervention is emphasized because pregnant girls and their parents experience in varying degrees emotional reactions to pregnancy and the problems it causes.

In the initial contact the worker attempts to explore some of the concrete plans which have been made on behalf of the client, such as: (1) whether prenatal care has been established; (2) whether a hospital for delivery has been arranged; (3) what the girl's plans regarding school or other activity during the period of her pregnancy are; and (4) whether she has, with her parents and the baby's father, considered some workable child care plans and individual responsibilities for carrying out these plans.

From the intake interview(s) a worker, with the client, will determine where and how 4Cs will intervene. After individualized services are planned with the client, an initial diagnostic formulation is made. This means that the frequency that a girl is seen and the length of her treatment varies from client to client and from situation to situation. The consideration of how to bring family members and young fathers into the treatment will also flow out of the diagnostic understanding of the specific situation.

Though we stress individualization of 4Cs services to meet the clients specific needs, certain characteristics in client families are observed:

1. FAMILIES WITH SOME STABILITY AND COHESIVENESS. These usually reach out to the agency and their main request is such specific help as educational plans for the girl. Though the family is having some relationship problems and/or social problems, they are able to mobilize their strengths and to

solve the crisis with resultant appropriate practical planning around the girl's pregnancy.

Frequently the parents in this category are struggling with a feeling of failure and the girl with guilt for having disappointed her parents. The main treatment focus with them is on intrapsychic issues and the goal is to restore the individual and family equilibrium. Some of these families become very active group members, willing in the group to air, for other members to consider, sensitive issues that they have worked out in their counseling sessions.

2. FAMILIES WHO GIVE THE INITIAL IMPRESSION THAT THEY HAVE "SOLVED" THE PROBLEM, WITH THE EXCEPTION OF SPECIFIC ASSISTANCE REQUESTS SUCH AS FINDING ADDITIONAL FINANCIAL RESOURCES OR MAKING HOSPITAL ARRANGEMENTS FOR CONFINEMENT CARE. Often, in reality, they have not faced the situation, evidenced by the fact that they have minimized all the implicit problems and by their reluctance to look at how realistic or workable their stated solution is. Since crises frequently occur when the baby arrives because they no longer are able to deny the realities of the situation these families usually reactivate their contact with the agency after the arrival of the baby.

Many of these parents choose to use parents' group counseling, rather than individual counseling which involves a closer relationship for information and clarification of their parental responsibilities. The mother is most frequently concerned with what she should expect of her adolescent daughter now that she is also a mother, how to control the girl's sexual activity, and how to solve the dilemma of the girl's use of birth control pills.

3. PARENTS WHOSE MANY UNRESOLVED EARLIER CONFLICTS ARE STIRRED UP BY THE GIRL'S ILLEGITIMATE PREGNANCY. They are very angry and punitive toward the girl and refuse to assist her with practical planning, while the girl protects herself by being regressive, nonverbal and passive-dependent. These parents try hard to detach themselves from the problem,

stating "she created the problem (pregnancy) and she has to take care of it." Initial focus with these parents is to provide an opportunity to ventilate their feelings. Only after some of their inner pressures are worked out and they perceive that they are accepted as concerned parents, are they able to focus on the immediate need for practical planning.

Because of their need to detach themselves from the issues at hand, they are frequently inaccessible for individual counseling at the intake phase. Some of them come to parents' group to find immediate relief from inner tension, only to find the group's focus and goals differ from their own. Depending on the degree of discomfort and the stress point, some of them seek casework service to gain awareness of how some of their own problems block their relationship with their daughter.

4. PARENTS WHO ARE VERY LIMITED OR VERY DISTURBED EMOTIONALLY. They simply do not have the capacity to cope with their adolescent girl's pregnancy. With this kind of family, the intervention must be to immediately help the family make a medical appointment, to follow up closely so that the girl keeps regular prenatal and postnatal checkups, and to see that the infant is properly and adequately cared for. Along with the close supervision of the home, the worker makes all efforts to mobilize family and community resources to meet the needs of this particular individual and family. Girls from very disturbed homes are sometimes very precariously defended and sometimes require psychiatric care during the postpartum period.

Many adolescents feel threatened in a one-to-one, client-worker relationship. Furthermore, not all pregnant girls need or want individual casework service. Therapeutic group work, as an integral part of the comprehensive care program, has become an indispensible technique at the 4Cs. For adolescents the peer group remains one of the major sources of support, further strengthened when the common problems of pregnancy and its effects on themselves and their families are shared by the girls. Within a nonjudgmental and accepting environment, they are willing to use the peer group as a catalytic agent. They are able to risk themselves, to test their negative feelings and effects of their behavior and action on the group. The group provides an opportunity to learn to communicate, to develop relationships with peers and the adult therapist, and to distinguish individual differences as well as the multiple issues in discussions. A therapeutically-oriented group promotes and improves ego functioning of sensitivity, self-awareness, and integration. The group serves as a clearly-defined structure which provides guidelines for young people who are bewildered by confusing and changing social values, such as the sexual revolution and/or sexual freedom. Although they may appear to resist any type of structure basically these young people are seeking reasonable guidelines and directions to follow.

An adolescent pregnant girl becomes more conscious of her physical self. She usually starts in the group with a discussion of her physical problems—a less threatening area—wanting to understand how she conceived a child and how the fetus develops in relation to the stages of pregnancy. Thus, the content of the maternal child health groups covers the anatomy and physiology of the reproductive system, physical and emotional changes during pregnancy, nutritional needs during pregnancy, prenatal care, labor and delivery, the postpartum healing process, family planning and child care, and optimal use of health care resources and follow-up services. In the process of understanding the fetal development as well as the stages of pregnancy, the girls begin to identify and accept their expected child and psychologically prepare themselves to become mothers.

It becomes clear that, underneath the pregnant adolescent's quest for information and knowledge about her physical self, is her desire to understand herself as a person, one who has a multitude of needs and wishes and who wants to prepare herself to meet some of her needs, to clarify and fulfill her appropriate responsibilities, and to achieve self-realization. As the process of group therapy moves from the initial resistance stage to the intimacy stage, the girls' distrust and fears are replaced by feelings of trust; they become free to explore their own feelings and the feelings, opinions, and/or evaluation of other members. This is the period when many girls reach out to the group leader/worker for individual help because they feel that their problems are unique or because they are not quite sure that they can trust themselves with other group members. A worker's perceptive and receptive response encourages them to test the group by bringing out the personal concerns that they once thought too unusual to share in the group.

Programs similar to group services to girls have been planned for parents of the girls and for the babies' fathers. Groups of parents have come to the agency for morning and evening meetings, planned to provide opportunities at times when the parents can come. After experimenting with a variety of approaches and requesting the parent's help in planning the kinds of meetings which they prefer, the monthly sessions have been basically educational in focus. The speakers have been psychiatrists to discuss adolescence, lawyers to talk about the rights of grandparents and minor parents, girls formerly in the program to discuss problems that arise after the baby comes. After the presentation of a specific topic, parents have been encouraged to discuss their reactions and concerns. The parents who have participated in groups tend to avail themselves more readily of individual service when the need arises than those who have not been involved in the group program.

Meetings of expectant young fathers have taken place. Each of these young men has come initially through the girl's wish to have him involved with the agency and after she has given sufficient information to locate him. Once contacted, the young man has been approached as a client in his own right, meaning that the focus of service is around those issues which are his concern. At first he tends to want very specific help with employment or vocational training. As his comfort with and trust in the workers grow, his role as an expectant father and his relationship with the girl and her family and requests for information about anatomy, labor and delivery, and birth control are significant subjects explored.

Group approaches have enabled 4Cs, with a small staff, to serve a large number of girls. The 4Cs provide services to about 1,000 girls a year. However, concern goes beyond helping a girl plan for delivery of a healthy baby. The agency is constantly aware that, because it is working with adolescents, a variety of other tasks need to be considered. Members of staff try, through a number of reaching-out techniques, such as home visits to group members, to individualize the girls and their situations.

Many families will attempt to deny that problems existed before the pregnancy and go through the total experience as if there is no change. Enrolling the girl in school seems to give the false assurance that the situation is normal. When such an attitude increases the girl's stresses, 4Cs is responsible for helping the girl and her family re-evaluate their planning. As an example, Anita, an eighteen-year-old, was enrolled in the summer session of the Tubman School program. Suspecting pregnancy after she missed a menstrual period, she went to the emergency room of a local hospital for a pregnancy test. When pregnancy was confirmed, her mother expressed lack of surprise, did not feel upset, and looked forward to a grandchild. She was glad her daughter would be continuing her education. Anita, on the other hand, was far more ambivalent, feeling at one time happy and at other times thinking she had done wrong. She appeared embarrassed to talk about the baby's father, a man ten years older than she.

Early in the pregnancy, Anita was hospitalized three days with a kidney infection. She repeatedly complained of dizzy spells, abdominal and leg pains, and vomiting. Her medical complications interfered with regular school attendance. When she failed to receive any credit because of her poor attendance, she was angry, saying it was not her fault but rather that of her poor health.

The nurse who became involved learned that in her prenatal period Anita had begun a pattern of referring herself to hospital emergency service complaining of a urinary tract infection. Although regular check-ups in the prenatal clinic indicated no unusual symptoms, Anita said she had infected tubes and infection in her womb, a misconception of her problems. She seemed unable or unwilling to explore possible emotional counterparts to her problem.

Anita lived with her widowed mother and five siblings. The family had a history of medical problems: an older brother was congenitally blind and her mother and an older sister had vague illnesses which interfered with their being employable. The mixed messages Anita received in this setting, both to complete school and to see herself as part of a sick family, added to the pressures she felt in her present condition.

The nurse assigned as her therapist agreed that Anita should not attend school during her pregnancy but planned instead a vocational program which in this case was more realistic. Beyond the concrete planning was an attempt to work on her self-concept as a sick person.

In the 4C's program individual services may be recommended at various points during the period a girl is known to the agency. For example with Anita, the referral came after she had dropped out of school before delivery. Some issues, if presented at the intake contact, suggest that a casework plan be considered. Two examples are the girl requesting adoption placement, who needs opportunities to explore the many facets involved, and a case in which the conflict between the girl and her parents seem to be blocking efforts to more adequately cope with the pregnancy. Sometimes a girl, who is receiving mainly group services, will be referred for casework services by the group leader who senses that the group is not able to meet her specific need. The group leader will sometimes reach out to a very quiet or nonverbal member who seems to be anxious and frightened in the group. At times individualizing this group member will indicate a problem in her situation which requires more intensive casework service. In the special school program, girls who have difficulties in adjusting to the program are referred by the school staff for more thorough evaluation. Symptomatic behavior in the school, i.e. frequent absences, numerous complaints of a physical nature, behavior isolated from peer groups, and learning difficulties might be reasons that school personnel would request 4Cs evaluation.

The period following delivery of the baby is a crucial point for many girls and their families. Girls who have been members of groups and those already receiving casework help are in contact with caseworkers during this time. Home visiting has been used as a tool, especially in this period, to clarify our diagnostic thinking and to build a relationship with a girl who has not been as accessible prior to delivery. The arrival of the baby is frequently a point to offer casework help, because, in many situations, plans made when pregnancy was first recognized shift when the new baby is a reality. Also, when the labor and delivery experience has been traumatic, e.g. a dead infant or some complications in the delivery, the girl and family may need additional support. Sometimes a young man who has denied paternity throughout the pregnancy may reenter the situation. Both he and the new mother may require services of professional staff to sort out their feelings and define their future roles in the life of the baby.

Sometimes the arrival of the baby or sorting out what role she will play in the baby's life will stimulate a girl to openly reflect on the question, "Who am I?" This question is felt to be universally considered during adolescence. Some clients, once the immediacies of the pregnancy are resolved, wish to move into treatment relationships where they can explore this question. Since the request does not come from every girl, some positive group experience frequently steers them in this direction.

It is understandable why the question is so pertinent in the case of Barbara, a seventeen-year-old high school senior. At ten months of age she was adopted by her paternal grandparents. Her natural parents were divorced—mother later died—but her father lived with his parents, Barbara's adoptive parents, all her life. The father lived in a somewhat irresponsible way and shifted his role, acting sometimes as a father, other times as a brother. The adoptive father died two weeks before Barbara was referred to 4Cs during her fourth month of pregnancy. Initially the family focus was on helping them work out an adequate medical plan and a reasonable financial arrangement. As the worker began to work with the girl, a pattern emerged indicating that Barbara and her adoptive mother were not communicating. Barbara and the baby's father were planning independently of the mother. The mother expressed feeling of being left out and fearful feelings of being left alone. (It is true that some of the communication problem related to both the girl and the adoptive mother's mourning the loss of adoptive father.)

In a few short interviews with Barbara, questions about her natural father began to surface. She was weighing the question of what kind of man she wished to marry. She talked with the worker about life goals and about college or other training. She talked of leaving her adoptive mother and she began to question how she related to a variety of people. The treatment plan for Barbara included joint sessions with mother and daughter to work on the breakdown in their communication. Barbara was seen weekly and was dealing with the questions of "Who am I now?" and "Who do I want to be?"

The importance of the treatment termination phase was particularly stressed in this program. The learning which had taken place during therapy was reenforced through reviewing with the client her beginning ability to understand and solve her own problems. Emphasis was placed on her leaving the program with positive feelings so that she might return if the need arose.

EVALUATION AND CONCLUSION

The need to study and demonstrate that services are reaching the clients in the ways stated by the aims and goals have been a major concern from the conception of the 4Cs program. There is an ongoing procedure for the collection of demographic and socioeconomic data on all clients. Aside from the compilation of these facts, two major studies have been undertaken. The focus of these research projects has been on the assessment of program effectiveness.

In August 1968, a study by Bedger,[8] in which 180 girls were interviewed, was published. The purpose was to determine, a year after termination of service, the status of clients who had participated in the 4Cs program during the school year 1966-1967 and to assist the agency in developing more effective plans and programs.

Some of the conclusions drawn from this survey are:

From the initial days of the Pilot Project in Chicago in 1963 until the period of the survey, May 1968, except for slight differences in the age of the girls because of variations in program emphasis, the client population served had not differed significantly.

---

8. Jean E. Bedger, *A Follow-up Survey of Teen-age Unwed Mothers,* Chicago, Florence Crittenton Association of America, Inc., August 1968.

The clients' opinions and judgments regarding the value of program were asked. The results showed that the services offered were well received, were adequately used, and were of great value to the clients and their families. Eighty-seven percent of the clients indicated that they would recommend the program, and many had already referred their relatives and friends to it.

Evaluation of the most helpful program components expressed by the sample possibly reflects adolescent interests and attitudes. To most school girls, school is very important. Although statistics from the past were not available, it appears certain that more girls (52%) remained in school and graduated from high school than before these special services were available. The value of small classes and the special attention from teachers, social workers, and nurses had made a great impression and impact on the clients. In many cases this had been their best learning experience.

Although the situation of pregnancy out-of-wedlock implies that medical, especially prenatal care, is needed, it is understandable that young people would not consider the clinic program most helpful. Experience shows that unwed teenage mothers, especially those who have had little or no previous medical supervision, need help and support during prenatal examinations and throughout the pregnancy and the postpartum period, even though they and their families may not recognize its importance and value. With the follow-up effort by 4Cs staff to assure that the girls maintained regular clinic care, there were significant results. The rate of premature births in this group was 1.2 percent and there was a 3 percent infant mortality rate. The Illinois State figures for 1967, which include all reported births, showed the percent of premature births as 7.88 and in Chicago alone 10.11. The perinatal death rate for Illinois was 29.76, for Chicago 35.04, and for our sample 30 per 1,000. Although this record reflects improvement over that of the general population, continual emphasis on close supervision of clients' prenatal and postnatal care is necessary.

Of the 180 girls interviewed, 50 percent claimed they had no problem at the time of the interview. The greatest needs expressed were for jobs and money; 22 percent were working at the time of the interview, and 86 percent of the clients wanted work. Many requested help in finding employment, but only 41 percent of those who said they wanted work had sought it. Most clients expressed concern for their financial status whether or not they were employed. Contrary to the most common belief, 14 percent of the baby's fathers were providing some financial support. In addition to the reality demands, a girl's wanting a job or needing money represents her struggle for independence. It is evident that the agency as well as the community at large must make more concerted efforts to provide job training and/or employment opportunity for this group.

There is a 4Cs philosophy toward research which views all studies as a further means of enhancing service to clients. From the findings of this survey 4Cs was convinced even more that its philosophy of comprehensive service was valid—that every teenage expectant mother needs and should have the opportunity to receive educational, medical, vocational, social, and psychological counseling and assistance with child care plans.

The clients in the study who attended school during the day had to provide some other caretaker for the child. Some young mothers cared for their babies when possible and at the same time continued their education and the tasks of adolescence.

An additional study[9] was undertaken to review knowledge about adolescence and relate the life styles of these clients to known theory. Along with other interests, this was a study to test the assumptions that (1) a greater number of those clients who receive comprehensive service would show positive changes than those who do not receive such service; (2) rating scales are useful to provide order in assessing characteristics of clients functioning before and after service; (3) although teenage unwed mothers

---

9. Jean E. Bedger, *The Crittenton Study: An Assessment of Client Functioning Before and After Services,* Chicago, Florence Crittenton Association of America, Inc., April 1969.

have been a high risk group medically and have been potential school dropouts, these characteristics can be altered; (4) functioning levels of teenage unwed mothers in most areas of greatest concern can be changed.

It was determined that our own scales, reflecting the specific nature of variables important in services to pregnant teenagers, would be designed to evaluate functioning in (1) relationship with family, (2) relationship with the baby's father, (3) plans for the baby, (4) client's future plans, and (5) environmental stress.

This study of 240 teenage pregnant girls and their families showed that 55 percent of them rated more positive in behavioral status. A connection between the involvement in casework, group work, educational and medical programs, and change in behavior was assessed. For example, at intake, communications between mother and daughter and father and daughter were inadequate, but results at case closing showed improvement. There was no significant change in the area of the clients' relationships to the baby's father; where the relationship was considered positive at intake it remained positive. When the young father was not supportive, the negative relationships were frequently improved at delivery or even before. However, the positive relationships over time refute the arguments and stereotypes that the relationships between unwed parents are casual and meaningless.

Casework intervention in the area of child care planning was probably more significant than any other area and reflected a 70 percent success story.

On this study scale, an assessment was made to determine whether the client is operating as an adolescent, an adult, or a combination of the two, recognizing that there is a struggle between life style and roles. One of the goals of the program was to help the client define her role and choose an acceptable or appropriate role for her own circumstances. In this study 68.8 percent of the girls were combining roles, but of these only 1.3 percent changed behavior patterns significantly and assumed the dual roles. This finding seemed to support the initial theory that the pregnant adolescent is in a conflictual situation. It was clear that adolescents do have difficulties carrying out their developmental tasks while taking on adult maternal responsibilities, and that they need the comprehensive services to learn to cope with the situation.

Environmental stress, which was frequently very serious, was lessened in some cases during the year. A certain amount of stress was eliminated as a result of the acceptance of the pregnancy. Help with planning, the continuation of education, and the delivery of a healthy baby tended to improve the attitudes of the family.

The Crittenton Study has many more facets to its report than can be described here. The summaries of the two major studies of 4Cs clients and program (1) confirm that comprehensive services to the population we served are feasible and that they have an impact on that population's ability to cope with the immediate crisis, the pregnancy, and its effects on the maturational process and planning for the future, and (2) attest to the value of continuous evaluation of the program and of its effectiveness to the client population and to the community.

CHAPTER XI

STAFFING OF TEENAGE PROGRAMS AND ATTITUDES OF STAFF

Myrtle White, Dorothy Chevalier and Ruth T. Gross

THE VIEW OF TEENAGE pregnancy as an isolated, purposeful act, symptomatic of deep-seated, conflictual emotional problems has yielded, in recent years, to the realization that a variety of causes may lead to this event in adolescence. From this broader perspective it is possible to identify a number of potential problem areas for adolescent parents:

1. The physiological stress produced by the superimposition of pregnancy on the growth processes of adolescence.
2. The emotional stress of the pregnancy occurring at a time when adolescent parents are attempting to master their own developmental tasks.
3. The conflicting influences and pressures exerted on adolescents by their peer groups, their families, and society.

These issues dictate the need for coordinated, comprehensive services offered in a manner consistent with the socioeconomic resources, the developmental levels, and the life styles of the adolescent parents-to-be.

PROGRAMS

Comprehensive health services must include readily available prenatal and general medical and dental care, education in nutrition, the physiology of conception, labor and delivery, venereal disease, as well as methods of contraception and family planning.

Counseling services should provide information about abortion, adoption, types of child care, marriage, single parenthood, legal rights of minors, continued education and/or employment, as well as opportunities for exploring and sharing feelings and experiences.

285

There have been a variety of organizational structures within which comprehensive medical-social-educational services have been provided to adolescent parents using government and/or voluntary funds. Often these programs have developed around hospitals or schools in recognition of the special needs of pregnant adolescents using hospital clinics or excluded from public schools. These programs tend to direct their services toward the beginning stage of parenthood, that is, to the successful completion of the pregnancy, but provide little by way of ongoing services to the adolescent as a parent.

As more young parents are raising their own children rather than relinquishing them for adoption or to be nurtured within extended families, or as communities have become more sensitive to the needs of these young family units, infant and child care centers and family service agencies are expanding their services to include medical, social, and educational programs for the young parents of the children under care. These programs reach only a selected number of young parents, however, as they are unrelated to the services provided the adolescents during pregnancy, and they require the young parents to seek nursery or child care or to perceive a need and then identify the appropriate available service.

A few new community programs are being developed which provide a full range of services exclusively for adolescent parents, not only during the pregnancy, but for a sufficient time thereafter to assist the young parents and the children to establish stable, satisfying, self-sufficient family units. These programs provide natural and flexible entrance and exit possibilities consistent with the individual needs of the adolescents. For one adolescent they may provide only abortion counseling and medical services; for another, prenatal services, schooling, child care, and young parents' counseling group; and, for a third, residential and infant care services while she is seeking employment and/or a living situation.

We envision the future possibility of community consortiums made up of government and private organizations assigning educational, medical, recreational, residential, counseling, vocational, and child care resources, as well as financial support under the direction of a centralized administration.

There will also be the need within communities for smaller community house facilities providing the full range of prenatal services for a given group of adolescent mothers and the ongoing education, social support, and recreational services key to the development of the young family.

The most common organizational structure, however, will probably continue to be a service developed within an already established community program, such as a hospital obstetrical service, a residential center, an adolescent recreational service, or a pregnant-girls' school, which then arranges for additional services to be provided by other community agencies. With this type of organizational structure, as with any of the patterns described, it is extremely important that program planning and the provision of services be on an interdisciplinary basis.

STAFFING

A basic program planning unit must at a minimum include a physician, a public health nurse, a social worker, educational and vocational personnel, and representatives of the adolescents for whom the program is designed. A variety of health professionals can effectively be used in providing the medical-social-educational or comprehensive health services described. Professional orientation is less important than the ability to exchange knowledge and techniques across discipline lines. The staff must be capable of responding to a wide range of adolescent concerns without excessive referral to specialists or artificial jurisdictional disputes.

It is crucial that, whatever the program's structure, it be designed so that a primary group of staff people are consistently involved with the adolescents, preferably in more than one setting or activity. Second, all groups, counseling sessions, and clinic services should be limited in size from ten to fifteen participants at any one time.

As an example of one possible staffing pattern, we would like to describe our experiences with a hospital-based program and school. This program is jointly sponsored by a federally funded

Children and Youth Project and the San Francisco Unified School District. The program is designed to provide continuing education to students, ages thirteen to seventeen, prenatal and general medical care for the mother, and sick- and well-child care for the babies through two years of age. There are about thirty-five students in the program at any one time, with school in session for five half-days each week. About 200 mothers and babies are under medical supervision provided through a weekly obstetrical and general medical clinic, specifically for these students and through a biweekly evening well-baby clinic to accommodate the young parents who have returned to school or work. Acute care for mother and infant is provided through the hospital's regular pediatric clinic and emergency room services.

The association of this program with the federally-funded Children and Youth Project makes it possible to provide a variety of staff members on a part-time basis and to change allocations or types of staff when indicated.

The following staff are currently engaged in this program:

San Francisco Unified School District

No.	Description	Time (Percent)
2	Teachers	100
1	Reading specialist	50
1	Vocational counsellor	20
1	Educational counsellor	20
1	Social worker	100
1	Public health nurse	100
1	Community health worker	100
1	Nutritionist	50
1	Occupational therapist	50
1	Psychologist	20
1	Pediatrician	25
1	Obstetrician	50
1	Program coordinator	20

The senior teacher, the social worker, the community health worker, and the nurse constitute the core or primary center team, which assumes responsibility for the ongoing operation of the center. The teacher is responsible for planning, programming, and coordinating all aspects of the academic program and the use of staff provided by the school district. The Children and Youth Project staff is responsible for ten hours of special activities which include group and individual social counseling, health care, infant care, nutrition, and an activity program directed toward the student's individual developmental needs. The same staff members are also responsible for the medical, supportive, and follow-up services of the program. For example, the nurse who teaches health education provides individual health counseling and public health nursing follow-up. The occupational therapist does developmental screening and programming and conducts activity classes. The community health worker is with the students in the center and in the obstetrical and well-baby clinics. She also makes home visits when indicated.

The intake process is considered critical to the proper functioning of the program. At intake the social worker interviews the adolescent, completes intake forms, contacts other involved agencies, begins a social evaluation, identifying potential problem areas, and initiates planning. At the point of intake, most of the families have already considered and usually rejected the options of abortion and adoption. Nevertheless, all options regarding the pregnancy are explored. The public health nurse also interviews the student on entry and begins to evaluate her ability to use health services and her level of understanding of pregnancy, delivery and infant care and development. The nurse may also use this initial contact to allay any fears or misgivings the student may have about her pregnancy. In instances where the patient has chosen a private physician for prenatal care, the nurse contacts him to inform him or confirm with him that his patient is attending the adolescent program and to encourage the exchange of information and concerns. She may also act as a liaison between doctor and patient to ensure that the patient understands and carries out instructions. The teacher reviews the student's academic experience and designs her academic program. Each student's situation is discussed by the total center staff at a conference shortly after her admission to the program. Problems are identified and an individualized plan is developed to help solve them and to increase the potential benefits of the program to the student.

The obstetrician in a special afternoon clinic sees each girl, who has chosen to come to this clinic, every other week until the ninth month, when he sees her every week. At the initial prenatal visit he evaluates the general health of the patient, orders prenatal laboratory work, prescribes medication and treatment as needed, and assumes responsibility for the total obstetrical care of the patient. Also in attendance at the special clinic is a pediatrician who does a comprehensive health assessment of each girl. She collaborates with the other members of the health team (obstetrician, nurse, community health worker) in making health care plans for the young mother during and after her pregnancy. The same pediatrician is in attendance at the evening well-baby clinic. Thus, the pediatrician's participation in the prenatal program affords the young mother-to-be the opportunity to know her baby's doctor well before her child is born.

The program coordinator position has been filled by a social worker and also by a public health nurse. Each has brought different professional orientations, approaches, and responsibilities to work productively with a common group of students.

ATTITUDES OF STAFF

Recruitment must focus on attitudes about adolescence, sexuality, and alternative life styles in addition to professional competence. Attention must also be directed to maximizing the potential value of each discipline in providing a combined medical-social-educational program from a shared base of general information.

To help the pregnant girl explore alternatives open to her she must be made to feel important and worthy as a person. If the prevailing attitude of the service person is judgmental or detached, the opportunity for realistic planning may be lost. On the other hand, if the expectant mother can be made to feel that she is entitled to and, indeed, worthy of a period in which to grow up and explore alternatives for a fuller life, she may then view the options as her opportunity to determine her own life style.

Adolescents are quick to pick up what they perceive as phony interest in them. The "let-me-help-you-help-yourself-because-I-know-better" approach is a big pitfall. The fact that the adult has already grown up and gotten his life together does not necessarily make him an acceptable role model for the teenager. A willingness on the part of the adult to share with the teenager some parts of his life that are pertinent, such as his own confusion and method of working through it as an adolescent, may set the stage for mutual respect. Sharing can be effective if it is offered with the attitude of caring and concern rather than obvious example-setting or comparison between what the staff sees as the ideal and what the student sees as important to him.

The adolescent's greatest need may be for a sense of belonging. The young mother is often rejected by family, peers, and, in some cases, by the father of the child. If the attitudes of those to whom she must turn for help (medical staff and social welfare agencies), are punitive the feeling of rejection is reinforced.

In acting as advocates for adolescents and as liaison with others who may be involved with them, staff attitudes are easily transferred. If they are positive, they may be effective in altering negative stereotypes. The carryover is especially important in areas such as labor and delivery, obstetric clinic, and the private physician's office. If there is lack of concern in these areas the trust which may have been built up by primary staff is seriously undermined.

Primary staff must carefully examine their own concerns and motivations for working with this particular group. Their feelings of adequacy and their sincerity and frankness in discussions about sex are often challenged by the teenagers. Single or childless staff seem a ready-made target for prying and ridicule. The degree of ease with which these subjects are handled by single staff members shows the adolescent yet another life style option, the choice of being single and childless without feeling deprived.

If possible, staff should be racially heterogeneous and reflect the ethnic backgrounds of the clients. This affords the adolescent not only a sense of identification but also the opportunity to see that adults, in spite of racial differences, are able to work together toward a common goal.

CHAPTER XII

APPRAISING YOUR PROGRAM

James F. Jekel and Lorraine V. Klerman

WHAT?

DESPITE THE POPULARITY of the term "evaluation" in the area of human services, serious efforts at evaluation are seldom attempted. Although the difficulty involved in doing it well and concern about what might be revealed may be obstacles, the greatest deterrent to routine program evaluation is probably lack of familiarity with its methods.

Program personnel tend to confuse two types of evaluation: evaluative research and program appraisal. *Evaluative research* is the application of scientific methods (including research designs, sampling methods, and statistical tests) to determine the value of specific kinds of human endeavor. This is a complex task that should be left to experienced investigators and not attempted in every program for school-age parents. Many administrators avoid taking a good look at their own programs because they believe this would mean doing evaluative research. This is not so. Evaluative research has its place, but it is neither necessary nor feasible for most programs.

Every program for school-age parents, however, does have the ability and obligation to describe its goals, services, and impact in a systematic manner. Such a *program appraisal* may not be overly simple, but it is possible without taking excessive time from the serving of young parents.

WHY?

The justification for program appraisal may become clear to service staff and administrators suddenly when a funding agency requests data about the population served, the kind and number of services given, the results achieved, and, perhaps, an estimate of cost-effectiveness. Or the need may appear gradually, when failures occur and staff begins to ask: "Are we really helping? Whom are we helping? Whom are we missing? What could we do better? Are we doing as well as the programs in other cities which reported fantastic results?"

Program appraisal has great potential for improving the ongoing effectiveness and often the long term survival of service programs for adolescent parents. Comprehensive programs tend to have a natural history with a beginning or developmental phase, a middle or a consolidation phase (both in terms of funding and program), and, all too often, an end when unable to survive, the programs must close. Program appraisal provides a tool to demonstrate accomplishments where they exist and to identify weaknesses so that they can be eliminated. It can also help to bring the need for programs for teenage parents more clearly to the attention of the public.

WHEN?

As an administrator begins to look for answers to the vital questions posed above, he may discover, much to his chagrin, that the existing records either do not contain the information he wants or have it in a form which is difficult to summarize. Frequently little or no additional effort would have been required to record the data in a more useful way. Another revelation may be the absence of unanimity within the staff regarding the program's objectives. For example, some staff members may believe that graduation from high school and avoiding subsequent pregnancies for a number of years are appropriate expectations for essentially all of the clients, and they may have been operating on this premise. Others may have been trying to assist the girls to define and achieve their own goals, even if this meant interrupting their education and having another baby. Thus it may become clear in retrospect that the program needed a better definition of service goals and staff responsibility at the outset. Program appraisal tends to force such definitions, since it requires precise and objective statements of program goals in terms that can be measured.

Inaugurating program appraisal measures at the beginning of a program need not take excessive time and has important advantages. First, it requires that program goals be stated clearly and discussed with the staff. Second, it enables records to be kept in a maximally efficient manner. Third, it permits early discovery of program strengths and weaknesses, so that adjustments are possible before the patterns of services become too firmly established or before the staff and public lose confidence in the program.

Programs which have been underway for some time, either without program assessment or with minimal attempts in this direction, may start program appraisal procedures at a later time. Under such circumstances, however, programs should not try to assess past accomplishments, unless there are urgent reasons, such as a demand from a funding agency. It is difficult to obtain complete and accurate data retrospectively, and the results will seldom reflect the amount of time and effort invested. A better way is to pretend the program is about to begin. A date should be set, such as the beginning of the next month or the new semester, on which the staff will start to collect information on every school-age mother admitted to the program, and data recorded from that point forward.

HOW?

Appraising a service program has three basic steps.

STEP I: Determine the program's goals in terms that can be measured using information that can be collected. There are at least three areas for defining specific program objectives: the population to be served, the services to be rendered, and the impact to be made. Who is eligible? How many and what proportion of the eligible population does the program expect to serve? What services, both qualitatively and quantitatively, does the program intend to provide? What changes or end results are expected in the clients?

Programs must be realistic about their goals and the amount and kinds of data that can be collected. A crisis intervention program (one providing services only during pregnancy, delivery, and the immediate postpartum period), might set an educational goal of assisting at least 95 percent of those who register in the program to remain in school throughout pregnancy and at least 80 percent of these to return to school postpartum. Graduation from high school is not a fully realistic primary program goal for a short term program, even though preventing the interruption of education during pregnancy appears to improve the possibility of graduation as well.

Similarly if obstetrical care is provided by the program, it would be realistic to expect good perinatal health for the mother and baby; but if long term pediatric services are not part of the program, a healthy child at two years of age should not be considered a program goal. Although counseling or special classes may improve the care the mothers give their children, this association is too tenuous to be established as a realistic program goal. Those comprehensive programs which offer pediatric care for the first year postpartum, however, should expect all infants served to be fully immunized and have no untreated defects at the end of that time.

The advantages of using short term objectives for short term programs are: (1) a shorter wait for some measure of accomplishment, and (2) long term contact with the client need not be maintained to determine achievement. If the long term data are easily available, such as health problems and subsequent pregnancies in hospital records or school achievement in school records, documentation of long term effects is interesting, but these should not be primary concerns in appraising short term or crisis intervention programs.

The following examples of program goals would appear to be reasonable expectations from an integrated crisis intervention program for school-age mothers:

A. *Persons served.* To serve about 50 percent of the known eligible school-age mothers in the target population during the first year of the program, 60 percent the second year, 70 percent the third year, and at least 75 percent the fourth year and thereafter. (These figures would vary from place to place.)

B. *Services.*

   1. To enable clients to begin prenatal care no later than

the fourth month of pregnancy and keep at least 75 percent of the scheduled prenatal visits.

2. To limit the clinic waiting time at the initial visit and at each subsequent visit.

3. To insure that prenatal care is given by the same person (or a small group, if a group practice approach is used) at 75 percent of the visits and that this individual (or one of these persons) delivers the infant.

4. To have all clients attend at least 75 percent of those school days for which they are eligible, with the exception of those clients with unusual problems that interfere with attendance.

5. To have every client interviewed at least twice by a social worker, and a home visit made if indicated.

6. To have all clients visited by their social workers in the hospital and/or on arrival at home following delivery to insure that adequate arrangements have been made for both mother and infant.

C. *Impact.*

1. To insure an acceptable level of maternal and infant health during pregnancy, delivery, and the immediate postpartum period. Despite the commonly held ideas about the dangers of initial pregnancies in young mothers, a recent study suggested that first infants born to school-age mothers were not at unusually high risk in the presence of good care, so a reasonable infant mortality rate for first infants might be 20 per thousand live births.[1] However, subsequent infants born to these mothers while they were still teenagers had a far greater risk of perinatal mortality.[2] The first school-age pregnancy also did not appear to carry abnormal risks of other obstetrical problems except for somewhat higher rates of

1. J. F. Jekel, J. B. Currie, L. V. Klerman, C. P. N. McCarthy, P. M. Sarrel and R. A. Greenberg, "An Analysis of Statistical Methods for Comparing Obstetrical Outcomes—Infant Health in Three Samples of School-Age Pregnancies," *American Journal of Obstetrics and Gynecology,* 112:9-19 (1972).

2. J. F. Jekel, J. T. Harrison, D. R. E. Bancroft, N. C. Tyler and L. V. Klerman, "A Comparison of the Health of Index and Subsequent Babies Born to School-Age Mothers," *American Journal of Public Health,* in press.

toxemia and prematurity. Aside from these two indicators, therefore, comprehensive programs should expect normal obstetrical results.

2. To provide sufficient contraceptive information and materials so that no more than 10 percent of the clients have *unwanted* pregnancies during the first postpartum year. If long term follow-up of clients is difficult, the goal might be to make sure that every client was offered contraceptives and had an adequate understanding of their nature and use.

3. To enable at least 85 percent of the clients to return to school postpartum.

These program goals will not be appropriate for all programs, but they do provide examples of goals that are relatively easy to measure (although not necessarily to achieve).

STEP II. Establish an ongoing data collection system that will provide the data needed to assess the goals established under Step I and is simple enough to be maintained by staff members as part of their regular duties. It is better to concentrate on collecting a small amount of data accurately and completely than to attempt to obtain a large amount of data and risk omissions and errors. Incomplete data will seldom be useful, whereas a small amount of high quality information directed at the most important questions will not only give important and dependable answers, but will also establish the habit of self-appraisal and the appetite for additional effort. One fairly simple data collection system that has been advocated uses a card for each client served.[3]

STEP III. Analyze the data frequently, preferably quarterly or semiannually, in order to monitor the progress of the program and discover problems early. Many persons worry about the complexities of data analysis, but the most useful kinds of analysis for self-appraisal are simple and merely require counting and calculating the percentages that have and have not achieved a particular goal. In order to find the answers to some appraisal questions it may be necessary to divide the population into

---

3. L. V. Klerman and J. F. Jekel, "Services for Teenage Mothers—What Do We Need to Know?" *Connecticut Health Bulletin*, 84:219-229 (1970).

groups by a characteristic such as age and determine the success rate in each group. A card system makes such tabulations simple. Cards are sorted into piles by the characteristic (e.g. age), and then each of these piles is sorted into groups by whether the goal was attained (e.g. return to school postpartum). By counting the cards in each pile an administrator can quickly develop the desired percentages. The next step upward in complexity of data processing (for those so inclined) would be marginal punch cards (sorted with a long needle). A still more complex level would include IBM cards and a sorter. Although analyses can be done more quickly with the more sophisticated techniques, conceptually they are the same as counting piles, and for early efforts in small and medium-sized programs, the card technique may be quicker and easier. Most of the self-appraisal questions asked by programs can be answered using the card-sorting technique.

WARNING

One of the natural temptations of program staff is to compare results with those of other programs. This is a kind of professional "rubbernecking" and should be avoided because it turns the problem of serving young mothers into a competition and usually one with unfair handicaps. A positive program comparison may produce unjustified complacency within the program staff, while a negative one may produce unnecessary pessimism or even panic. Programs with poor results seldom report their findings, so that the published literature represents a biased sample containing only those with the most favorable outcomes. Moreover, program comparisons are meaningless unless one is certain that the study populations were comparable (and that is very difficult to determine) and the criteria of measurement, the quality of data, and the time intervals were the same. Subtle differences in populations studied can make profound differences in the findings. If comparisons are to have any meaning, the differences observed must be due to variations in the programs and not in the populations served.

Instead of looking at other programs with different goals, methods, populations, and problems, administrators should concentrate on comparing their results with their program goals.

This method is more likely to improve the program and maintain staff morale and to be convincing to funding agencies.

SUMMARY OF PROGRAM APPRAISAL

1. The goal of program appraisal is careful description of the population served, the services given, and the results achieved.
2. Start program appraisal early.
3. Set clear and realistic program goals.
4. Develop an ongoing data collection system designed for easy use.
5. Analyze the data frequently.
6. Compare results with program goals, not with the results of other programs.

FINDINGS FROM EVALUATIVE STUDIES

A brief look at some evaluative research may place program appraisal in a broader perspective.

Few well-controlled evaluative studies of comprehensive programs for young parents have been reported.[4] Research usually has focused on some of the services of a comprehensive program and found slight reductions in the rate of subsequent pregnancies,[5-7] a high probability of returning to school postpartum,[8, 9] and good infant health at birth.[1]

A recently completed longitudinal study of two comprehensive programs showed that even a demographically homogeneous population of urban school-age pregnant girls may contain a wide

4. M. Baizerman, C. Sheehan, D. L. Ellison and E. A. Schlesinger, "A Critique of the Research Literature Concerning Pregnant Adolescents, 1960-1970." Mimeographed report to the Maternal and Child Health Service, 1971.

5. F. F. Furstenberg, "Preventing Unwanted Pregnancies Among Adolescents," *Journal of Health and Social Behavior,* 12:340-347 (1971) .

6. J. L. Rauh, L. B. Johnson and R. L. Burket, "The Management of Adolescent Pregnancy and Prevention of Repeat Pregnancies," *HSMHA Health Reports,* 86:66-73 (1971) .

7. J. B. Currie, J. F. Jekel and L. V. Klerman, "Subsequent Pregnancies Among Teenage Mothers Enrolled in a Special Program," *American Journal of Public Health,* 62:1605-1611 (1972) .

8. Marion Howard, *The Webster School,* U. S. Department of Health, Education, and Welfare (Children's Bureau) , 1968.

9. J. J. Dempsey and G. P. Ravacon, "The Use of Life Table in Expressing Follow-up Data," *Perspectives in Maternal and Child Health,* Series B, Number 5 (November, 1971), pp. 1-10.

range of capability, motivation, and potential for achievement.[10]

The programs had a positive impact on the clients for up to one year postpartum in the areas of infant health, mother's education, and child-spacing. This impact diminished over time and by a little over two years postpartum was still noticeable only in the area of education.

The individual components of the clients' postpartum life, such as education, employment, marital status, source of income, and child-spacing, were not randomly distributed; rather they tended to form several fairly distinct life patterns. Thus during the first postpartum year, educational status, not acceptance of contraceptives, was the best predictor of whether the client had a rapid reconception.[11] By two years postpartum the most common life style was a young unmarried mother living in her parent's home, attending school (or graduated), and possibly employed, but still partly dependent on her parents economically. Another large group was married and economically independent, but most of these mothers had interrupted their education and/ or had another child. A third group (about 15%) was unmarried, had dropped out of school, had become pregnant again, and was largely or totally dependent on welfare.

SUMMARY

Each program must appraise its own services and accomplishments using its own goals as the standard for judgment. Program goals should be expressed in measurable terms which are realistic in the context of the program's services. Three kinds of information should be used in setting quantitative goals for achievement: the type, intensity, and duration of services; the character and problems of the population served; and the findings of evaluative research studies as they become available. Program appraisal is not difficult if goals are reasonable and measurable and if plans are made early to collect information for this type of evaluation.

10. L. V. Klerman and J. F. Jekel, *School-Age Mothers: Problems, Programs, and Policy* (Hamden, Connecticut, Shoe String Press, Inc., 1973).

11. J. F. Jekel, L. V. Klerman and D. R. E. Bancroft, "Factors Associated with Rapid Subsequent Pregnancies Among School-Age Mothers," *American Journal of Public Health*, 63:769-773 (1973).

AUTHOR INDEX

SUBJECT INDEX

A

"Abnormal Pyridoxine Metabolism in Toxemia of Pregnancy," 151
Abortion, 75, 113-116, 163, 228, 230
  decline, 15
  elective, 80
  illegal, 15, 113
  incomplete, 93
  induced, 4, 15, 16, 30, 58, 60
  induced, increase in, 17
  legal, 57, 113
  legal elective, 114
  legally induced in New York City (Table II-VI), 76
  spontaneous, 21, 49, 58, 60
  therapeutic, 193, 238
Abortion counseling, 286
Abortion deaths, 15
Abortion death ratio, 16, 17
Abortion-on-demand, 82
"Abortion in New York City: The First Nine Months," 16, 75
Abortion ratios, age-specific (selected states), (Table III-XII), 114
Abortion ratios, legal age specific (Table III-I), 115
Abortion recidivism, 209
"Accidents and Social Deviance," 204
"Adaptation to the First Years of Marriage," 163
Adolescent
  dietary habits, 152, 153
  heterosexual behavior, factors governing (Table III-II), 86
  meal pattern, 153-154
  motivating to select good diets, 154-156
  pregnant, 164, 171
"Adolescent Attitudes Toward Abortion: Effects on Contraceptive Practice," 209

Adolescent Contraception, female, social psychiatry view of, 203-231
Adolescent family and the community health nurse, 187-202
"Adolescent Maternity Services: A Team Approach," 187
Adolescent out-of-wedlock pregnancy: an overview, 206
Adolescent pregnancy clinics, Community health nurse's duties in, 194
Adolescent prenatal clinics, coordination of and teaching in, 195
"Adolescent Primigravida, The," 126
Adolescent sexual activity and contemporary attitudinal change, 203-208
Adolescent Sexuality in Contemporary America, 204
"Adolescent Trap, The," 83
"Adolescents Who Attempt Suicide: Preliminary Findings," 86
Adoption, 38
Adoption agencies, 197
Adult education, 197, 198
Advisory Boards and Committees, serving on, 197
AFDC on reducing punishments related to illegitimacy, the effect, 37-39
AFDC and illegitimacy in the United States, 31
Age of consent (VII-I), 232, 234
Agenda for a City: Issues Confronting New York, 77
Aid to Families with Dependent Children, 48
  benefits
    annual cost, 31
    change in (Table I-VI), 32
    illegitimacy, and, 33-37
  effect on illegitimacy, 31, 32
American Academy of Family Physicians, 230